CULTURE**SHOCK**!

A Survival Guide to Customs and Etiquette

RUSSIA

Anna Pavlovskaya

Н. РЙГЬТ
4/08

Marshall Cavendish
Editions

This edition published in 2007 by:
Marshall Cavendish Corporation
99 White Plains Road
Tarrytown, NY 10591-9001
www.marshallcavendish.us

Other Marshall Cavendish Offices:
Marshall Cavendish International (Asia) Private Limited. 1 New Industrial
Road, Singapore 536196 ▪ Marshall Cavendish Ltd. 119 Wardour Street, London
W1F 0UW, UK ▪ Marshall Cavendish International (Thailand) Co Ltd. 253 Asoke,
12th Flr, Sukhumvit 21 Road, Klongtoey Nua, Wattana, Bangkok 10110, Thailand
▪ Marshall Cavendish (Malaysia) Sdn Bhd, Times Subang, Lot 46, Subang Hi-Tech
Industrial Park, Batu Tiga, 40000 Shah Alam, Selangor Darul Ehsan, Malaysia

Marshall Cavendish is a trademark of Times Publishing Limited

ISBN 10: 0-7614-5414-4
ISBN 13: 978-0-7614-5414-4

Please contact the publisher for the Library of Congress catalogue number

Printed in China by Everbest Printing Co Ltd

Photo Credits:
All photos by the author except pages 120–121, 164–165, 204–205,
220–221 and 224–225 (Photolibrary)
▪ Cover photo: Age Fotostock/Richard T Nowitz

All illustrations by TRIGG

ABOUT THE SERIES

Culture shock is a state of disorientation that can come over anyone who has been thrust into unknown surroundings, away from one's comfort zone. *CultureShock!* is a series of trusted and reputed guides which has, for decades, been helping expatriates and long-term visitors to cushion the impact of culture shock whenever they move to a new country.

Written by people who have lived in the country and experienced culture shock themselves, the authors share all the information necessary for anyone to cope with these feelings of disorientation more effectively. The guides are written in a style that is easy to read and covers a range of topics that will arm readers with enough advice, hints and tips to make their lives as normal as possible again.

Each book is structured in the same manner. It begins with the first impressions that visitors will have of that city or country. To understand a culture, one must first understand the people—where they came from, who they are, the values and traditions they live by, as well as their customs and etiquette. This is covered in the first half of the book.

Then on with the practical aspects—how to settle in with the greatest of ease. Authors walk readers through topics such as how to find accommodation, get the utilities and telecommunications up and running, enrol the children in school and keep in the pink of health. But that's not all. Once the essentials are out of the way, venture out and try the food, enjoy more of the culture and travel to other areas. Then be immersed in the language of the country before discovering more about the business side of things.

To round off, snippets of basic information are offered before readers are 'tested' on customs and etiquette of the country. Useful words and phrases, a comprehensive resource guide and list of books for further research are also included for easy reference.

CONTENTS

Chapter 7
Culture and Travel 196

Chapter 8
Learning the Language 236

Chapter 9
Business in Russia 248

Chapter 10
Fast Facts on Russia 270

INTRODUCTION

Writing a guide is difficult. Writing a guide about Russia is next to impossible. An unenviable but noble task of any guide to any country is to thoroughly acquaint the reader with its history, culture, way of life, traditions, customs and sights, as well as to give useful information about various aspects of life. A guide must be true and specific. It must encourage a traveller to start for the unknown. It must serve like a compass in a strange world. All this is extremely difficult in the case of Russia. Life here is changing so rapidly and drastically that any guide will become outdated before it is published. Finding one's bearings with its help is like using a compass in a region of iron deposit.

Only one thing in Russia is changing slowly and reluctantly—it is the Russian people. It is about them, their character, mentality, habits, likes and dislikes, their manner of behaviour and communication, that is worth writing about nowadays.

The main principle that any foreign traveller setting out for Russia must bear in mind is that it is the Russian people that make Russia. In his days, Joseph Stalin—the father of peoples as he was called in the country—introduced a motto still widely spread and used in Russia: everything depends on the personnel. Any leader in Russia knows how true it is. Not infrequently, some hopeless projects work thanks to the enthusiasm of personnel, while very promising ones fail because of wrong partners. Find the right person or a group of people and your problem is settled. It will work by itself.

Times change, black becomes white and vice versa, 'those who were nobodies have become somebodies' as the revolutionary hymn had it, and state and ideological values have been replaced with their exact opposites. In the space of one century, Russia has on three occasions made fundamental changes not only to the state system but to life as a whole. But whichever system they were living under—an autocratic system, developed socialism or undeveloped capitalism—the people have remained the same, amazingly saving their traditions, ideas and relations to the surrounding world. Furthermore, slowly but surely, they are refashioning the latest new world in their own way, and in such a way that it is starting to look very much like the old world.

As it is impossible to foresee all the difficulties, especially while the social life is changing so rapidly, one ought to rely on personal contacts and communication, on which the whole country depends. While a whole lot of services is at one's disposal in Western cultures, in Russia, all of these may be quite successfully provided by just one person: an acquaintance, your business partner's wife, a concierge in your block of flats, a woman on duty in your hotel, an old woman who lives next door, etc. This kind of people, if they like you, will share anything with you—from their richest experience to some cash to borrow. Feminists will be glad to know that under the circumstances, it is women who are most useful, efficient and reliable, particularly in all kinds of down-to-earth problems. Like heroines of Russian folk tales, they save the hero from the most dangerous situations with the help of a magic mirror or a clew.

Don't be afraid of coming to Russia. Many foreigners who have visited come back to Russia again and again, finding in this world something which is lacking in their own. Russia is a country of enormous scale and a successful business here often opens up more possibilities than in other countries. Not surprisingly, the head of Coca-Cola in Moscow, when asked by a journalist whether he wanted to go home, answered that he did not want to as it is much more interesting in Russia than in other countries and each day you have to take up new challenges. Russia is a country with a startling culture full of works of art and historical monuments. Any contact with them will remain in your memory for a long time. And, if you are lucky, you may eventually get to know and make friends with the Russian people and try out their legendary hospitality and heartfelt openness for yourself. And even if none of the above meets with success, there is always Russian nature, glorified in Russia's famous classical literature and which has still retained its God-given freshness (not least 'thanks' to the decline in agriculture).

Before setting off on this journey through the enigmatic Russian soul, there is one other word of advice. It is well known that your own state of mind is extremely important when travelling. If you arrive stressed and with doubts, expecting unpleasant moments and dirty tricks at every step, then something will surely happen to you. If your soul is clear of all obvious aversions to the surrounding world, then everything will probably be fine and neither bad weather, nor everyday annoyances nor foreign traditions will spoil your mood.

Writing a book that includes everything about contact with Russians would be extremely difficult. Russia, like any other country, has many different facets. Americans like the scale of things in Russia and the Russian soul, but are irritated by the lack of service. The English are drawn to Russian culture, but the inability to stand in a queue makes them indignant. The Germans like Russian hospitality, but do not welcome the dirty streets and public places. Italians like Russian friendship, but are not comfortable with the familiarity. The Chinese like the Russian countryside, but cannot understand why things are done so slowly. In a word, everybody has their own Russia. But an attempt to generalise and write some sort of overview of the main characteristics of Russian life is, of course, possible.

This work is unique because of the information that it brings together. Its author is Russian, a historian and specialist in inter-cultural studies. At the same time, a wide range of material—from surveys to diaries and memoirs—from foreign (not Russian) sources has also been included. This has made it possible to do something which it is very unusual: join together the views of both the internal (Russian) and external (foreign) worlds.

ACKNOWLEDGEMENTS

First of all, I must acknowledge the influence of my parents on all my education, books and researches. My mother, professor of Linguistics Svetlana Ter-Minasova, and my late father, professor of Russian Literature Valentin Fatushchenko, have always been more that just good and caring parents. I consider them to be my colleagues, advisers and friends. My brother Andrei (a historian and film director) and my sister Maria (a philosopher) have always provided me with great support.

I would like to thank my friends and colleagues from Moscow State University with whom we spent lots of time travelling around Russia and discussing the Russian national character, its ways and peculiarities, among them Nikolai Borisov, Irina and Andrei Rootsinsky, Tatiana Ivanova, Andrei Zabrovsky, Vladimir Elistratov, Anna Skorik, Tatiana Tarabanova, Elena Zhbankova, Natalia Ivannikova, Galina Smirnova and the late Ivan Kruglov.

This book would not be possible without help (although often unconscious) of my friends from different countries of the world: Peter Czap (USA), Keith Rawson-Jones (UK), Sebastian Andre Zelechowski (France, my brother- in-law), Anna and Michel Rentien (France), Judith Walker (UK), Elisabeth Millar (UK), Michael Pushkin (UK), Marvin Loflin (USA), Katia Shtefan (USA), Judy and Eugene Zeb Kozlowski (USA), Francesca Fici (Italy), Joanna Woods (New Zealand), the late Nina Kristesen (Australia) and many others. Their remarks and comments on Russian life gave me a new perspective and new vision of my country. My special gratitude to Amanda Calvert and Timothy Seaton, who not only translated the main body of the text but made some very helpful notes as well.

And last but not least, two persons made a great contribution to my work. My husband Igor, a historian, is my first consultant, adviser and critic. He is also a photographer who makes illustrations for my books (including this one). And my son Ivan—a great patriot of Russia. Our long discussions and disputes helped me better understand my country.

MAP OF RUSSIA

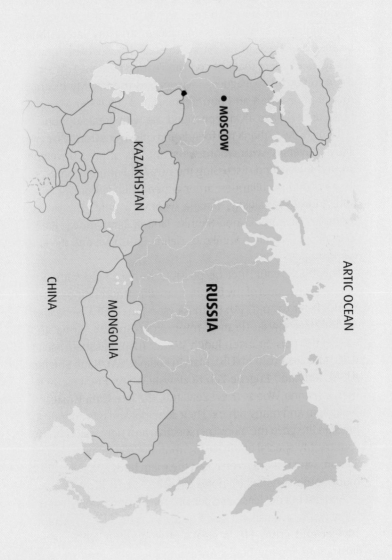

FIRST IMPRESSIONS

CHAPTER 1

'Russia can't be understood with the mind,
And can't be measured with a common yardstick:
It has a peculiar character—
In Russia you can only believe.'
—Fyodor Tyutchev, Russian poet

THE MYSTERIOUS RUSSIAN SOUL

Life in Russia has never been plain sailing. The weather conditions, geographic location and unique way in which politics have developed have created difficulties throughout Russian history. Freezing temperatures or droughts have from time to time destroyed harvests, resulting in inevitable famine. Likewise, Mongols from the East and Germanic tribes from the West pillaged the land and killed many people. Then there were the revolutionary waves within the country which led to collapse and ruin. In *Chapaev*, one of the popular old Russian films about the civil war, a sad peasant remarks, "The Whites came, and they stole. The Reds came and they also stole. What is a peasant to do?" Life is difficult in any case.

It was even harder for those observing from the outside to make sense of this far from simple life. Russia has never fitted well into the boxes which foreigners know and love. It appeared that the country was just a mass of contradictions: barbarians and high culture, obedient subjugation to a strong government and revolutionary movements, poverty and the aversion of the people to wealth and the luxury of the courts and temples. The only way to explain all of this was to resort to that 'mysterious or enigmatic Russian soul'. The fact that it was impossible to solve this puzzle irritated some and enthralled others, but whatever the reaction, there were few who remained unmoved by Russia.

The veil of secrecy, which had surrounded Russia since ancient times, had not made it any easier to understand the country. Winston Churchill called Russia 'a riddle wrapped in a mystery inside an enigma'. This quotation quickly became famous, as it neatly summed up the general relation to Russia.

After the fall of the Iron Curtain, people flooded both out of and into Russia. Many people's first reaction was surprise. It turns out that the Russians are not so different from the rest of the world: they have two arms, two legs and a head, they love their children, respect their elders, have long faces when they are sad and laugh when they are happy. The second reaction was doubt. Are they really so similar after all? It turns out that ideas which are well known in the West (democracy, market economy, even freedom) take on a completely different form in Russia. And people are sometimes sad or happy for reasons impossible to comprehend. This acquaintance with the new Russia ended up reaffirming the traditional view of the mysterious Russian soul that is so hard to understand.

However, and at the risk of disappointing people, there is no particular enigma in Russia. There is just a country and its people, which have developed along their own historical path, in their own geographical and climatic conditions, in line with its own social and political traditions. We just need to move away from familiar labels and stereotypes and understand, in a more abstract way, what is behind any particular phenomenon. It turns out that Russians are not good or bad, just that in some ways they are 'different' and in some ways like everybody else. But any attempt to understand another people is already to accept it, with all its quirks, habits and foibles. Furthermore, travelling in Russia is not only easier than expected, but sometimes even pleasant.

Thus Russia has always been a mystery for foreigners. And the mysterious always attracts and frightens at the same time. At different historical periods, Westerners 'discovered' Russia again and again, each time revealing some 'new' aspects. In the 19th century and even nowadays, a Westerner going to

Russia is looked upon as half-mad and half-heroic. Even now at the time of mass media, many foreigners are surprised to realise that Russians have the same joys and sorrows as the rest of the world.

Historically, there have been two directly conflicting views about Russia in the world. The first is distrust, verging on hostility. Many generations have been brought up to fear the threat of Russian (Soviet) aggression, accustomed since childhood to the terror of this invisible enemy. Now that this threat has been reduced to almost nothing, Russia has become a sort of consolation prize for the West, a place where everything is worse. If one day you are feeling down in your own country, you are dissatisfied with your government's actions or the way the economy is developing, just think about Russia. You are sure to feel better.

But there is another point of view. Some people are enraptured by Russian life, culture, the special spirituality and the relations between people. Some of them, dissatisfied with their own lives which are more and more domineered by machines and technology, tired of a world where sincere feelings and emotions are often suppressed for the sake of business and profit and fed up with the abundance of individualism in all spheres of human communication, turn to Russians now with admiration, then with derision. Russian people, in their opinion, preserved the sincerity of feelings and behaviour. Here is how an American woman poet Edna Dean Proctor describes Russian national character (1866): 'The Russian nature, with favourable conditions, is like forest and steppe in summer, full of peace and grace and charm... But it has also the strength and terror of steppe and forest; and under the winter of injustice and tyranny and cruelty, its impulses, its energies, its affections, become pitiless blasts and devouring wolves.'

However strange it may seem, both love and hate towards Russia lead to the same result. Firstly, they both give birth to curiosity. Secondly, to a lack of objectivity. Both those who seek in Russia the personification of evil and those who dream about its special spirituality are blinded to the real Russia, the way it actually is, with all its virtues and all its drawbacks.

How Far is Russia?

One of the most widespread reactions around the world when people learn that you have come from Russia is to exclaim "Oh, that's so far away!" Little old ladies in provincial England (and England is the European country furthest from Russia) are surprised to learn that the flight is only about three hours and that some people even manage to drive to England (only 2,300 km separate the Russian border from the English border). America is both further and harder to get to, but nobody would have that sort of reaction were they to see an American in Europe. We are talking about a divide that is more profound than kilometres and the difficulties of geography, a curtain that is more impenetrable than the Iron Curtain. This is cultural incomprehension. Those strange Russians cannot possible be so close, they are somewhere a long way away over there, in the lands of permanent snow called Siberia.

However, it is not all that bad. Many of those who actually make it to Russia begin not only to love the country, but also to understand it. As with any culture and any people, Russia has its charm and its attraction. This strange, mad, crazy, ever-changing world opens itself willingly to those who come here without arrogance and prejudice. Russians love it when they are loved and will respond with the most genuine and all-consuming feelings (as is characteristic of that passionate Russian nature so celebrated in classic literature and shown in cinemas).

ACQUAINTANCE WITH RUSSIA AT HOME

People's acquaintance with Russia usually starts at home. Above all this is through the mass media, which does not usually pay much attention to the life of ordinary people. Russian mafia, public scandals, beggars on the street, the rich throwing their money around—this is the image of the 'ordinary' Russian that is created by the mass media. Cinema bends willingly to the whims of the time. Over the years, James Bond films have portrayed a number of different Russians: evil KGB agents, voracious women, bandits, mad professors…

Russians abroad are a topic in themselves. They can be divided into those who live abroad permanently and those who have come temporarily to work, relax or travel. Russian émigrés, who are often an important source of information about the country that they have left behind, are an interesting and distinctive category. And it is with them that you can start to tell the difference between Russia and other countries. Nowadays, people travel freely around the world, and the number is increasing as world globalisation gathers pace. Some go for an interesting and well-paid job, others to find a spouse, yet more simply want to see the world and try something new. Nevertheless, they remain loyal to the land of their birth which they have left behind, knowing that at any time they can return to it.

In Russia, emigration is not simply a desire to leave and go somewhere, it is first and foremost a rejection of your motherland, an unwillingness to live there. In the past, it turned out that leaving the country not infrequently meant that a Russian was unable to return. People often left not because they wanted to go somewhere, but because they no longer wished to live in their own country. Russians have always had a characteristic naïve belief that somewhere there must be a better life. Religious people thought it in the world beyond, Soviet citizens in communism, and some looked for it abroad.

Having left their country and burned their bridges, many find it difficult to put down roots in the new soil. This sometimes give birth to a desire to please their new fellow-countrymen and lead to interesting results. Many émigrés talk about the Russia that people want to hear about and repeat worn-out stereotypes. They often pour abuse on the world they have left behind, as it is important that they themselves believe that the motherland they left deserved to be abandoned.

But there is another category of émigrés. The nostalgia and melancholy for their home, so typical of the Russian character, leads them to idealise the Russia they left. Everything that was bad, and which was once so important that it led them to take the serious decision to leave, is forgotten and they are left with a rose-tinted idyll comprised of touching memories from their childhood and youth. These people remember only the best moments, which are made more beautiful by separation, and their desire to defend what they have left behind often becomes quite bellicose.

Meeting Russians who are abroad only temporarily can often be more fruitful and useful. More often than not, Russians who are working or studying in other countries make friends, are

The opinion of émigrés is very important when the rest of the world forms its impressions of Russia. Their words are listened to carefully, as this is the opinion of 'real Russians', who have at some time actually lived that strange, enigmatic life and who have managed to escape from it and tell the truth to others.

very communicative and break down the usual stereotypes about enigmatic and strange Russians. Tourists, though, are another matter. They either run around in a noisy crowd, leaving behind a vague impression of excitement and bad manners, or shock everybody with their demands and the money they throw around.

Nowadays, the situation has changed significantly. Since *perestroika* (the policy of reforming the economic and political system practised in the 1980s under Mikhail Gorbachev), a new generation of Russians has grown up who feel themselves to be citizens of the world. They do not have the usual Russian complex of constantly feeling some sort of haughtiness on the part of foreigners to them, mixed with distrust. These new Russians feel comfortable in the elite clubs of London, on the streets of Paris or at home in Moscow. They find spouses in various countries, but often spend a lot of their time in Moscow. They do not have a desperate curiosity or desire to leave for a better world. They feel fine everywhere. But these are a minority of well-off people who have the possibility to travel freely and converse on a regular basis with foreigners.

ARRIVING IN RUSSIA

There is a popular saying in Russia, 'Better to see once than hear a hundred times'. However much you may have heard or read about the history of Russia and the Russians, it is all no more than an enigmatic and abstract idea until you have actually visited the country. The reality that confronts tourists and those who for whatever reason are travelling through Russia is always both simpler and more complex than what

they imagined. On the one hand, it is not so frightening. Bears do not roam the streets, KGB agents are not following your every footstep, and temperatures of 20 degrees below zero do not occur year round but only in the height of winter, and even then not that often. On the other hand, the world around you and which particularly now, in this new era, seems so normal (Coca-Cola, high prices, foreign cars, supermarkets, mobile phones) is nevertheless very strange (you only have to travel a few kilometres from the centre of Moscow to notice the difference). Furthermore, even in Moscow, there is much that differs from the typical Western way of life to which the civilised world is accustomed.

The first thing you should be wary of is drawing generalisations from first impressions. There are two reasons for this. The first is that for historical and cultural reasons, the places that are most accessible to the majority of tourists and travellers are the large cities, Moscow and Saint Petersburg. And, more often than not, their central parts. Most people judge the real Russia on the basis of central Moscow and central Saint Petersburg, and the view from the window of the Moscow-Petersburg train. This is not, however, an entirely unfaithful portrait. Moscow, as the capital of the Russian state, is quintessentially Russian and contains the main virtues and drawbacks of Russian cities. On the other hand, as with every other large city, Moscow is extremely cosmopolitan, and you can find everything that you would find in any other large city. Furthermore, any Russian who has been successful has a desire to go there, as living in Moscow is the surest indicator of success (to climb any higher, you have to have a villa or castle in Europe).

The second reason is that Moscow is not only a collection of the richest in Russia, but also the poorest. All the refugees, poor, aggrieved and unhappy also want to go there, hoping for a better life in the chaos of conglomerate. The streets are filled with the destitute and beggars, as well as strange people of indeterminate look. The further you go from the capital, the less chance you have of meeting this picturesque rabble.

This is an old tradition. In the 19th century, travellers who made it to far-off Russia left picturesque descriptions of those whom they considered to be Russian 'peasants': drunks in rags and torn clothes. These city outcasts actually had very little in common with real village dwellers.

The first thing that awaits any foreigner arriving in Russia is passport and customs control. In most cases, this is at Moscow's main airport, Sheremetyevo 2. This is not the second airport but the second terminal. Sheremetyevo 1 (i.e., terminal one) mainly handles internal flights, while Sheremetyevo 2 is for international flights. Other options are to go through customs by car at the land borders with Finland, Belorussia and Ukraine, or arrive at a different airport. But Sheremetyevo nevertheless remains the main gateway to

Even before you have set foot on Russian soil, there is a strange Russian tradition that awaits you, particularly if you have flown on Aeroflot where the majority of passengers are Russian. As soon as the aircraft has touched the ground, a round of applause breaks out. Whether it is people expressing their joy that the danger is past, or congratulating the flight crew, or simply that they are happy about this small miracle of travelling is hard to say. People simply applaud, and that is that.

Russia. It should be noted, though, that this gateway has not aged well, and is not really up to its high calling. Talks about the need to rebuilt Sheremetyevo have been going on for several years. The airport was constructed in the days of the Iron Curtain, when only the lucky few from the Russian side and the brave few from the other side used its services. At that time, it fulfilled its obligations just fine. Nowadays, with travel in either direction a usual and daily occurrence, the number of passengers is clearly too much of a burden for this ageing airport.

Too many people, too little space and, yes, very badly organised. In addition, the new economic situation in the country has greatly increased the prices of the entirely mediocre goods and services at the airport. There are chaotic queues everywhere. From time to time, one or other service will suddenly become unavailable. For example, luggage trolleys. All of a sudden they simply disappear, and large crowds fuss around in a disorderly way in the middle of the arrivals hall, waiting for the lazy employee who, with complete indifference, wheels in 10 or 15 of them from time to time.

This author, who has travelled frequently, has on a number of occasions become a participant in the general grab for trolleys and has watched how well-dressed and intelligent ladies have suddenly lost all control of their European lustre and have grabbed hold of the cherished handles in an iron grip. And then, all of a sudden, the problem resolves itself and lines of the longed-for trolleys are everywhere. Trying to explain the timing or reasons for these unexpected difficulties is impossible, it is simply one of those secrets of this enigmatic country.

In other Russian airports, there may be other difficulties. At Domodedovo, for example, they have increased the security measures in the wake of the terrorist atrocities in Moscow. All those departing are subject to a careful and thorough search. Everybody must take their shoes off, and their coat, belt and other items of outerwear, as well as anything metallic. And this is all correct and justifiable. But the badly-organised line often turns into a noisy, chaotic rabble with everybody trying to squeeze in front of the others. On top of this, you have to put your items in plastic trays: small ones for shoes and large one for items and clothes.

And these too can be in short supply, with people fighting and arguing over them.

For the rest, passport and customs control in Russia is much the same as anywhere else in the world. More often than not, you simply walk through and answer a few simple questions. In spite of what many are expecting, nothing special happens. If your passport and visa are in order, you have nothing to fear; you will not have any problems. Customs and border control officials around the world are not known for being excessively polite and usually assume that any traveller is in violation of border rules (I still remember fondly an old Englishman at Heathrow, the only one in my many years of travelling to Britain, who smiled and wished me a pleasant journey). Russians are well acquainted with this groundless fault-finding when entering another country, when you have to answer for the colour of your passport. In comparison with what usually awaits them in airports all round the world, Sheremetyevo is a pleasant and refined place.

But it goes without saying that chaos and confusion reign here too. First you run to queue up for passport control. Here, as a rule, there are two types of booth: one for citizens of the Russian Federation and one for everybody else. Queues spring up everywhere and people are let through everywhere,

irrespective of the passport they hold. Moreover, Russian citizens are checked no less rigorously than everybody else, which really irritates the Russians and helps to calm the foreigners.

Then comes the luggage hall, where there are the not infrequent fights for trolleys. After that the customs, usually a formality, assuming that you have not declared anything. They are not trying to catch foreigners (they are more interested in foreigners when they fly out of the country, to see if they have any works of art) but their own citizens bringing in goods to be resold.

FIRST IMPRESSIONS

So here you are in Russia. On the other side of the glass barrier, which separates two worlds, stands a large and confused crowd waiting to meet those who have arrived. There are close friends and relatives with a welcome kiss, employees with greeting signs, and taxi drivers with their endless questions. If you have nobody to meet you, it is better to organise a taxi in advance before you fly, because there is a better than evens chance that the drivers at the airport will make the best of your helplessness. Some foreign travel guides still contain the claim that you can get anywhere for a pack of foreign cigarettes. That is the long gone past. A taxi ordered in advance will take you from Sheremetyevo to the centre of Moscow for about 1,500 rubles, while something found on the spot will cost at least twice that.

If you have flown to Russia from the West, you immediately run up against an interesting phenomenon: the trip to Russia has taken some time out of your life. The difference between Russia and London (Greenwich) is three hours, and with most of the rest of Europe two hours. So for example, if you have flown from London, departing reasonably early at 11:00 am (in other words, you were at the airport at 9:00 am) and the flight is 3½ hours, your plane will land in Moscow at about 6:00 pm, and by the time you have cleared all the formalities it is well after 7:00 pm. Thus, the whole day has gone by travelling, and on top of that you have lost three hours out of your life (you 'get them back' of course on the way home, but that is another matter). Morning, day and evening get mixed together and mixed up, creating an impression of unreality.

There is one obvious problem: the language. In many countries, even exotic ones, at least the alphabet looks familiar. Not only is Russian not much like other languages, the alphabet is completely different, and those letters that do look the same are pronounced differently. The Russian letter 'в' is pronounced 'v', 'p' is pronounced 'r', and so on. If you do not know the basics of Russian, not only will you not be able to explain what you want, in most cases you will not even be able to tell what is in front of you: a café, shop or hairdressers? Even standard international words such as 'restaurant', 'taxi' and 'bank' sound almost the same but look different when written in Russian. Here they are in order: ресторан, такси, банк. Not everybody recognises even these, all of which strengthens the feeling of confusion, muddle and some sort of mysticism surrounding your arrival.

It should also be noted that until 1918, Russia still lived by the old Julian calendar. In other words, travellers arriving in Russia not only lost a few hours, were unable even remotely to read a single sign, but had also landed two weeks in the past. Thus, the famous revolution of 1917 actually took place on 25 October (and hence its well-known name, the October Revolution), which was already 7 November in most other European countries.

The Soviet government quickly 'caught up' with the world and switched over to the widely-used Gregorian calendar. Only the Russian Orthodox Church refused to follow suit and follows the old dates to this day. So it is that Christians all round the world celebrate Christmas on 25 December, whereas Russians celebrate it on 7 January. The so-called 'old New Year' takes place on the night of 13–14 January. Today, there is an increased interest in the country in new types of holidays. Therefore many (mainly atheists) celebrate all the dates and so the holidays, both old and new, carry on throughout the year.

Outdoor Advertising

The foreigners who came to Russia before *perestroika* were surprised (and some were enraptured) by the chastity and strictness of the streets. Only very few banners with ideological slogans were hung up (such as 'We are heading for victory of the Communism!') and these were of the simplest design. Nowadays, advertisements have filled the cities and streets of Russia. The road from Sheremetyevo to Moscow has even more than usual. This is a road travelled by people with money and placements are particularly popular amongst advertisers. In Sheremetyevo, even the booths where the border guards sit and the floor in front of the passport control are covered in advertisements (I am not even going to mention the walls and luggage collection point).

The appearance of a large number of advertisements has met with a mixed reaction and resulted in a number of effects. If in other countries they have appeared over a period of time, in Russia they have appeared all at once. Not so long ago, bright adverts were considered vulgar and a capitalist evil. Now, there is not a single pole on the streets which has not been adorned with all sorts of advertisement of varying quality. As often happens in Russia, they have gone in at the deep end. There are now so many adverts that it is sometimes impossible to read what exactly is being advertised, as they cover one another.

Posters and advertisements can be found everywhere on the streets of Moscow.

Most Russians are irritated by advertisements. There are too many of them, more often than not advertising goods that only a narrow circle of the rich can afford, and some are worried about the moral aspect. For example, in a country which has traditionally held that 'being rich does not make you happy' and 'money can't buy happiness', one of the adverts that irritates people shows a young woman looking haughtily at those around her. A large slogan explains the reason for the haughty gaze: 'If you love me, prove it'. She is surrounded by items of gold. This is an advert for a jewellery company. In a word, if there is gold, you are in love, and vice versa.

The Mysterious Vandal

At one point, somebody started covering a series of advertisements for underwear (showing half-naked women) around Moscow with red paint. The police hunted for the vandal, but he was able to hide from them for quite a period of time, while destroying new adverts each night. When he was finally captured, it turned out that he was a priest in one of the Moscow churches who had decided to fight evil single-handedly. "Well, children are looking at this filth," he said, when he appeared before the courts. Many Muscovites sympathised with him.

The main roads leading into Moscow are also crammed with adverts on all sides. Some even consider this to be dangerous, since it distracts drivers' attention.

First Acquaintance with the Locals

Those who have come to Russia for the first time get to know the country in a superficial way and only meet Russians on the street or in public transport. They often complain about the particularly 'gloomy' nature of the Russians, the lack of smiles in the crowd, the introspection. The reason for this is not to be found in the peculiarities of the Russian character, but in the specifics of their behaviour. In Russia, it is not usual to smile at passers-by. At best this will be thought of as some sort of stupidity, but smiling at a stranger in certain circumstances, in a dimly lit doorway for example, could even be dangerous.

There is a saying in Russia that 'laughter without reason is the sign of stupidity'. When the first McDonald's opened in Russia, the employees were taught to smile at clients, which caused a lot of problems, or as one of the young employees put it, "People think that we're complete idiots". The serious, concentrated face that Russians wear on the street is not a sign of any particular glumness, but just a tradition that considers smiles to be something private and reserved for those close to you.

Hospitality

Getting to know real live people usually dispels the impression you have of the faceless, cold and reserved crowd. It is no accident that the famous Russian hospitality has become the country's calling card. Talkative, benevolent, generous, open, sincere: these are the qualities in the Russian character noted by foreigners who have had the opportunity to visit somebody's home. Many even complain that a trip to Russia often turns into an endless banquet, with enormous quantities of food and drink.

For the Russians, food really is more than simply satisfying a physical need; it is also a specific and important ritual. Eating together is a sign of friendship which takes your relations onto a new level. In the olden days, this was called 'breaking the bread'. People who have shared bread could no longer feel enmity towards one another (a bit like the Red Indian peace pipe).

Furthermore, a well-laid table is a sign of respect. Even during the toughest times, when nothing was available at all (the late 1980s and early 1990s) and when the shop shelves were as empty as the people's purses, you could be sure that a table set out for good friends would be groaning under the weight of food. This exasperated many foreigners. Why such reckless luxury when you do not even have the basic necessities? Why so many nibbles when the guests do not need them? Some considered it a sign of absurdity, others a desire to cover up the actual situation in the country. But it is all much simpler. In those days, foreigners were a rarity and they were to be shown respect, and from a Russian point of view, a well-laid table is the best way of doing so. And that is why a Russian host will be offended if a guest eats little. It is not because they begrudge the food which may go to waste, but because their show of affection and respect is being turned down.

And finally, Russians are convinced that eating (and, particularly, drinking) together helps to relieve any tension between people who do not know each other (especially if they belong to different cultures), to remove any embarrassment and to establish contact. Once you are sitting round a table, the conversation becomes more trusting and candid and people become more honest and open.

So when you come to Russia, you need to be prepared for the fact that there will be a lot of food, of all different types and in all sorts of unexpected places. This does not, of course, concern tourists who are travelling in a group on a set programme. In this, the Russians have quickly learned the lessons of the business-oriented West: food should be expensive, not too plentiful and usually cooked 'in pseudo-local style'. But there can be Russian surprises here too, and while travelling out to the countryside, the company may have arranged for Russian *bliny* or Caucasian *shashlik*. The desire to feed guests has even made its way into the tourist business in Russia.

Service

The first impressions you get from your acquaintance with Russia are often spoiled by the service, which is far from being as it should. In this instance, tourist groups are better off: everything is arranged for them in line with the established rituals and the inbound operator keeps an eye on service, whereas those who have to talk to people in the Russian service industries themselves do not always have a pleasant experience. And probably the most important thing is the attitude of the Russians themselves. Historically, it has always been that traders and waiters did not hold a particularly honoured place in society, and this caused a reverse aggressive reaction on the part of those providing such services. From time to time, it is very important for them to show that they are no worse than their clients and they do not allow themselves to be bossed about simply because they are working in the service industry.

Sometimes this takes on ridiculous forms. Imagine an expensive shop: lots of goods, wonderful design, everything thought out down to the last detail. And it is filled with shop assistants whose main aim, it would seem, is to scare off all the customers with their replies.

An older man is choosing a suit. "What do you think, does this fit me well? Or should I try another one?"

"At your age it's so hard to choose something suitable."

Or a lady who is on the large side can hear quite clearly the comment that there is no point in people like her even bothering to look through the collection. And any request to look for something less expensive will simply draw the most contemptuous of looks. Or in a food shop that looks like any other supermarket in the world, where it is usual to see a group of shop assistants engaged in a lively discussion about the latest news and completely ignoring the shoppers' attempts to get their attention. Or a waiter in a restaurant who may simply disappear for some unknown period of time, particularly if a football match is being shown on television or if one of the restaurant staff is celebrating a birthday.

Russian culture retains a certain asceticism in questions of household items, and so many of the questions asked by clients or guests seem like rather capricious childishness to the Russians. Ice is put in drinks mainly to spoil children, a leaking shower does not stop anybody from washing, and if there is not enough toilet paper, well, you should be more economical.

To be fair, we should note that the situation is starting to change. First and foremost, this is noticeable in the expensive hotels and restaurants, which will be much the same as they are the world over, and maybe even slightly better (everything needs to be taken to the limit, after all). And inimitable Russian service does have its advantages. You have asked a shop assistant to bring you some sausage. Where else in the world would you be told, in a half-whisper, that it is probably better to choose something different as it is not fresh? Or if you ask for biscuits, you hear the reply, "Take *pryaniki* instead, they're better."

However, coming face to face with the sadly well-known Russian bureaucracy can be a pleasant surprise. Years spent comparing the bureaucracies in many leading countries such as the USA, France and Italy have led this author to conclude that their Russian colleagues are no worse, and in some cases better, than their foreign counterparts. Yes, there are delays, endless papers and indifferent bureaucrats who are tired of their life of responsibilities. But even here, there is still room for the wonderful human factor. If you find a way to get through to the official who is considering your request, then you can consider all your problems solved. And note that despite the widespread opinion about the ease with which you can buy Russian bureaucrats, there are a number of different approaches you can take. You can move them to pity, shame them into action, make them your friends and, of course, in some instances simply give them a bribe.

Looking Round

What else catches your eye when you first get to know Russia? The amazing spaces, the size of the country, the endless horizons. Of course, these are simply empty syllables for those who spend all their time in Moscow and Saint Petersburg. But if you travel around the country itself, you cannot help but be impressed. Furthermore, the population is concentrated mainly in the towns and the ongoing process of urbanisation shows no signs of letting up. Feelings of emptiness and being lost in this huge land are a constant companion for those travelling in Russia.

Many foreigners are surprised by the abundance of the land. On the one hand, it is very pleasant. For the most part there is freedom; you can walk where you like and set up a tent without having to ask permission. On the other hand, it is sad. Agriculture is not exactly flourishing in Russia at the moment and uncared-for fields and untended forests have become a common sight.

One American who was cycling with a group from Moscow to Saint Petersburg summed up his view on the Russian village life he had witnessed along the way as follows: "And this is the superpower that we struggled against for so many

A water pump such as this is a typical source of water in small towns and villages.

years!" In Russian villages, life changes very slowly, and that is always the way it was. Water is brought from the pump, houses are heated using wood fires, the toilet is a small shack round the back of the house and the shop (if there is one) only has the bare necessities. And all that only a few dozen kilometres outside the capital.

In order to calm the cyclist, I can only say that Russia has always been strong as concerns the spirit of its people, and not necessarily their material well-being. The appearance of the villages and the unsettled state of life deceived both Napoleon in 1812 (he decided that he could cope with such a people) and Hitler in 1941. Leo Tolstoy wrote in his famous novel *War and Peace* that the French army was crushed by the 'bludgeon of the people's war'. So external appearances can be deceptive.

Winter

The most widespread stereotype about Russia concerns the cold, snowy winter and everything that goes with it.

The image of Russia as a cold and snowbound country is characteristic in literature from all periods, and is still with us today. Travellers in the 19th century who published the diaries of their travels undoubtedly bewitched their readers with phrases such as 'here you can feel the breath of winter' or 'outside the window, Russian men were walking in their indispensable fur hats which protect them from the cold'. This later phrase was penned by the famous English author Lewis Carrol, who came to Russia in July.

As for later periods, you only have to think back to films about Russia such as the famous *Doctor Zhivago*. The characters love and suffer against the backdrop of endlessly deep snowdrifts and beautiful icicles. Cinema actively uses and thereby reaffirms this ingrained impression of permanent snow and cold conditions in Russia. Most films and even cartoons (think about Disney's *Anastasia*) take place in the winter, which means that you can recognise the place straightaway. Of course that's Russia, the land of eternal snow.

There was also a characteristic reaction from American students, who had never been to Russia, when they were shown a series of slides from Moscow (this took place in one

One of Russia's lovely villages in winter.

of America's central states). Their surprise knew no bounds, they had never even imagined that Russia was so green. According to them, they associated Russia with the colour white but never with green.

This association is also linked with all the other attributes of winter which are considered to be an inseparable part of Russian life: fur, coats, fur hats, large shawls and even vodka (overindulgence in which is often put down to the cold weather).

The Famous Russian Weather

I was once visiting one of America's northern states in the winter and was faced with a very steadfast reaction to my presence. When I arrived, the weather was quite warm, and did not differ that much from what we were having in Moscow—around –5˚C. Every American, from professors to girls I knew in passing in the shops, would greet me with a phrase, sometimes joking, sometimes not: "You probably feel uncomfortable and ill at ease in this weather. You won't get this sort of weather in Moscow in January." (Actually, the temperature had gone up and Moscow was covered in slush). Soon, there was a fall of snow, the temperature dropped suddenly and the greetings turned to, "Congratulations, I guess you feel at home now, don't you?" They repeated these phrases with amazing consistency and right the way through to the spring. You could predict what an American would say upon meeting me, depending on the temperature outside. This can seem incomprehensible and troublesome if you do not know that one of the favourite stereotypes connected with Russia is frost, cold and winter.

Western observers are surprised that Russians love this cold and snow, look forward to a winter and have a great amount of holidays, festivals and games with snow. An American boy John Q Adams, who later happened to become the sixth president of the United States, visited Russia in the 18th century and was shocked by the 'barbaric' way of Russians and their passion for snow. Here is how he described the Russian bathhouse (1781): 'They bathe themselves at first in very warm water, and from thence they plunge themselves into the snow and roll themselves in it...' And then follows the conclusion '...this nation is far from being civilised...'

Winter really is a beautiful time of year in Russia, and Russians really do love it. The whole world is covered by fluffy

There are winter joys to be enjoyed in Russia, a ride down one of the snow-capped slopes being just one of them.

white snow, which means that even the long nights are not entirely dark. During the day, the snow reflects the sunshine and everything sparkles and glistens. The light frost gives you the feeling of freshness and this time of year is considered to be healthier from a medical point of view. Children and adults get out on their skis, skates or sledges, build forts or throw snowballs. But this is the ideal. Over the last few years, the increasingly frequent warm spells mean that snow swells and darkens, the air becomes damp and the temperature hovers around its most unpleasant and unhealthy zero.

Nevertheless, winter is a great time for travelling to Russia and you should not be afraid to come. You simply need to choose the right clothes. Often, you come across unhappy tourists wrapped in thin garments and with leather gloves on their freezing hands. Winter coats, hats and fur gloves or woollen mittens are not simply a pretty part of Russian life, they are a 'bare necessity'.

Vodka

Drunkenness is another phenomenon that is considered to be an important characteristic of Russian life. Unfortunately, foreign guests are often justified in commenting that many

shops and kiosks which supposedly sell food actually have nothing to sell, although you will always be able to find a few types of vodka and other alcoholic drinks in them. And 24 hours a day at that!

The Russians really do drink, and the drink of choice is vodka. It should be said that in terms of quality, vodka in Russia is better than everything else. Great caution should be taken when purchasing wine, brandy, cognac and beer, and then only in reputable shops. Good-quality vodka can be bought almost everywhere, you just need to beware of the cheap brands. Russians drink for many reasons, in joy and sadness, from melancholy and boredom, after a hard day's work or when there is nothing to do, to warm up or to chill out. More often than not, drinking goes hand in hand with a good conversation: going out to the countryside with friends, heading off hunting or fishing, meeting up to discuss the latest news, meeting by chance after work, etc. And in the course of a year, you can find any number of reasons.

The political situation in the country and the government's policies play an important role in all of this. It is well known that one of Mikhail Gorbachev's least popular reforms was the anti-alcohol law. Unfortunately, the results of it were much more important and destructive than could have been expected. Beautiful, historic vineyards in the south of Russia were destroyed, a loss which was irreplaceable and, most importantly, senseless; there was an unhealthy hullabaloo when half the country, from workers to professors, stood around in queues for vodka; the production of moonshine took on unprecedented proportions; the distribution of poor-quality, illegally-produced alcohol had a greater detrimental effect on the nation's health; and the dissatisfaction with the state's policies led to agitation and disaffection in society and prepared the ground for social conflicts.

Nowadays, the situation is completely different, which is another extreme. Proclaiming a market economy in the country could not fail to lead to an enormous increase in the production and sale of alcoholic drinks. As a result, they are now available everywhere and to all. On top of that, people now have the strange conviction that drinking in public places and on the street is a celebration of freedom and that the whole free world does exactly that. So it is entirely normal to see young girls drinking gin and tonic from a can 'on the hoof' or well-dressed businessmen swigging beer at a bus stop nowadays.

However, we should not overestimate drunkenness in Russia. It is one matter to relax with some friends over a couple of shot glasses, or to warm up when you have walked home in the snow, and entirely another to be a clinical alcoholic. Not everybody drinks, and those who do don't drink all the time. Women do not drink much, and many do not drink vodka or other strong drinks. To drink doesn't necessarily mean to get drunk. In Russia, there has always been a great esteem for those who can drink alcohol and stay sober and not lose control of themselves at the same time. There are alcoholics of course, and you will come across them on the streets of major Russian towns (a problem in any large city in fact). Most importantly, though, is that over the last few years, almost all the state-run medical institutions where you could take alcoholics for treatment at the State's expense have been shut down.

The way in which people drink is also different. In Russia, it is not the done thing to pour yourself a couple of fingers of whisky and then pace up and down the room with it discussing business. Or to drink wine over lunch for the taste, in which case the drink complements the food. Or to spend an evening with a glass of port and a good book. In the West, people drink often and little, in Russia less often but more. And they will always drink around a table, taking a bite to eat after each shot (in this case, the food complements the drink).

Russian Fairy Tales

Fairy tales can tell you an enormous amount about a people and its character traits. In particular, this is typical for Russian fairy tales. Fairy tales are the starting point for the formation of a view of the world, of good and evil, and about moral values. And they have always been popular in Russia. Even during the rationalist and materialistic times of the Soviet Union, folk tales had huge print runs and the country's best directors brought them wonderfully to life on the screen, as well as creating ballets, operas and other performances based on them. Fairy tales in Russia are like a linking thread through the eras, passing on certain national values from generation to generation.

Another important feature of fairy tales is their universality. They were loved and are loved by all sections of society. Peasants, who formed the overwhelming majority of the population, recounted fairy tales through the long winter nights. Aristocrats heard them retold by their peasant nannies. The intellectual and artistic elite used folk elements in their works. And today, both in the poorest families and in the homes of the new Russian oligarchs, the same fairy tales are told. They are a special social unifier in Russia, teaching general ideals.

The same can be said for the various age categories. Fairy tales have always been loved not only by children but also by adults.

The national characteristics of fairy tales become particularly obvious in two instances: when they are interpreted by people of other cultures and when they are compared to fairy tales belonging to other peoples.

One of the favourite fairy tales in Russia is *Morozko*. The subject is simple: a poor stepdaughter grows up in the home of her weak father and evil stepmother who has her own stupid and greedy daughter. The stepdaughter is very unfortunate. She tries to please everybody but nevertheless gets in the way and, what is worse, irritates everybody with her mild nature. When the stepmother's patience runs out, she decides to get rid of the tedious girl and sends her out into the forest, into the cruel frost.

There, the girl sits under a tree and is preparing to die quietly when she is found by Grandfather Frost (Morozko) who is wandering through the forest. He asks her "Are you warm, little girl? Are you warm, beautiful girl?" She answers him, barely audible "I am warm, father, I am warm, *Morozushko*." He increases the frost and again asks, and she, weaker than before, answers in the same way. As a result, Grandfather Frost takes pity on her and rewards her with presents. The stepmother sees all this and soon leads her

own daughter to the woods. Grandfather Frost comes by and asks his question "Are you warm, little girl? Are you warm, beautiful girl?". And in reply he hears "Oh, very cold, I have no strength left, and I shall freeze." Grandfather Frost got angry and froze the stepmother's daughter to death. And that's the simple story.

This Russian fairy tale has a German equivalent: Frau Holle. The story is very similar, but the values are different. In the German version, the good girl works well and is neat and clean, she tidies well in Frau Holle's house and is excellent at fluffing up her feather bed. On the other hand, the bad girl is lazy, dirty and neither can nor wants to do anything, for which she is punished.

The reaction of American students to this story is very interesting. They just could not understand what the point of it was. The first girl tells a lie, deceives the old man and is rewarded. The second is truthful and open, she is cold and says so. And she is punished. And if that is not the mysterious Russian soul, what is?

Every Russian person understands that the heroine is modest, quiet and gentle, in other words, embodies the favourite national qualities. She does not want to burden the old man with her problems and accepts her fate as it is, without grumbling and complaining. Her truth is in her patience and humility. While the stepmother's daughter is egotistical, thinks only about how cold she is, makes a lot of noise and shouts and does not deserve to be indulged.

The heroines of Russian fairy tales are wise, hardworking, loyal and modest. Sometimes they are beautiful, but more often than not this is not mentioned, since this is not of great importance. The heroines of European (French, for example) fairy tales are often beautiful. Because of their beauty, they are forgiven anything: cruelty, stupidity, emptiness or betrayal of the hero. The clever women in such tales, as a rule, personify the evil and their main desire is to deprive the heroine of her main asset, her beauty.

Russian heroines are wise, they often save the hero by getting him out of the most difficult of situations, they give him advice and do his work for him, and not infrequently they are able to work miracles.

The hero may do stupid things (burning the frog's skin) or turn betrayer (as with Finist, the bright falcon), forgetting about his love and devoting himself to another. But the heroine forgives him and keeps true to the end. At the same time, she does not get in the way and remains in the shadows. For her, love and marriage are always fated, which cannot be changed. A beautiful bird flies to a meadow, lets fall a feather and turns into a beautiful girl. The hero creeps up and steals her feather. She does not see him but asks him to show himself and says as a spell, "If you are an old man, be my father. If you are a young girl, be my sister. If you are a young man, you will be my husband." And she keeps her word, because there is no escaping destiny.

Ivan the Fool

Ivan the Fool is a frequent hero in Russian folk tales. He looks unremarkable and does what are at first glance stupid and unnecessary things, without any desire for wealth or fame, but at the end of the tale receives as a reward a beautiful princess and sometimes even half a kingdom in addition. At the same time, his older brothers, who are clever and practical, get into stupid situations. Ivan the Fool's strength (and this shows the special folk ideal) is his simplicity, his candour and his lack of a mercantile and pragmatic nature. He gives his last crust of bread to a hungry little hare, an action that is pointless from the point of view of common sense, and then in a difficult moment it is the hare who brings him an egg, which is deadly for evil Kashey. That is how charity is rewarded. Nobody takes Ivan the Fool seriously, and that is his strength. He is naïve, compassionate, impractical and of few words, so 'clever people' think he is an idiot, while for the people he is a hero.

The international subjects of folk tales give wonderful examples of the ideas prevalent in society. The subject of the ancient Roman legend of Eros and Psyche has echoes in many Russian fairy tales. The tale called *Alenky Tsvetochek* (The Scarlet Flower) is particularly close. Without question, both works have the same main basis and are undoubtedly similar despite time and space gap between them. What is interesting is the difference, the interpretation of the subjects which reflect the national characteristics of the two peoples. In the first case, the main problem for Psyche is her beauty and trustfulness, her enemies the goddess Venus and her envious sisters. At the gods' wishes, she is sent to a mysterious palace, where an invisible soul lives who instantly starts up an intimate relation with her. When, set upon by her sisters, she lights up his face while he is asleep, he turns out to be the most beautiful young man on the earth: Eros. Rescue comes from the God of Gods, Zeus, whom Eros who has fallen in love manages to convince. The basis of love here is beauty, and rescue is in the hands of the gods.

In the Russian version, the heroine gets herself into trouble by dreaming about the secret Scarlet Flower. She also finds herself in a beautiful palace, whose master (it is hard to imagine that they, like Psyche and Eros, would have ended up in one bed on the first night) is invisible to her. He talks to her, tells her interesting stories, preys on her pity, and tries to win over the girl's feelings by intelligence and decency. Only the sisters seem to be international: they are envious and evil. In the light of day, the hero turns out to be a real monster, and it is he whom the heroine loves with a tender heart. The basis of love here is fate—the idea that they are destined to be married—and the eternal principle of the Russian woman: 'he may not be that good, but he is mine'. Hence, the heroine is rescued by her devotion and steadfastness.

Bears on the Streets

Fur, caviar, *samovars* (decorated Russian tea urns) and enormous shawls have all been considered to be an integral part of Russian life for centuries. To the joy of visitors, some of them really still exist. You only have to travel a few kilometres outside Moscow to be convinced that duck-down shawls are still widely used and that there are many families in which tea is always given to the man in a tea holder. Some of the attributes of Russian life have disappeared naturally but are being cultivated in the country either for commercial reasons (since foreigners are willing to pay good money for them) or as an observance of traditions and ceremonies. Nowadays, the folk festivals (and not those for foreigners, but for themselves!) will always include a *troika* (pulled by a team of three horses) sleigh, a *samovar* with *barankas* (round cracknel) and sometimes even a bear on a chain.

The first impressions, which are often stereotypes already existing in the traveller's mind, are far from always being untrue and indeed they often contain much that is justified. The first impression, which is very sharp and real, sometimes gives a better picture of the surrounding world. What is important is the mindset with which you judge other people and their world. It is important to remember that each nation has been formed in specific historical and cultural conditions, which determine its behaviour and actions.

For example, a Russian returns from America or Great Britain and says, "Everything is great, but they are so stingy. They invited me round for a coffee and gave me a cup of coffee and a biscuit, nothing more. And at the party there was only beer with crisps and nuts." British students living in Russian families are often irritated by the persistent looking after them. There are constant attempts to feed them and on top of that, they are offended when you politely turn them down. "Well, why should I eat patties and potatoes in the morning if I prefer cereal and tea? Why do I have to justify myself all the time?" Foreign students may also be forbidden from returning home late. According to Russian traditions, children live with their parents until they get married and are subject to constant surveillance.

Of course, much of what people expect from Russia turns out to be a lie. Bears do not wander the streets and many Russians can live without a hard frost. But Russian hospitality, fur hats with earflaps, excessive confiding and openness with half-strangers live up to expectations.

OVERVIEW OF LAND AND HISTORY

'The severity of the climate, the marshlands, forests, and deserts, which make up a large part of the country, put man in a struggle against nature. What the English call comfort, and what we call *l'aisance*, is hardly to be found in Russia.'
—Madame de Stael, French writer and publicist

THE RUSSIAN REGIONS: UNITY IN DIVERSITY

Russia has thrown itself far and wide across the map of the world. One part of it lies in Europe, the other in Asia. The European part is significantly smaller in terms of size, but the Asian part has a far smaller population. Even today, having lost much of its territory, you cannot help but be impressed by its size: Russia is still the largest country in the world. The population of Russia, according to the 2002 survey, is about 150 million.

Russia is spread over 11 time zones, so as the inhabitants of Kaliningrad are just looking forward to their lunch break at 1:00 pm, many of those on Petropavlovsk-Kamchatka are already asleep. Russia also has a wide variety of climatic belts, from the Arctic tundra to the Caspian deserts. You could fill a whole library with books about the diverse geography and nature of Russia. There are endless plains, high mountains, the impassable *taiga* (swampy, coniferous forests), and the bleak steppes (large areas of flat, unforested grassland). The population is spread out very unevenly: most people are concentrated in the cities, and everybody else gravitates towards them. So it is that vast tracts of land are completely uninhabited. Throughout history, this has attracted invaders to Russia: either the Germans, who started worrying about the senseless waste of it all, and now the Chinese, who have decided to resolve their housing problems at Russia's expense (the difference between them and the Germans is that the Chinese are doing it quietly and without tanks).

Living in Isolation

The spread of the country is so wide that it is easy to get lost. At the beginning of the 1970s, Soviet society was stunned by the news that a group of hunters in the Altai had come across a family that had for decades been living completely isolated from the outside world. They knew nothing about the political changes in the country (they were still convinced that Russia was ruled by a *tsar*) or technological advance and were simply living in Russia as though on a desert island. They had been born in isolation and had never seen any other people. This discovery, though, had a sad ending. As once happened with the American Indians, the contact with modern civilisation brought with it a number of infectious diseases, which quickly put an end to these unusual recluses.

Despite this geographical and natural diversity in Russia, there is an exceptionally unified culture. You can take a plane in Saint Petersburg and fly for nine hours. Or jump on the famous Trans-Siberian train in Moscow and travel east for seven days. Or set off on a long (multi-day) car ride through the roadless Russian hinterlands. And everywhere you will meet a world that is surprisingly like the one you have already seen, the Russian world. The background will change—mountains, sea, enormous pine trees, slender silver birches—but the life of the people will be surprisingly similar, the same houses, the same standard of living, the same peculiar ways of life and traditions and, most importantly, the same people.

Try comparing a medium-sized town somewhere outside Moscow and one in Siberia, thousands of miles apart. It would be impossible to distinguish them. The shops on the main square sell exactly the same range of products, there is a similar service going on in the church opposite it, old women are sitting on the streets chewing seeds and glance up at the passers-by with identical expressions on their faces. Even the name of the square and streets around will be the same: Lenin Square if it was not renamed after Soviet times (if it was, it will be Central).

The main village shop is similar from one Russian town to another.

The cultural diversity of Russia has been preserved by some of the so-called minority peoples (minority in terms of numbers, of course) who have retained their ethnic traditions: Chukchi, the Evenk, Hakasi and others. But their way of life has been subjugated to a general Russian influence, and for the most part, the traditions which have been preserved have to do with faith or national costume.

Surprisingly, there is no particular internal conflict in Russia between north and south (as in Italy or Norway, for example) or east and west (as in Germany). Those conflicts that exist (between the towns and the villages, or the capital and the provinces) have nothing to with geography and are the same in the various regions.

All of this, of course, does not prevent different areas of the country from developing in different ways (Russia is nowadays divided into 89 regions). Each region has its own natural and climatic conditions, its natural resources, its neighbours (with whom one needs to ensure good relations) and its priorities. This is no political idyll. Many parts of Russia would happily accept independence if it was offered to them. But that does not change anything on the various levels of culture, daily life, local people, their views and

Trying to unify the country is an ancient tradition. It has much deeper roots than simply the Soviet period, to which it is often ascribed. The Soviet state simply copied it, as many other things, from the previous administration against which they had so actively fought.

relation to life and the world, traditions and habits. This unity is undeniably there.

This unity has happened quietly and naturally as Russians have settled on the land. Heading off to live in far-flung areas, they took their way of life with them and carefully guarded it, handing it on to their children. The state, as it grew stronger, supported this tradition. One obvious example is education. The state education system in Russia was laid down in the 18th century and immediately set the principle of unity as the cornerstone. The programmes, textbooks and requirements were developed into a single keystone for the whole country. Of course, specific local features were taken into account. Thus in the 19th century, the languages which were obligatory at secondary schools were as follows: French and German (in the central European regions), English (in the Archangelsk *guberniya*), Greek (in the southern *guberniyas*) and Chinese (in the Irkutsk *guberniya*). But the overall thrust was towards a unified education system.

During the Soviet period, this tradition was further strengthened. The Ministry of Education, located in Moscow, regulated the education process in all four corners of the Soviet Union with an iron hand. Foreigners were surprised and wrote ironically about the system, saying 'a pupil in the fifth class can, in the middle of the school year, move to Moscow from Novosibirsk, go to school there and not notice the change. Fifth class students there will be having the same lesson, reading the same text books, and even the subject matter will be the same'. And it was really like that. Not only was there a single programme for everybody, but it was linked to the same dates for everybody, with the same homework and examinations at the same time. It was that strict.

Over the last 15 years, the situation has changed somewhat. Freedom, and the certain amount of chaos that goes with it (for a start the Ministry is in a permanent state of reorganisation, and now it is called a Committee, now an

Agency, and of course they do not have any time to discuss questions of education), means that the unified education system in the country has weakened. Educational institutions have, in places, been given the opportunity to choose the subjects and course materials for themselves. The results are predictable: confusion and a decline in education standards. Nowadays, many teachers in regional schools miss the unified education plan, programmes and textbooks. They feel helpless, standing in front of the 21st century avalanche of information and books.

Russia's surprising unity of culture, despite its obvious geographical diversity, is the result of a centuries-old history. It has come about gradually, as Russian peoples have spread to the south, north and east, and is a particular feature of Russia as a single, unified state.

MOSCOW—THE HEART OF RUSSIA

The capital has a very specific place in Russian life, whether it was ancient Moscow or Saint Petersburg (when Peter I moved the capital there). In 1918, the newly-installed Soviet power moved the capital back to Moscow and restored its previous importance. The capital city draws the Russian people like a giant magnet. This enormous country has always lived with the vague feeling that all the very best is concentrated in the main centre. And for a large part, this really does correspond to the reality.

In Russia, there is a particularly vivid contrast between the capital cities (Moscow and Saint Petersburg) and the provinces. The centralisation of state power and economics which has taken place during Russia's history has meant that the country's main wealth, materially, culturally and spiritually, has been concentrated in the capitals. Most important was that the main cities were not only materially better off, but that the general educational and cultural level of society was also higher. The state has always tried to smooth over these differences by creating theatres (and good ones at that), setting aside funds for the development of universities and libraries and creating museums in all the far-flung corners of the country.

View of Moscow from Sparrow Hills.

But the problem has nevertheless remained. Above all, people still consider that all that is best in Russia is located in the capitals. It has always been a cherished dream of all Russians to live in Moscow. Children moaned to their parents about it and it was a sign of the summit of a career and the height of success. Over the last few years, Europe and America have become the 'promised land', but for many, Moscow still remains the preferred land. There is now a certain amount of ill feeling in Russia, a widespread impression that Moscow is pumping money from the whole country and is living a rich and successful life while the rest of the country is in poverty. This is not entirely justified. The difference between rich and poor can be seen all over the country, and Moscow is no exception.

It is well known that all capitals are more cosmopolitan than the provinces, where you can feel more of the national roots and traditions. This is characteristic not only of Russia, but throughout the world. Furthermore, Moscow has sucked in the main characteristics of national life and its life reflects all the specific features of the Russian world. Not without reason did N M Karamzin, the famous Russian historian and writer at the end of the 18th century, write that he who has seen Moscow has seen Russia.

Thus, welcome to Moscow, the ex-capital of the Soviet Union, the present-day capital of the mysterious CIS (Commonwealth of Independent States). Moscow has been called 'the heart of Russia', and it is true and fair. Indeed, Moscow is that vitally important part of the body without which the normal functioning of the organism is impossible. It is here that the 'mysterious soul' of Russia is hidden.

The city has been planned and built in a 'rings-and-radii' way. Moscow has been growing like a tree, adding rings from century to century. The rings were crossed with transversal streets. The city still has Boulevard Ring, Garden Ring and Moscow Ring-road. An American traveller to Russia noticed that Moscow looks like a whimsical web from the air.

Moscow has always been divided into evident social areas. In the 19th century, some districts were meant for nobility, some for merchants, some for students, etc. Nowadays, it is divided into 'prestigious', 'non-prestigious' and 'sleeping' areas.

The 'prestigious' and, consequently, most expensive districts are located first and foremost in the centre, as well as in the south-west and the west of the city (for example, Leninsky prospect, Kutuzovsky prospect, Krylatskoye). Over the last few years, the amount of so-called elite real estate has markedly increased. Expensive, beautiful buildings with expansive flats are popping up one after the other with incredible speed. Even more surprising is the fact that they are quickly snapped up. Russia is still trying to get to Moscow, and any Russian who has managed to earn a more or less tidy sum wants to own property in the capital.

In stark contrast to this luxurious and expansive flats are the so-called *communalkas* (or communal flats), some of which still exist. There were significant numbers of them after the 1917 revolution and also after the Second World War. Several families were housed in one large apartment, each family having its own room. The kitchen, corridor, bathroom and toilet were all shared. The number of rooms (and people living in them) was sometimes very large.

Living in such conditions was not easy. Large queues for the communal areas in the morning, arguments in the kitchen and neighbours always keeping an eye on you were

all a characteristic part of communal living. One room frequently housed a number of generations, parents with grown children, grandparents, as well as other relatives who had come to stay. And it hardly needs to be said that any sort of private life under such conditions was very difficult indeed. But people survived, and having escaped the nightmare remembered the good old days with nostalgia, because as well as the arguments and obvious difficulties, there was friendship, people helping each other out and special neighbourly relations.

Even not so long ago, *communalkas* were still fairly widespread in Moscow. Some are still in use today, although they are slowly but surely becoming a thing of the past.

Under Nikita Khrushchev, there was a large-scale plan to try and solve the housing problem and phase out the *communalkas* during the 1960s. Areas grew up in Moscow which were called *kruschoby* (a Russian play on words, combining *tryschoby* (slums) and the surname Khrushchev). The most famous of these is Cheryomushky. They were put up extremely quickly and intended for those who had a particularly acute need of accommodation. These five-storey buildings have now become the symbol of the squalor and inhumanity of such living conditions. Tiny little kitchens, no corridors and with paper-thin walls, which means you could hear everything that is going on in the neighbouring flat.

But at that time, to have your own, albeit small, flat was a great joy. Having suffered through the difficult post-war years, people moved from the *communalkas* into these tiny living spaces and felt as though they were rich. The kitchen was small, but it was theirs; the toilet was tiny, but it was not shared with neighbours. Nowadays, these areas which used to be on the outskirts of Moscow are not far from the centre of the ever-expanding capital. The old *khruschoby* are being demolished and large modern blocks built in their place. Some of the new flats are inhabited by those who had been living there previously; the rest are put up for sale.

In addition, Moscow also has what are called the 'sleeping districts'. This is the name for the places where accommodation is built on a mass scale. They all look the same as each other, have a relatively spread out infrastructure, more often that not quite poor ecological conditions and are overcrowded. The standardised concrete houses, built in the 1970s–1980s, were far from being the jewel in the city's crown. As similar as two peas in a pod, they did, however, go some way to solving the housing problem in the ever-expanding city.

Fate and Russian Housing

There is an old Russian film, which is still very popular, called *The Irony of Fate*. In it, the hero, a Muscovite, having gone out for a drink with his friends on New Year's Eve ends up in Saint Petersburg. In his drunken state and not realising where he is, he climbs into a taxi and gives his home address. Having arrived, he opens the door with his own key, sees his own furniture, and goes to bed, supposing that he is in his Moscow flat. To his good fortune, the owner of the Saint Petersburg flat is a young, beautiful and single woman, so the end of the film turns into a real New Year's fairy tale. But the film is also a biting comedy about the tendency in Russia to build towns to a standardised plan.

Similar standardised and ugly buildings can be found throughout the country, and strengthen the impression that the country is a unified whole. They were built to the same blueprint in all (more or less) large towns.

The housing problem remains permanent in Moscow. The population is growing year on year, and there is a catastrophic lack of accommodation. And one of the the downside is that people want to have the new and expensive blocks as close to the centre as possible, which has a detrimental effect on the look of the city.

More about Moscow

Moscow is situated in latitude 55044' N (roughly the same as Copenhagen and Glasgow) and longitude 380 E at an average altitude of 130 m (400 ft), on the river Moskva in the European part of Russia.

It is in the temperate continental climatic zone; the average temperatures in January are -10–3˚C, in May 7–11˚C, in July 8–17˚C. The average annual temperature in the capital is 4–5˚C, which is 4˚C below the average annual temperature in Glasgow, while the annual amount of precipitation in Moscow is 640–670 mm (in Glasgow it is three times as much).

Moscow is the largest city in Russia. The Moscow Ring-road, the latest of Moscow rings, built in 1960 is 109 km (68 miles) long. It encircles the territory of 900 sq km (347 sq miles). Since then, the territory of the city has been growing, and more than 200 sq km have been added up to now.

By the official statistics, the population of the city is about 9.5 million people. This figure, however, is rather relative. Moscow has always attracted Russians. Some part of the population has been drawn by culture and education. At the time of shortages, Moscow was best provided with goods. And at all times, the level of life and living conditions in Moscow have been far better than in provincial cities and towns.

However, seeking refuge in Moscow has been done at some enormous, almost catastrophic scale since the time of severe international conflicts in former republics and various regions of Russia. The international spirit of Moscow has made it the most attractive place for refugees. Some bolder experts claim that the real population of Moscow is twice as many as the official data; more moderate ones talk about

1 million extra people who are not officially registered. All this results in an ever-growing problem of overpopulation, a shortage of accommodation, an abundance of labour force, difficulties with supplies, etc.

In addition to all that, representatives of different nationalities—especially those exiled by force, alien, and those without any means—are often responsible for the growth of the criminal wave in Moscow, which used to be one of the safest world capitals.

By the official statistics, 90 per cent of the Moscow population are Russians, followed by Ukrainians, Jews and Tartars. However, the data is relative too, if one takes into account not only the number of unregistered people inhabiting Moscow, but also numerous international marriages so habitual of the Soviet times.

A 'typical' Muscovite can have a Ukrainian grandmother and a Jewish grandfather, and the proverb 'scratch a Russian and you'll find a Tartar' is well known far beyond Russia.

Furthermore, the overwhelming majority of Muscovites speak Russian as their first language. It is the mother tongue of the Muscovite Armenians, the Muscovite Georgians and the Muscovite Tartars. Those who have chosen Moscow as a place to live are also Russian in the way they live and in their cultural traditions. Until recently, those coming to the capital have willingly given themselves over to its rhythm, partly keeping their national traditions such as their eating habits and their favourite national dishes.

Nowadays, there are some changes. The population changes have become so noticeable, and ethnic conflicts have become so acute throughout the country as a whole, that it is now possible to talk about the development of specific, closed communities in Moscow, such as the Chechens, the Uzbeks, the Azeris and others. But this process is only just beginning, so it is difficult to predict how it will turn out in the future.

SAINT PETERSBURG

If Moscow is called the heart of Russia, then Saint Petersburg is its head. Second in size only to Moscow, this city is still called the second capital of Russia (and it actually was the capital from 1712 to 1918). The rivalry between the two cities is still going on after some three hundred years. Moscow (which was founded in 1147) has always been considered to be a traditional, patriarchal city, which conserves the national way of life and traditions. Even though it lost the status of capital for two hundred years, it nevertheless remained the religious and cultural centre of Russia.

Saint Petersburg was founded by Peter I as a distinctive symbol of the new life. It was built by foreign builders in the European style and has always been considered to be the intellectual centre, slightly cold and 'high society', but better educated and more civilised than the bread and salt (gifts traditionally offered to arriving guests) hospitality of Moscow. Saint Petersburg was an imperial city from the moment it was founded, a concentration of state and political power. And this was one of the reasons why the Bolsheviks decided to move the capital back to Moscow in 1918, to a city which did not have so many close ideological ties with the overthrown imperial house.

The city on the Neva has changed its name on a number of occasions. Peter I gave it the name of Saint Peter, his heavenly protector, and it was called Saint Petersburg in the German manner which was fashionable at the time. During the First World War, the last Russian Emperor Nikolai II renamed it Petrograd in the Russian style, as a result of rising anti-German feelings within society. After the death of Vladimir Ilyich Lenin, the leader of the Soviet state, in 1924, the city received a new name: Leningrad.

With the beginning of *perestroika*, the question of what to call the city came to the fore again. Renaming the city was a painful and expensive process. A survey carried out at the end of the 1980s showed that the population was roughly divided in half. Some voted to return to the old name, believing that a city of such glorious historical traditions should regain its old name, Saint Petersburg, which in addition had no links with the years of Soviet power. Others pointed out that under the new name, Leningrad had gone through a glorious and heroic period and so returning to

This sign in Saint Petersburg has been kept on a wall since the Second World War times. It reminds people of the siege of Leningrad and it says: 'This part of the street is especially dangerous during shelling.'

the past was pointless and even insulting to the memories of several generations of Leningraders. In particular, they referred to the events of the war years, to the siege and fortification of Leningrad which cost hundreds of thousands of lives. Nevertheless in 1991, the city was given back its original historical name, and nowadays it is once again the city of Saint Peter: Saint Petersburg. Most people call it 'Peter' for short.

The district still keeps the name 'Leningradskii', thus on the one hand illustrating the contradictions between the capital and the province in Russia, and on the other the inclination to compromise, inherent to modern Russian politics.

Saint Petersburg is now in fashion. Vladimir Vladimirovich Putin, president of the Russian Federation, was born and brought up there, and many of

Saint Petersburg is home to an enormous number of Russia's artistic treasures. Over a long period of time, the best works of art have been collected here, beautiful and ornate houses have been built, and wonderful theatres and fantastic museums have been opened. It is no surprise that the number of tourists visiting Saint Petersburg is growing year on year. And it is not only popular amongst foreigners. Russians come too, flooding to it in order to get a feeling for the history and culture of the country.

his Kremlin companions also come from there. Grandiose festivals, extra funding and a large number of official state functions have all graced the city and enhanced its reputation over the last few years. The age-old rivalry with Moscow is still alive, although it does not stop them living peacefully side by side.

THE RUSSIAN VILLAGE

For a long time, Russia was an overwhelmingly village-orientated country. Census of 1897 shows that less than 15 per cent of the population lived in towns. And these town dwellers were, for the most part, people who had recently come from the villages and who had arrived in the towns after the emancipation reforms of 1861. Nowadays it has become fashionable in Russia to search out one's noble roots, but it is important to remember that the vast majority of modern Russians have a peasant background, and that it is precisely the village life, with its traditions and mentality, that lie at the heart of the modern Russian character.

It is interesting that despite this, very little is known about the life of the Russian peasants. Russian literature, which is famous the world over, is mainly written by the nobles about life of the Russian nobility, and the diaries and memoirs which have survived also belong to that circle. The realist writers who were interested in village life mainly paid attention to its shortcomings. Historians of the soviet period wrote about the 'dark, forgotten and ignorant' peasants, in order to illustrate more clearly the changes in their lives after the revolution. Modern textbooks describe the acts and lives of famous historical figures. The real day-to-day life of the Russian peasants, their thoughts and feelings, are almost unknown.

According to old traditions, the sources of all the achievements of Russian culture can be found in folk art. The great composers derived motifs from its melodies, writers the themes and language for their works, and painters found their colours and choreographers their movements and fluidity of shapes. But the common people—the creator of that artistic initial source for the talent of Russia, the people who were praised in the 19th century and for whom many were killed in the 20th century, and for whom reforms were pushed through and revolutions carried out—still remain one of Russia's enigmas.

The little which is known shows that the life of the Russian peasant was not dark nor ignorant nor dismal. Villages have lived by their own unwritten laws since ancient times. The basis of this life was the land and agricultural work. They were protected by communal relations, which we shall talk about in Chapter Three. The ancient historical traditions were the basis of the peasant's existence.

There were a number of crucial moments in the life of the Russian village. The first was during the time of the great *tsar*-reformer Peter I, who made fundamental changes to the system and way of life of the Russian nobility. From that moment on, there was a gap between the Russia of the cities, courts, state apparatus and traders on the one hand and the villages and peasants on the other, which grew ever wider with the years. Until that time, almost everybody in the country had the same way of life and customs, and the only significance was in the amount of wealth. Some peoples' clothes and utensils were richer than others, but they were the same in form, everybody had the same festivals and traditions, there were similar relations within families, and so on. After Peter's reforms, the nobility went one way, increasingly towards the European style, although with a Russian flavour to it, while the peasants retained the old Russian traditions and customs.

Another turning point was the abolition of serfdom in 1861. From that time on, Russian villages slowly went into decline and cities began to grow. Having been freed, the peasants were able to go to the towns and streamed there to work in the large number of new factories and plants that were opening. Peasant families shrank, grown children made their own houses and lived and worked separately. Peasant land holdings grew smaller. Discord and worries and uncertainty about the future of both themselves and their children disturbed the peasants. All this finally led to a fall in agricultural production and the collapse of villages.

The first task of the Soviet government was the industrial development of the country. The flow of people to the cities took on a previously unseen scale. This was helped by the new government policy towards villages: wholesale collectivisation, resettlement and sometimes the liquidation of the prosperous peasants. Cities grew and developed, a new, more comfortable and active life started in them while the villages continued to live out their own century with its old foundations, which were poorly adapted to the new times. The young people left for the cities and the villages aged, in the literal and figurative senses. *Perestroika* finally 'finished off' the Russian village, which was already practically without the means to survive and hopelessly out of touch with modern life. Figures from 2001 showed that more than 73 per cent of Russians are now in urban populations.

The way of living in contemporary Russian villages still retains much of the country's historical past. In some instances, cultural traditions for example, the fact that these foundations of the nation have been saved is a good thing. But Russian villages, particularly in terms of everyday living, are out of date, and so much so that they are pushing the younger generation away in search of a more modern and comfortable life.

Russia is an enormous country. Many of the villages and communities which have lasted all these years have become forgotten in its vastness. In most of them, water is brought from the well, as it always was, homes are heated by log-burning fires and food is prepared on a log-burning stove, where water is also warmed for washing (for both people and clothes). Washing machines, dishwashers, microwave ovens and other technological advances, which are supposed to make life easier, are practically inaccessible in Russian villages. The unheated toilet is outside, which is particularly unpleasant in the winter. The shop, if there is one, sells only the essentials.

There are no cultural events. In Soviet times, there were attempts to support villages. Clubs and cinemas were opened, but today, without government support, they are all but empty. There is practically no way to earn a living under the new conditions of the market economy, and so many simply live off what they can grow: potatoes, onion and cabbage. Is it any surprise that young people from the villages (and not just the young) are desperate to get out at any price?

However, the desire to lead a simple village life in harmony with nature is still alive in the Russian people. More than that, it is growing noticeably, as people get fed up with city life. In 100 years, Russia turned from being a village-based country to a city-dwelling one, but the people still retain, albeit subconsciously, a memory of life among the forests, fields and rivers. Ask the city-dwellers if they would like to move to a village. Most of them would answer categorically 'No'. But there are increasing complaints about being tired of city life and a nostalgia for fresh air and boundless space.

And people are still drawn to the land. In the 1980s, as part of a programme to solve the food supply problem that had arisen, there was a widescale giveaway of land parcels to Russians. The principle was simple: feed yourselves. The result surprised many people. Russians snapped up these small land parcels of between 4 and 6 *sotkas* (A *sotka* is equivalent to 100 sq m), built small and primitive cottages on them (they did not have the money to construct anything grander) and, with great enthusiasm, set about tending the land in their spare time. Professors, teachers, doctors, people who professionally had no connection with the land, brought forth miracles from their plots. They grew stunning tomatoes, exotic southern plants and simple northern plants. This love of the land, which was at one point ascribed to Russian peasants, had suddenly and unexpectedly burst forth in their urban offspring.

We should also note that many village traditions have infiltrated urban life. Old habits claim their own and many Russians live in the city by the same rules as those in the villages, trying to retain the specific features of village life. Many know nothing outside their own area, and rarely leave it.

It is no accident that the Moscow courtyard, so feted in songs, films and literature, is in many ways an imitation of the patriarchal village life: everybody

One female villager who lived in a Moscow *communalka* kept rabbits in her room. When her neighbours complained, she answered that they reminded her of her home village, and on top of that, with typical village practicality, planned how each of them would be eaten and then sewed into fur hats. Village life, which is disappearing in its natural surroundings, is alive in Russian cities.

knows each other, they are always ready to help and to share their joys and sorrows. Nowadays people are being crowded into large elite blocks of flats, which may well be more beautiful and more convenient, but the old Moscow courtyard is remembered with nostalgia and longing.

Travelling about Russia outside the towns is very difficult. There are none of the usual conveniences and comforts. Often there are not even roads and you have to walk. But those who have set themselves the task of understanding the mysterious Russian soul will be unable to do so until they have visited Russian villages.

THE PECULIARITIES OF THE RUSSIAN STATE

The Russian state is usually considered to have been founded in 862. It is this date which has come down to us in the *Russian Primary Chronicles* (called *Tale of Bygone Years*), dating from the early 12th century and which contains many ancient tales and legends dating from much earlier. It tells that once upon a time, the Slav tribes gathered together and decided to 'seek a prince who may rule over us, and judge us according to custom'. They set off to the Varangians (as the Norman-Viking warriors were called in ancient Rus) and said to them "Our land is great and rich, but there is no order in it. Come reign as princes, rule over us." So it was that Rurik came to Novgorod with members of his armed force. His successor Oleg later captured Kiev and made it the capital of Rus.

This legend has given birth to many arguments, which have still not died down. In the 18th century, German historians working at the Russian Academy of Science first drew attention to this episode. They created a theory, confirming it with the legend in the chronicles, about the supposed lack of independence of the Slav peoples who needed a strong (and preferably German) hand which would bring them into order. At that time, there were a lot of representatives of the renowned German race and this theory was right in line with the political situation. It was called the 'Norman' theory.

However, indignant voices were raised in protest. One of the first passionate opponents of the Norman theory was the

great Russian scientist and founder of Moscow University, M V Lomonosov. Those who wanted to show the originality of the Russian state presented a number of arguments: that it was a fake which was of a later date, that Rurik was a Slav, and some even contended that he was not a person but a war booty. Contemporary researchers found a politically correct way round the question, stressing that even if there was a Rurik, he did not really have much to do with the creation of the Russian state.

Whatever the truth of the matter, the legend exists and has a right to exist. Regardless of whether it is true or not (although at that time it was quite common to find Norman warriors ruling foreign states—one only has to remember that a while later William the Conqueror captured England, and nobody is accusing the English of lacking political independence), the legend reflects certain concepts and views of the Russian people. And from that point of view, it is more important than the historical reality.

By analysing the legend, we can come to a number of important conclusions about the character of the Russian state. Firstly, it shows that the ruler of Rus was taken to be the person who managed to create order out of disorder. Secondly, it underlines the fact that he was chosen by the people, and not just by some of them, but by all, in other words he represents everybody's interests. And finally, it emphasises the enormous role that the state leader plays in Russian life.

These ideas have been developed over the ages. In the general consciousness, the leader and the state are inseparable concepts. It is no accident that in most books about Russian history, the different eras are determined by the years for which one or another leader was in charge. And it is really not important what he was called: Great Prince, *Tsar*, Emperor, General Secretary, President…

There are a number of particular features which have determined the course taken by the history of the Russian state. Succession or continuity undoubtedly has a great place in the Russian world. It is no accident that all chronicles started with the Biblical story and gradually brought it up to the time of the chronicle writer. In Rus, the year was—for a long time—counted from the creation of the world, and only at the beginning of the 18th century did they change over to counting from the birth of Christ.

Continuity gained particular importance during the period when the centralised state was being created. In the mid-12th century, the ancient Russian state, with its capital in Kiev, started to break down into independent principalities (although Kiev formally retained its title as the capital of all Rus) which were forever at war with one another. The situation was further aggravated by the Mongol invasion of Rus. The process of unifying the Russian lands was slow, painful and accompanied by the struggle against foreign invaders.

Then, completely unexpectedly, the young Muscovite principality took on the initiative to join the Russian lands. Three Ivans played decisive roles, and each of them made good use of the idea of the succession of state power. Ivan I (approximately 1283–1340), called Kalita (means 'money bag' in old Russian) and who ruled in the first half of the 14th century, was a careful and cunning leader. He was able not only to subjugate the other principalities to his power, but also to gain the favour of the Mongol khan, who allowed him to collect dues from the population himself. This meant that the Muscovite principality became rich, and with the money collected, he purchased lands from his neighbours. He also convinced the metropolitan (then the head of the Russian Orthodox Church) to come from Vladimir to Moscow, thereby making Moscow the spiritual centre. And it was under Ivan Kalita that they started to build the oak walls around the Kremlin and the first stone cathedrals in the Kremlin: the Assumption Cathedral and the Archangel Cathedral (Uspenskiy and Arkhangelskiy *sobor*).

Ivan III (1440–1505) was a great state figure, a wise politician and a diplomat. And it was under him that Rus finally rid itself of the Golden Horde. He had already named himself the 'Great Prince of Muscovy and of All Russia', and was referred to in a number of documents as the Sovereign and the Tsar. During his reign, the main lands were unified, including the freedom-loving Novgorod, and a new name for the country appeared: Russia. The process was called 'gathering of the Russian lands'.

For Ivan III, who was trying to strengthen state power, it was extremely important to show the connection with the state traditions which had gone before, and to make reference to the historical basis. Moscow was referred to as the 'Third Rome'. Both Rome and Constantinople had fallen because they had deviated from the true faith. Moscow was designated as their successor and the main centre of Orthodoxy (according to Russian tradition, 'there cannot be fourth', as God loves trinities). The Muscovy princes claimed to be none other than the descendants of the brother of the Roman emperor Augustus.

Ivan's second wife was Sophia Paleologue, the niece of the last Byzantine emperor. Constantinople had already fallen in 1453 and the Muscovy prince thereby considered himself to be the successor to the Byzantine tradition. In order to strengthen his power, many ceremonies and traditions were borrowed from the Byzantine court—which on the one hand underlined the succession of Muscovy, and on the other were very attractive to Russian people, with their magnificence and beauty. From Rome and Byzantine, the two great empires of the past, Russia borrowed the symbol of state (the double-headed eagle, which became the coat of arms of the Russian state), Monomakh's hat (*tsars'* crown) and more. Ivan continued to build up the Kremlin. He enclosed it in massive brick walls, rebuilt the Assumption Cathedral, tore down and rebuilt the Archangel Cathedral, and erected the Annunciation Cathedral (Blagoveshchenskiy *sobor*). Italian craftsmen were invited to work on the construction, which also helped to strengthen the idea of a connection between Russia and the West.

Finally there was Ivan IV (1530–1584), who was called Grozny (the traditional translation into English, Ivan the Terrible, completely fails to capture the Russian meaning of the name, which is much more to do with respect and esteem than terror) and who became the head of a united, centralised state. He was crowned head of the kingdom, secured the title of *tsar* once and for all, and continued to strengthen his power. Towards the end of his reign, Siberia started to be conquered, taking Russia out towards new shores.

The importance of succession and tradition in state power is also underlined by the fact that throughout the entire time that there has been a monarchy in Russia (more than 1,000 years), there have only been two ruling dynasties, the Rurikovichs and the Romanovs (and they were closely tied). Compare that to the European monarchies!

The question of legality was also very important when it came to supporting state power. The people had a clear idea about who was the rightful leader and who was an imposter. Often, it went against official legislation. The leader had to be a direct descendant, crowned in church as *tsar* and related to the ruling dynasty. Any violation of this rule inevitably produced discord and legends about rightful rulers being miraculously saved.

No less important than ridding themselves of the aggressors was the question of quickly restoring the rightful state power. How was that to be done? There was only one solution, and it recalls the period of the beginning of the Russian state. They had to start all over again and 'call', as they once had, a new ruler. In 1613, Zemski Sobor (first Russian parliament introduced in 1549 which may be translated as the 'Assembly of the Land'), which represented all the different levels of society, gathered and chose a new sovereign: Mikhail Feodorovich Romanov. The new ruler was only 16 years old and had none of the experience or skills of Boris Godunov, but he had been recognised as the rightful *tsar*, had blood links with the former dynasty and was selected by the whole nation.

The Time of Troubles

The most famous example from Russian history is the Time of Troubles. Ivan the Terrible, who married seven times, had five sons and three daughters. Only three of his sons survived infancy: Ivan, Fyodor and Dmitry. The eldest son, Ivan, died from wounds inflicted by his own father in a fit of rage. Dmitry died in unexplained circumstances (according to the official story, he ran onto a knife that he was playing with in the courtyard). Fyodor ruled until his death in 1598, but had no heirs. Thus, the direct line of inheritance was broken.

Boris Godunov, the brother of Fyodor Ioannovich's wife, came to power. A wily politician and far-sighted state figure, he tried with all his might to consolidate his power but was never accepted by the people, who were suspicious of the rightfulness of his claim to power. During his reign, Grigory Otrepyev appeared, a pretender claiming to be Tsarevich Dmitry, who had been miraculously saved—the rightful ruler of Russia. Despite the absurdity of this claim, he was accepted by many and False Dmitry (as he has become known in history) came to Moscow and was crowned *tsar*. Then there came False Dmitry II, and Russia was invaded by foreign aggressors, including the Poles and the Swedes. Having reached its apogee under the last Muscovite rulers, under the imposters the Russian land collapsed and fell into neglect. In a word, troubles in their full sense.

Many such examples can be found throughout Russian history. The Russian Empress Catherine the Great came to power under suspicious circumstances, and nobody doubts that she played a role in the assassination of her husband. She did much that was good for Russia, but throughout her life she was plagued by pretenders, both male and female.

Even the famous rebel Pugachev, who led an uprising in 1773, claimed to be Catherine's husband Peter III, who had been saved from death.

In 1825, again in mysterious circumstance, the Russian Emperor Alexander I suddenly died. His direct inheritor should have been his brother Constantine, who had refused the throne even before Alexander's death. He preferred family happiness with a commoner wife to the burden of the Russian throne. Power passed to the next brother, Nikolai. But the rightful order had been broken and not long afterwards, legends started appearing amongst the people about a wise old man living in far off Siberia. Supposedly Emperor Alexander had not died, but had decided to retire from the vanity of life and be a hermit. So, legends and discord have surrounded any violation of the legal (from the people's point of view) claim to the throne.

Any state power is supported by ideas. For Russia, the spiritual basis over many centuries have been the Russian Orthodox Church. Faith supported the special position and power of the Sovereign in Russia. Under Ivan III, the ceremony of anointing according to the Byzantine style was introduced (for Ivan's grandson). From the time of Ivan the Terrible onwards, it was a compulsory part of the ceremony when a new Sovereign came to power. Each new ruler of the Russian state had to go through this church ceremony. It was the day when he officially came to power, and that day was declared the main secular all-Russia festival in the country.

There was a profound idea behind this. The *tsar* became God's appointed sovereign and state service was considered to be a type of religious deed of penance. Consecrating state power in the church not only consolidated power in the eyes of the people, it also conferred a certain responsibility on the Russian *tsar*. In addition, it determined the special status of the Russian ruler. Historically in the East, the sovereign was worshipped; he was God, who could do anything. In the West, the king was, above all, a person, a politician and a state figure. In Russia, he was in the middle—a person whose power had been sanctified from above, which confers on him special demands and responsibilities. His power was, from the outset, limited by a more powerful force. But at the same time, that put him in a special situation: a revolt against the *tsar* is a revolt against God himself.

'MASTER OF THE RUSSIAN LAND'

During the first all-Russian census taken in 1897, Emperor Nikolai II, in answer to the question about his occupation, wrote 'Master of the Russian Land'. This phrase, more than any other, reflects the role that the ruler played in the life of the Russian state.

The Russian people have always had an ideal of a strong and fair ruler. Soviet historians referred to this phenomenon with the ironic phrase 'faith in the good *tsar*'. However, faith in a higher form of justice really is an important part of the Russian character. The ruler is always right. If something is not going right in the state, that means that those surrounding the ruler are wrong, they are impeding him, hiding the truth from him and harming the people. This entourage has been different at different times: *boyars* (members of the aristocracy), nobility, civil servants, bureaucrats; but from the people's point of view, it is they who are guilty of all the ills in the state. And it is from this that is born the desire to go straight to the top, to knock until they are heard on the ruler's door in their search for the truth, to open his eyes so that he punishes the guilty.

There are many examples of this. The emancipation reform of 1861 was not understood by most of the serfs. They were given personal freedom, but were ordered to redeem the land on which they had been working since time immemorial. The serfs could only come to one conclusion: the emperor's real manifesto had been switched by some evil-doing civil servants, and the sovereign had to be warned. Another time, the Stalin repressions. There is a huge archive of letters to Stalin in

The relationship between the ruler and the people, in its ideal form, is like that in a family. A father can be strict, but he is fair; he punishes but he loves and protects his family. This is reflected in the language: 'father-*tsar*' and 'our father' were what the people called the *tsar*, and they referred to themselves as 'we, the sovereign's children'. And this is why they strive for a strong leader who is, in the people's understanding, the same thing as a strong state.

which people who were suffering under the repressions tried to inform the leader about the evil deeds which were going on behind his back. And they believed, as did the serfs, that he would sort everything out and restore justice.

People often see in this evidence of some sort of slave mentality in the Russian nation, which is pleased when it is ruled by a strong leader. But if you look at the specific features of Russian history and geography, you can find many reasons why this ideal has taken a hold in Russia. One of them is the size of the country. In order to keep it together as a single whole, you need a strong, centralised power, otherwise chaos inevitably ensues and the country falls apart. An unstable economy and the difficulties of agriculture (in some regions there is drought, in others frost, and some areas have poor soil and others marshes) mean that regions are dependent upon each other. In order to control a single economy and to re-distribute, integrate and interfere in regional policies on the basis of the general good, a strong centre is required. Also, Russia has for many years been a multi-cultural country, and under such circumstances, you need a middleman, a peacekeeper who can stand over everyone and enact a single state policy with regard to such questions. And finally, Russia, in between the West and the East, has always been exposed to invasion. For many centuries, war was an integral part of Russian history. From this comes the ideal of a *tsar* as a warrior, protecting his people and his homeland. There are lots of reasons, but the output of the matter is simple: a weak central power in Russia will inevitably lead to chaos and breakdown in the country.

Based on this, it is easy to understand many of the 'mysteries' of Russian history and the current problems. Take, for example, Ivan the Terrible. For modern readers, he is a symbol of tyranny and violence. The well-known executions that were carried out during his reign, the persecution of those who did not agree with him and the suppression of the unruly. But in folk songs and legends, he is presented as a ruler beloved by his people. Whom did he persecute? The rich, the *boyars*, those who oppressed the people. He strengthened the state and marked his rule with military victories. This was also important for the people.

Elections have never held great interest for the Russian people. Firstly, people in Russians do not like choices. When a flood of various products poured into the country as the market economy developed and shop shelves were filled with all sorts of brands, many people complained that they were not happy. Why did they need so many different types of cheese, smoked sausage and toothpaste? How could you choose from the multitude? And if you make a mistake in doing so? Many were even nostalgic about the former times, when purchasing a pair of shoes or a good cut of meat (with difficulty, through acquaintances, or after standing in a long line) made a person happy, revived the ancient feelings of the hunter feeding himself and his family.

There are similar feelings towards political elections. It is one thing when there is an urgent need, as during the Time of Troubles in 1613, when the rightful dynasty was broken. Or when elections are simply a festival of strong power, as they were during Soviet times, when elections were for one party only and were accompanied by celebrations

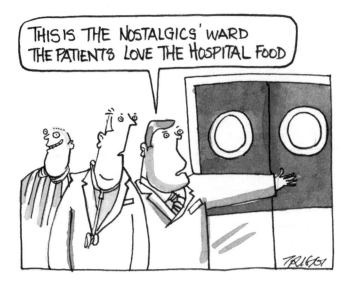

and festivities and the sale of deficit, unfindable items in the stalls at the voting booths. Following the arguments and debates of political candidates (and then having to choose one of them!) arouses no interest at all in Russia. On top of that, there is very little faith in the elections. Popular opinion is that 'they will nevertheless choose who they need, without our help'.

The fact that Russia wants a single and strong power does not mean that that power is total. For example, Henry VIII of England single-handedly introduced a new church which completely changed the spiritual life of the country. In Russia, there was a tiny attempt to reform the existing church in the 17th century and that led to a split which exists up to the present day. The so-called Old Believers still do not accept the changes. A strong central powering Russia has always combined with self-governance, from varying types of democratic structure: the Boyar Duma, the peasant commune, the *zemstvo* (the elective district council) and so on.

Soverign Rights

Serving the sovereign and serving the state has always been one and the same for the Russians, and love of the ruler has been a show of patriotism. Not so long ago, a taxi driver, someone who is not at all familiar with historical and political niceties, when talking about the last Russian Emperor Nikolai II exclaimed, "He did not have the right to abdicate!" So it was that almost one hundred years after the event, a man who had grown up in a completely different era considered the *tsar's* decision to be a betrayal, that he had not behaved according to the responsibilities that had been invested in him by fate, history and God.

Ideals are surprisingly alive. The Soviet period kept many of the ideals from the former times that it had discarded, although it was entirely different. In particular, the faith in a strong leader. Everything had changed—the ideology, the form of government, the ruler—but the feelings remained. The people are still waiting for their hero. Only a ruler who does not compromise, who is strong and decisive will gain the respect of the people.

THE BAPTISM OF RUSSIA

The *Russian Primary Chronicles* have preserved a wonderful legend about how Russia was baptised in 988. Of course, the choice of a faith was determined by a number of factors, including economic, political and international. But the author of the chronicle, a monk and a man of faith, wrote that the ruler at the time, Prince Vladimir, chose a religion for Russia based on some extremely important principles.

According to the story, representatives from various religions came to see him and tried to convince him that their religion was the right one. Vladimir liked the Muslim representative, because he said that you could have a number of wives (Vladimir was famous for his love for women). But he did not like the other rites at all, particularly the ban on drinking wine. If you believe the legend, the prince uttered a phrase which has since become famous: "Drinking is the joy of Russia. We cannot exist without that pleasure." He told the representatives from Rome that since their faith had not previously been accepted in Rus ("our fathers did not accept it"), it was not needed now either. And Vladimir finally turned down the Jews with the words, "How do you want to teach others while you yourselves have been rejected by God and are scattered all over the place? If God loved you and the Law was yours, you would not be scattered across foreign lands. Or do you want the same to happen to us?"

He listened to the Greeks attentively, but nevertheless had his doubts and decided to settle the question democratically, by calling the *boyars*. They decided that they themselves needed to take a look before deciding. And they went out to various areas, before gathering together again to talk about what they had seen in other lands. The *boyars* did not like Islam because of the lack of joy and kind-heartedness in the services. The Catholic Church was not beautiful enough. But what most astounded them was the Greek service. This is what one of the *boyars* said to Prince Vladimir, "We knew not whether we were in heaven or on earth, for surely there is no such splendour or beauty anywhere upon earth. We cannot describe it to you: only this we know, that God dwells there among men, and that their worship

A Russian Orthodox church.

surpasses the worship of all other places. For we cannot forget that beauty."

So it was that a number of factors played a deciding role in the choice of a religion for Russia. The most important was beauty. And nowadays, services in Russian Orthodox churches are very beautiful. They are a sort of theatrical performance, taking the 'spectator' off into another beautiful, higher world, even if only for the length of the service. Everything in the service is important: the external factors, such as the icons, the beautiful trappings, the sumptuous robes of the priests, the songs and even the smells. Furthermore, those who pray in church are not simply spectators; they are participants in the whole great secret which takes place. You cannot sit down, you cannot relax, you cannot daydream and not for a single second can you switch off from what is going on.

It is also interesting to note the role of the head of state. It is he, according to the legend, who determined which faith his people would take. Baptism did not come up against any noticeable protest from the people. The Orthodox Church was accepted in Rus relatively peacefully, and in 988, it became the state religion.

THE ROLE OF RELIGION IN RUSSIAN LIFE

The Russian people have traditionally been seen as very religious. Religion made its way into various areas of Russian life: the state, family life and public affairs. Nothing of any importance was started without first saying a prayer. Foreign travellers in the 19th century were amazed by the abundance of crosses and icons in Russia. When construction work was undertaken, a cross was erected and then the building. Moscow used to be called the city of *sorok sorokov* (which means '40 times 40') referring to the number of churches in it. They were so numerous that there was not a single point from which a cross could not be seen, so that it was possible to pray at any moment.

Churches were built both along all the major roads in Russia and on the tops of hills, so that they were visible from afar. And to this day, despite the destruction that occurred during the Soviet era, while travelling you only need to look around and somewhere you will undoubtedly see a church, shining over and protecting travellers on their long journey.

People observed the periods of fasting, which are fairly strict in the Russian Orthodox Church and account for

Religion has always played an important role in the lives of Russians. In the past, churches and crosses could be seen everywhere in the country.

If you went into a house, you had to cross yourself in front of the icon, and before eating as well. Traditionally, Russians celebrated not a person's birthday but their saint's day (or name-day), in other words the holy day of the protector saint. It was only in Soviet times that this was changed to the person's birthday. Religion was the yardstick for measuring value. If you did something wrong, people would say "You have no cross", and if you did something good, "that's God's way!"

more than 220 days in the year. It is forbidden to eat not only meat and milk products, but on many days also fish and oil. Furthermore, during periods of fasting, it was forbidden to have any form of entertainment. Theatres were closed and balls were not held. Abstinence is an important test of the soul's strength, a moral rejuvenation, a feat. Today, these traditions are coming back, at least as concerns food. Many people limit the food they eat during periods of fasting, and in addition to this, there is the widespread idea that it is also good for your health.

The popular ideal was never the great or the rich Rus, but the holy Rus. It is no accident that in 1943 during the Second World War (a very difficult time for the people, with the war dragging on, enormous losses and forces weakened), the Soviet government headed by Stalin took the decision to indulge religion. Churches were reopened, priests came back from exile and this was an important step aimed at raising morale amongst the people in order to comfort them and give them hope.

It is possible that one of the main reasons why people so easily understood and accepted communism was that it reminded them in some way of a form of religion, at least from the outside. Icons were replaced with portraits of the rulers, work was praised in the name of a happy future, today may be hard but at some point later on you will be happy. Even the idea of the immortal soul was kept. After the death of Lenin, the slogan 'Lenin lived, Lenin is alive, Lenin will live' was put around and what is that if not immortality?

Many of the particular features of the Russian character and culture are linked with religion. For example, humility, a specifically Russian concept which cannot be translated directly into any other language. It is linked to a certain

Russian passivity and fatalism. In this life, you may well have to endure suffering, but great happiness awaits you in the next life. This belief led to the idea that there was no point in struggling and resisting and gave patience. It is interesting that the Russian Orthodox Church's main festival is not Christmas, as in other branches of the Christian church, but Easter, known for its victory of life over death.

Religion is also linked to the idea that the spiritual is predominant over the material, which is characteristic of Russian culture. Life on this earth is short, and you cannot take earthly riches with you into the next life. They only lead to sin and that means material well-being is evil. It doesn't mean that the Russians have a negative feeling towards riches, or that they do not love money, but that they are afraid for their eternal soul. From this, you get the fantastic scale of Russian charity throughout history. Each and every merchant who got rich immediately gave money for the construction of a church, and the more the better, or to some other cause pleasing to God.

For all the deep religious feelings, many pagan elements have remained in Russian traditions, which have intertwined with Christianity and successfully co-existed with it for many centuries. This shows one of the most important qualities of the Russian character. A Russian does not struggle against new phenomena but accepts them as inevitable and slowly re-shapes them into the old and accustomed ways. This is why many Western traditions which have been borrowed in Russia have been filled with a more national content and are now changed beyond all recognition.

This is what happened with pagan ideas. When they converted to Christianity, the Russians filled it with many pagan ceremonies. The pagan spring festival was joined with Shrove-tide, which comes before the Great Lent; and the summer festival became Whitsunday, when churches are decorated with birch branches and multi-coloured threads are tied to them when making a wish. The ancient tradition of worshipping your ancestors has become the so-called 'parents Saturdays', and funeral feasts remind of magnificent pagan funeral banquets.

Over the last few decades, Russia has been overcome by a wave of mysticism and all sorts of fortune-tellers, prophets and healers. The difficult conditions in which people live are fertile ground in which superstitions flourish. There are even some political figures and businessmen who will not set out on a new enterprise without having their horoscope read.

A Russian's religious feelings are often internal and subconscious, coming to the fore in moments of crisis. In the 19th century, when many countries were undergoing a wave of atheist ideas, the Russian intelligentsia felt a particularly sharp yearning for religion and searched it out. And it is possible that it was precisely the undermining of religious feelings in Russia that led to the crisis at the beginning of the 20th century.

The Russian Orthodox Church Today
Despite the decades of official atheism in Russia during the Soviet years, religion continues to play a noticeable role in

people's lives. They can be divided into a number of groups, depending on their attitude towards religion. Firstly, there are those who truly believe, for the most part those of the older generation, although over the last few years there has been a significant number of young people joining. Secondly, there are those who attend church because it is fashionable, as a peculiar form of their desire for the past, for their roots, and here you mainly meet members of the intelligentsia and the well educated. Among the older generation, you can also find 'militant atheists', those who have retained the ardour of the 1930s–1950s, and for whom religion is only associated with stagnation and backwardness. Most of the population are on the whole indifferent to religion and sometimes go to church 'just in case, who knows, it won't do any harm', and also in times of trouble (there is an old saying, 'until the thunder sounds, a man will not cross himself').

In any case, most of the population takes this question fairly seriously, for the most part preferring not to discuss their beliefs but rather keep them to themselves. There is absolutely no tradition in Russia of going to church on

Women must cover their heads when visiting a Russian Orthodox church.

Sundays as some form of social outing. You go to church to pray, sometimes in a small group, but usually on your own. The question of faith is something very private for the Russians and is not discussed with others. Over the last few years, the church—as the collection of national traditions and moral support—has been attracting young people.

The most influential church in Russia remains the Orthodox Church. Those attending a Russian church stand throughout the service, sometimes for a number of hours. When entering a church, men take their hats off while women must do the opposite and cover their heads. It is not acceptable to enter a church in revealing clothing, in shorts or sleeveless dresses, and in some churches women are not allowed in if they are wearing trousers, although there is a more relaxed attitude towards tourists. If you want to ask a saint for something, you must buy a candle at the entrance and place it in front of an icon. Of course, during the service, it is not the done thing to talk out loud, take photos and video, or openly look at the parishioners.

DIFFERENT VIEWS OF RUSSIA'S DEVELOPMENT

One of the most important problems of Russian life is the question of self-definition. What is Russia, what sort of a person is a Russian, and what future is in store for them? Russians have been worrying over these far from simple questions for centuries. But if we look through the vast amount of work produced by Russian philosophers, writers and government figures, it would seem that, in essence, their search for the truth turns around one single question which we can sum up as follows: Russia and the West. It is the interaction between these two principles that is the cornerstone of Russian social and philosophical life.

For many centuries, the discussion centred around Europe alone. Can Russia be considered a part of Europe and are Russians European? How should we react to European influence which, far from diminishing, has actually increased over the years? And finally, how do Russians perceive the European nations, which are in constant interaction with them but at the same time are so distant and alien?

At the end of the 19th century, the concept of Europe transformed into the concept of the West. For the Russians, the West is not just what lies immediately to the west. The concept includes firstly Europe, but without the former socialist Eastern European countries. The Russians have never considered Poland, Bulgaria and others to be the 'real' Europe. Possibly now, in the new geopolitical conditions of the United Europe (and the most obvious effect of this for ordinary Russians is that they now have to obtain a visa when travelling to these countries), the situation will change. Secondly, a century and a half ago, the USA became an integral part of the West. Finally, far-off Australia is also—in Russian eyes—the West, because of the specific nature of its civilisation. This varied West has become the yardstick and definition of values for the Russian individual.

At the beginning of the Soviet period, the new government came up with the slogan 'Catch up with and overtake America!' in all the main areas of industry. For all its recent history, Russia (or the Soviet Union, depending on which period is under discussion) has been trying to do just that: catch up and, preferably, overtake somebody. Why this is so important, why we cannot just develop and travel along our own natural path, improving something here, perfecting something there, is one of the secrets of the Russian soul. No, everything must without fail be better than our neighbour's. Or at least the same. Otherwise we get no joy or fulfilment out of working.

In the 19th century, Russian educated society was split into two camps: the Slavophiles and the Westerners. The Slavophiles believed that Russia should develop along its own distinctive path, trying wherever possible to avoid European influence. They believed that this was the only way to retain our unique traits, the most important of which are the particular spirituality of the Russians, a deep religiosity, and a stable state. For the Slavophiles, Peter I, also known as Peter the Great, had done more than anybody to destroy Russia, by steering the country up the European stream and destroying traditional Russian customs. For them, the ideal was the pre-Petran patriarchal society. In their own way,

The great Russian writer Nikolai Gogol, who because of his ideas can almost be considered a Slavophile, wrote his thoroughly Russian works while he was—in his own words—'in the beautiful distance', or to be more precise, in Italy.

the Slavophiles loved Europe and often pondered the fate of their motherland while sitting somewhere warm like Rome.

The Westerners, as their name suggests, looked towards the West with confidence. They believed that only reforms and re-education based on the achievements of Western civilisation could help Russia out of its crisis. Science, rationalism, capitalism, freedom, such were the ideals which decorated their banner. However, the real Europe frequently failed to correspond to their representation of it. One of the early Russian émigré dissidents, Vladimir Pecherin, who fled to Europe in the 1830s, noticed that the people there had sufficient problems of their own, and that living there as a homeless, poverty-stricken émigré was not at all pleasant.

Actually, the Slavophiles and the Westerners had much in common. They both clearly felt that the country was in need of change, and agonisingly searched for the way out of the complicated situation, while trying to steer clear of the revolutionary upheavals. They were both brought up on German philosophy, loved their country, travelled around Europe with pleasure and were politically naïve. Their ideas became the icing on the cake of Russian philosophy and literature, but were far removed from real life.

However paradoxical it might be, and for all their abstractedness and idealism, these ideas turned the country upside down. Russians have for centuries loved ideas, and the further they are removed from reality, the more likely they are to find a sympathetic audience and even become embodied in real life (Marxism-Leninism being a good example). Russian society is to this day divided into two stable camps, which we could conditionally call Slavophiles and Westerners as before, although they have over the years lost much of their strength and love of peace, their idealism and their abstractedness. Today, the question of which path to select for the future development of Russia still for the most part depends on the solution to the main problem: should we take the Western path, or some other?

RUSSIA BETWEEN THE EAST AND THE WEST

Russia's geographical situation is the main factor that stops Russians from believing they belong to Europe. As everybody knows, the country straddles two continents, Europe and Asia. Moreover, the larger part of the country lies in Asia, while most of the population lives in Europe. The question as to whether Russians are more Asian or more European has worried people for a long time. Europeans usually see them as Asians, while the Asians do not accept them as one of their own.

So it is left to Russians to think of themselves as something special, not like the rest, simply Russian. There are times when this is a pleasant situation of which they can be proud, saying, "See how unique we are." At other times, like now, it is a source of irritation. "Everywhere people are people, but we are not like others and live like nobody else." Sometimes, Russians like to consider themselves powerful, wild eastern warriors. The famous Russian poet Alexander Blok, a man who was tender-hearted and physically not very strong, wrote the bloodthirsty lines, 'Yes, we are Scythians! Yes, we are Asiatics! With slanting greedy eyes!' But usually, they want to be part of the world, albeit the old but pleasant and comfortable world.

Among the Russian émigrés who fled the 1917 revolution, there arose a distinctive trend of thought, which was named Eurasian. Its followers believed Russia to be a special place which combined the characteristics of the East and the West, but which at the same time was a particular and unique phenomenon. They did not think that the Western path of development was right for Russia, nor was idealising Slavic principles and values. Rather, Russia should recognise its own particular destiny and fate. The ideas of the Eurasians have lost none of their pertinence, even today, and their followers in Russia speak out for the recognition of the special position and situation of Russia which are different from other countries.

Since ancient times, Russia has been the boundary between two worlds. This, naturally, had its inevitable effect on the country's destiny and the character of its people. On the one hand, there were constant invasions from two sides, from the west and from the east, which meant that the country was permanently on a war footing. On the other hand, Russians became firmly convinced that they had spent their whole lives standing on guard, protecting the boundaries of Europe and saving it, with their own blood, from the threat from the East. The great Russian poet Alexander Pushkin, who has retained his status as a prophet in his own land and whose words the Russians have learned to trust without question (despite the fact that the 200th anniversary of his birth was celebrated in 1999), wrote 'A mighty destiny was set aside for Russia. Its boundless plains swallowed the Mongol force and halted their invasion on the very edge of Europe. The barbarians did not dare leave an enslaved Russia at the edge of their empire and returned to the steppes of their East. Formative enlightenment was saved by a tattered and dying Russia.'

And Alexander Blok, in a poem composed in 1918, wrote 'We, like obedient serfs, held the shield between the two hostile races of Mongols and Europeans!' In this, he was also alluding to the fact that the Russians did not intend to play this role any longer and that those living in Europe were now on their own.

THE ATTITUDE OF RUSSIANS TO THE OUTSIDE WORLD

The attitude of Russians to the world around them can be summed up as unflagging interest. Their evaluation has changed (at different times, there were periods of fear, reverence, unease and admiration) but the interest in what was going on over there has remained to this day.

For a long time, the concept of a 'foreigner' in Russia was very complicated. On the one hand, it meant a 'potential enemy'—to use the military term—who presented a very real threat both to the country as a whole and to individual citizens. And this was not only the line taken by the official press; life itself supported the theory at every step.

The Enemy is Around!

In the 1970s, none of the inhabitants of the beautiful and quiet town of Tarusa were surprised by the events which occurred to one of the local shepherds. One warm Saturday evening, he went missing and the neighbours, whom the shepherd's worried wife had woken up in her alarm, were unable to find him for two whole days. Finally he appeared, crumpled, with a little wisp of hay in his hair, and recounted the following story. On Saturday evening, he was making his way home to help his wife with the housework, minding his own business, when he came across two foreigners (or 'Mericans' in one of the more detailed accounts). They grabbed him, forcefully opened his mouth and poured in a large quantity of an unknown liquid. Thereafter he remembered nothing until waking up in a strange hayloft two days later with a stinking headache. All of Tarusa believed in his story, even the wife of the poor man, although she did express some doubts about the part in which he had offered to help with the housework (this was obviously the least credible part of his tale). And from that moment on, everybody knew that the enemy was not slumbering and they had to be on the lookout.

There was another side to the problem. For Russians, it was impossible to lose face in front of foreigners. Even during the darkest days of the food shortages, the ordinary Soviet family would welcome infrequent and unexpected foreigners in a fashion no worse than that in which Ivan the Terrible welcomed English ambassadors. Tables strained under the cornucopia of victuals, although the family had to gather together all its resources and make use of all their connections (the only disappointment being that, as during the reign of the *tsar*, not one single foreigner was able to eat even a tenth of what was offered), wine and vodka flowed freely and there was a 'cultural programme' consisting of a cousin—specially invited for the occasion—singing 'Moscow Nights'.

These strange beings, the foreigners, were nevertheless enticing. They were the living embodiment of a completely different world which was far off, inaccessible and therefore secret and alluring. A trip from Moscow to Vladivostok (some 9,000 km) was considered normal, whereas going to neighbouring Berlin (1,850 km), even the socialist part, was an 'event'. Above all, Russians wanted to know what the people there were like, what they ate, how they lived and worked, since the man in the street had little or no idea about such things.

Some information about that other world did however make it through, although it was extremely meagre pickings. There were a few lucky people, almost like celestials, various diplomats and journalists who travelled around the world and brought back information, which was then spread in the form of verbal folklore amongst friends and acquaintances. However, their circle of friends abroad was, as a rule, a closed circle limited to the Soviet embassy and other Russians, which meant that they only very rarely saw real life. The official publications of journalists in the press were usually limited to articles such as 'Their Morals and Manners', which was—of course—instructive, but gave a rather one-sided view. In the Soviet times, there was a standard expression about 'the putrid effect of the West', about which the wits joked, 'It's decaying, the West, and rotting, but doesn't it smell good!'

Excellent programmes such as *Travellers' Club*, hosted by the popular Soviet TV presenter and traveller Yuri Senkevich, tended to concentrate on the exotic and showed the lives of those peoples who, it seemed, belonged to a long-forgotten past. The main body of information about far-off countries came to the Russians through literature, via the favourite novels and short stories of foreign authors. So it was that in Russia, the various countries and people had their own special signs: the Paris of *The Three Musketeers*, the London of *Sherlock Holmes*, the Germany of *Three Comrades*, and the America described by J Fennimore Cooper and Jack London. The rest of the world was covered by the books of Jules Verne (who had made the outrageous mistake of confusing Latin America and Africa). In schools and institutes, Russians studied the Queen's English or German based on the interrogation techniques used by the military, neither of which was that useful for everyday life.

In this situation, real live people remained completely unknown to the Russians. They were either pitied (as a result of the 'Their Morals and Manners' articles or Soviet films about their lives) or envied (as a result of vague stories about lands flowing with milk and honey), but in general Russians did not spend too much time worrying about them. Then, having comfortably hidden themselves behind the Iron Curtain, Russians no longer even considered them to be neighbours.

But that was before. What is it like now? Now everything has changed. The world is large, beautiful and inviting; it has opened up to the Russians in all its variety. For some it has opened wider, and for some less, but nevertheless for everybody. And through that wide open door flowed a stream of Russians eager with curiosity, some to work, some to study and some to 'find happiness and rank'. The noticeable demand from the West for Russian brides got a heartfelt response from the locals, who headed off to their newly-wed husbands in clans: parents, children, ex-husbands, grandchildren, in short, anybody they could get their hand on.

> One ecstatic mother of a newly-married couple wrote in the mid 1990s from the USA: 'We all came to the wedding, my husband and I, my younger daughter, my sister with her two cousins, and the school friend of my daughter. And all of us have stayed here.'

The flow of tourists also grew noticeably. Inevitably, they used the mass of tourist companies which were appearing, which made holidays even cheaper, which led to an increase in the flow of tourists, which increased the number of travel agents, which made holidays cheaper, etc. It was no longer necessary to have a relative abroad or to find a job that allowed you to travel. People could just save the necessary sum of money or take out a loan, or get it as a present from a son who had gotten rich quick, in order to go and have a look how they actually are over there. Many travelled and continue to travel, using their last (and also first) money. Russians have never had the philosophy of 'save now for your son's education, then for medical care in old age, then for something else useful, and then we'll go travelling on whatever is left over'. First of all in Russia, everybody remembers well what happens with money which has been put aside for a rainy day. Secondly, for a long time there was (and still is) a latent fear to the effect 'And what if that door is suddenly slammed shut again, and once again I didn't see Paris, and they say it has changed so much since the time of *The Three Musketeers*, but looks awfully like a scene out of the film *Sabrina*'.

One of my student acquaintances exclaimed in a fit of honesty "I have been to Petersburg and yes, it's beautiful, but then, I've been everywhere: Italy, Cyprus, Turkey, Spain, but nowhere is it that beautiful." Oh well, 22 is not that late to start getting to know one's own country...

This new life has brought with it new challenges. The language that everybody had studied at school and university was, it seemed, hopelessly out of date. "But we can still use it, they'll understand," the Russians thought. It turned out that foreigners are exactly the same as the Russians: two legs, two arms and one head. It turned out that life over there is not quite so dipped in honey as it had seemed, and so the idea of going there for good lost its appeal. It also turned out that it is not at all bad there either, so travelling abroad is both pleasant and interesting. Modern children often have a better idea of the Egyptian Pyramids than they do of the palaces of Saint Petersburg.

However, the main discovery is that despite Europe opening its arms to Russian tourists, it nevertheless remains a mystery to them. Going on a wonderfully-arranged tourist excursion (and there is now something for every taste) does not differ that much from watching a television programme or a film. You see all the main sights, which you have known for years from postcards and books, and eat pseudo-local specialities in faceless restaurants catering to the masses. The only thing you really get to know is your coach (or liner, if you are on a cruise), immersing yourself thoroughly in the problems of that small but complex organism called the tour group. Of course, knowing who will again be late getting to the bus and hold up the entire group, who will get drunk in the evening and will want to have a tête-à-tête, complaining about everything and everyone and missing home, and who did not sleep in their own hotel room (and, more to the point, knowing which room they did sleep in), all this is very instructive and not without its own interest, but you hardly need to travel all the way to expensive Europe for it.

Russians relate in the same way to holidays at resorts, which usually boil down to sitting on the beach or by the pool in the company of those very same compatriots (see above) and only rarely venturing out on excursions. Real life and the people are, as they always were, hidden behind the hotel wall or the coach window. Of course, these sorts of trips mean that you can say "I've seen the Coliseum", or the Eiffel Tower, or the Pyramids, but behind that phrase hides the stuffiness, crowd, noise and secret dream of coming back to the hotel in the evening for a cold beer. But can many of them really say, "I saw an Italian", or a Frenchman, or a Spaniard (not counting souvenir sellers)?

RUSSIA AND THE REST OF THE WORLD

The relations between Russia and the countries surrounding it go back a long way. The window on Europe was sometimes thrown wide open, sometimes left ajar, sometimes shut altogether (with the Iron Curtain fixed behind, just to be sure). However, even in these circumstances, there was still a door. The temporary breaks in contact which occurred from time to time did not stop the Russians from creating their own peculiar and specific images of other nations. These images found widespread expression in international jokes that are very popular among Russians. They all start the same way: 'There was a Russian, an American, an Englishman and a Frenchman' (or German, Spaniard, etc.). Then they are put into a situation in which they all behave in accordance with the peculiarities of their national character (or, to be more precise, in the way that they should behave, according to the Russian image of them). The English are stand-offish and official, the French flippant and full of love, the Americans pragmatic and not very bright, the Germans very well organised and dull and the Jews cunning. The Russians themselves are usually rude but kind-hearted drunks (in the modern versions) or organised along party lines (the Soviet period) or characterless romantics (pre-Revolutionary times).

There are endless such jokes. Here is a favourite one:

As an experiment, representatives of various nationalities were sent to uninhabited islands. On each island, there would be two men and one woman. There are then any number of versions about what the international commission saw when they visited the islands, say five years later. On the Spanish island, there lived a happy family, with lots of noisy children running about. The question about the woman had been solved quickly and simply: Jose had killed Juan in honest one-to-one combat and had married Laura. The French were also living in peace and harmony. Jean, Jacques and Louise lived as a single family, which suited them just fine. On the English island, the two men were playing golf and the woman was sitting under a tree reading a novel. "No, we do not talk with the lady," the Englishmen said to the surprised commission, "we haven't been introduced yet." On the Armenian island, there were two houses, children running about and two happy families. To the question about how they sorted out the situation, the Armenian replied "There was only one thing to do, we had to get a second one!"

There are two versions for the Russians. In the pre-Soviet version, there were three deeply unhappy people living on the island. Olga loved one of them, married the other, and everybody suffered. On the Soviet island, there were two well-fed, strong and healthy men playing chess in the hut. One introduced himself as the head of the collective farm (*kolkhoz*), the other as the secretary of the local party organisation. "And how did you decide what to do about the woman?" asked the commission. "Ah, you mean the people? The people are out in the fields." As yet, there is no version about modern Russia.

A Joke About Elephants

The representatives of various nations were asked to write a book about elephants. One month later, the English representative came to the jury and presented a beautiful book, bound in a leather cover, entitled 'Elephants and the Trade in Ivory'. The French brought the elegantly published 'Love Among Elephants'. The Germans carted in a multi-tome epic called 'Introduction to the Life of Elephants'. The Americans presented a pocket book entitled 'All you need to know about Elephants'. The (Soviet) Russians presented a book, bound in red and with the name embossed in gold 'Russia—Birthplace of Elephants'. The (pre-Soviet) Russians sent a note on a platter reading 'Had a terrible headache, and the guests kept interfering'. These jokes are practically endless since each nation can be represented in some way or another.

Russia and England

England and Russia are connected by ancient and varied links. It is well known that there were two Anglo-Saxon princes (the sons of Edmund II Ironside, killed in 1016) at the court of Yaroslav the Wise in Kiev. The daughter of the last Anglo-Saxon king, Harold, fled to Rus via Denmark, where she became the wife of Vladimir Monomakh. Historians are still arguing over whether she was the mother of Yuri Dolgoruky, the founder of Moscow, or whether he was the son of the prince's second wife.

At one time, there was a lot of noise surrounding the proposed matchmaking between Ivan the Terrible and Elizabeth I, Queen of England. In Rus, it was rumoured that the English had 'ruined the *tsar*', who was neglecting Russian women and making advances to a foreigner. As became obvious later, Ivan the Terrible loved Russian women very much and had not forgotten about them at all, and the matchmaking was more likely to be simply one of those curious moments in history. And it must be said that there was a big difference between the Russians and the English. Amusingly, in one of his letters, Tsar Ivan tries to rebuke the English queen: 'Of all the documents that I have received until now, at least two should have borne the same seal! But all the documents have different seals. This does not correspond to the norms by which a Sovereign abides. No state will believe such seals. Each Sovereign in a state should have a single seal.' As we can see, even then Russians thought that it was important to have the right papers with the proper stamp, and the English were acting with unforgivable flippancy.

The era of Ivan the Terrible was a turning point in the history of Russian relations with England. From that time on, there were substantial economic reasons for the relationship and consequently mutual interest grew noticeably. English goods have always been highly rated in Russia. We know that Russian craftsmen of the 19th century placed fake English marks on their goods. The magazine *Moskvityanin* wrote in 1851 that 'English letters lacking any sense' were often placed on Russian items, and that such items were not only in great demand in Russia but were also 'exported to Persia', where English letters were also a guarantee of high quality and a good price.

The English were considered the masters of upbringing. Having an English nanny or governess was very fashionable in the 19th century, and children were entrusted to them at a very young age, when it was necessary to bring them up properly.

Horses and the English

As well as their children, the Russian aristocracy also entrusted their horses to the English, rightly thinking that the English were excellent trainers and jockeys. The trainer of what is probably the most famous horse in Russian literature, Froo-froo (which broke its back at the most inopportune moment in the life of the heroes of Tolstoy's *Anna Karenina*), was a typical representative of his nation as the Russians saw them at the time. He was a 'dry Englishman', who talked 'without opening his mouth'. At any critical moment, he was 'calm and haughty' and when he was happy, he simply 'wrinkled his lips, in order to show he was smiling'.

England has never historically been a place to which Russians travel en masse. The Russians regard the English more with respect than with love. In France, the Russians amused themselves and joined in with the fashionable trends; in Germany, they relaxed and went for treatments; in Italy, they immersed themselves in the beautiful and cherished aesthetic feelings. The majority of those who went to England were diplomats, business people, scholars and political figures. The historian M P Pogodin wrote that 'in France life is more fun, in England it is more free, in Italy more pleasant and in Germany more calm'. Judging by the statistics of Russians visiting Europe, freedom is the least important of these values for them.

Nowadays, many people go to England to study. English, having become the global language, has brought much money to the land of its birth. Russians concerned about the education of their children try to send their beloved offspring at least once to practise the subject which is of such importance for their future, in the belief that even the air of Albion—a poetic term used by the Russians to refer to England—will fill their progeny with some reserve of knowledge and skill. Those

Recently, a younger generation of Russians have recognised London as the youth capital, and having been there described it as 'Cool!'

who have more money at their disposal prefer to send their children to English schools or colleges for longer-term education. The prestige of an English education and upbringing is still very high. In his heart of hearts, every well-off Russian dreams of a son who is a gentleman or a daughter who is a lady.

In another category entirely are the 'Russian-intellectuals', who look down on the beaches of Cyprus and Turkey, who are not attracted by the Finnish countryside or the mass immersion in Italian art, and who talk about former socialist countries using phrases such as 'Chickens aren't birds and Bulgaria isn't abroad'. For them, England is mostly all London, with its wonderful shops and restaurants, famous museums and fashionable theatres. They are not only rich snobs (although they frequently are) but also people who grew up on a diet of English classics and who now have the chance (which before they could not even dream about) to see with their very own eyes the world which had formerly only existed in their imagination.

In a word, although it is not the first choice for mass tourism, England undoubtedly has many fans, as can be seen by the long queues waiting every day outside the British embassy. Moreover, as opposed to many other places, there is no 'off season'. People wait in line in the rain, in the snow and under the baking sun, trying to fulfil their dream and get to that far-off country which is so well known and at the same time such a mystery.

Russia and Germany

It is hard for the Russians to talk about the Germans. Probably the only thing more difficult is to talk about themselves. Firstly, there is too much that links us. They are our closest neighbours in Europe, as well as having ancient and close historical ties and the same passions—philosophy, literature and music. And at the same time the most intense pain. On the one hand, we have not yet decided whether it is actually the Germans who created everything in our lives, from the state to the education system. On the other hand, many Russians feel fear and disgust at the staccato sound of the German language. Maybe this has stayed with us from our grandmothers and grandfathers who lived through the war, maybe it is from films about the war which we continue to watch, and maybe there is just something genetic. The negative reaction to the sounds of German is harboured somewhere within us on the subconscious level.

At the same time, it is with the Germans that the Russians have had the closest links over the last few centuries. There are even the so-called 'Russian Germans'. Germans arrived in Rus a long time ago, primarily to trade. German settlements with their own world—traditions, celebrations, the way of life, architecture and even graveyards (cemeteries)—appeared in Novgorod, Pskov, then Moscow. As of the beginning of the 18th century, their numbers started to increase rapidly and their aims and objectives diversified. They became involved in politics and the running of the state, promoted European culture and science in Russia, became doctors, teachers and soldiers, and from the time of Catherine II even tilled Russian soil. Historians also talk about German 'domination' at separate periods of Russian history, about how they tried to become rich off gullible Russians and tricked them.

There were those, of course, who were out for fame and fortune. But it is well known that many Germans served Russia faithfully and truly, and considered Russia to be their homeland. Many German surnames have gone down as a part (sometimes famous part) of Russian history: Bering, Fet, Benckendorf and Shletser, for example. Russians gladly married Germans (for example the great Russian scholar M V Lomonosov, who married a German girl, which never stopped him from fighting with a Germanic influence on science in Russia, and the thoroughly Russian poet F I Tyutchev). The Russian landowner Yakovlev also loved Germans and the result of his union with his German sweetheart was the champion of freedom, Alexander Herzen.

Russian Emperors and German Wives

A surprising example of the Russian-German union is the Russian emperors. The first to take a German princess as his wife was Prince Alexei, son of Peter I and heir to the Russian throne, when he married Sofia Charlotta von Braunschweig (this was understandable, as Germans were the height of fashion at the time). The first to place a German on the throne was Peter I himself, who first made his lover his wife, and then upon his death, the empress.

During the following two centuries, many German principalities tirelessly supplied the Russian Empire either with empresses or with wives for the emperors. When Alexander II tried to place his Russian lover on the throne after the death of his German wife, there was great opposition and she remained only a morganatic wife, without any rights to the Russian throne. Interestingly, these royal personages who had German blood were probably more 'Russian' than the Russian. And not only those such as Alexander III or Nikolai II who embodied, so it would seem, all the virtues and shortcomings of the Russian national character, but even the pure-blooded German Catherine II or Pavel I, who was a lover of German traditions.

Such close links between two nations could not fail to lead to attempts to understand each other. Russian literature, an important and often even accurate source of our knowledge about other nations, has dedicated many pages to German figures, who are, as a rule, either comic or satirical (to be fair we should note that this can also apply to Russian characters, so there can be no talk of a prejudiced relationship).

One great example is the character of Schiller, a master tin worker living in Meshanskaya Street, who was created by Nikolai Gogol in *Nevsky Prospekt*. 'Schiller was a German through and through, in the fullest sense of the word. From the age of twenty, from that happy time when Russians are still living on the never-never, Schiller had already set out his entire life and did not, under any circumstances, make any exceptions. He would get up at seven o'clock, take lunch at two, be accurate in everything and drunk every Sunday…' Germans fill the pages of Russian classics, from the kind-hearted Carl Ivanovich in Tolstoy's *Childhood* to the energetic Stolz by Alexander Goncharov and the purposeful characters of Leskov, but they are always pedantic, organised and do not put up with chaos.

For the Russians, Germans were for a long time the main Europeans in the outside world, and it was from their country that we started to know that strange other world which was enticing and frightening at the same time, in other words, Europe. It was on the German border that the first contact, and clash, of the two cultures occurred.

Often, this first meeting with Europe was a disappointment. There was too little that was exotic, the links were too close and there were too many Germans in Russia. It was because of this that Berlin, the first large German town on the road and which, according to many, looked like Petersburg, caused a 'sour impression', as Dostoevsky put it. Interestingly enough, modern day travellers consider Berlin to be much more 'their own' than the other European capitals. It is closer and more understandable to the ordinary Russian. Maybe it is just that a beer and fried sausages are nearer to Russian taste than the cuisine of other nations.

Russia and France

France holds a special place in Russian hearts. Over the last few centuries, any Russian with self-respect has wanted to go to France at least once during their lives. Until you have been to Paris, you cannot consider yourself as having travelled abroad. If you have a lot of money, then it is to France that you should go in order to have a good time (and the Russians like having a good time) and to spend money. This stereotype grew in the 19th century and it still holds firm today.

However, when Russians are in France, they usually prefer to talk to their compatriots, and so their impressions of the French are somewhat vague. However, this does not stop Russian girls from actively increasing the population of France by becoming model French wives and good-natured mothers. On a warm summer day in the centre of Paris, you so often hear Russian that you get the impression you are in the centre of Moscow. During the Soviet period, Vladimir Vysotsky, the well-known bard and singer who married the French actress Marina Vlady, sang in his song, 'Our infiltration across the world is particularly noticeable here, far away, In the public toilets of Paris there is graffiti in Russian.'

Russia and Italy

Italy has always enticed the Russians. Art lovers, romantics, artists, pilgrims and ordinary tourists all want to go there, each for his own reasons. Some want to immerse themselves in the beautiful, others go to see holy relics, some to relax from the stresses of life, or satisfy their exacting tastes, or finally just like everybody else, to be able to return home and say to their neighbour in an offhand way "When I was in Italy…" It is interesting that Italy was always particularly close to the Slavophiles, and it was here, more than anywhere else, that they liked to reflect on the destiny of their country.

For most of those who go to Italy, it is an enormous open-air museum, where each stone has its own history, each church in every little village has its masterpieces, and each ruin is ancient. Works by the great masters, each of which would be the pride of a good European museum, are seemingly scattered carelessly about the country. Here it is possible to immerse yourself in the beautiful, relax to music and opera, and admire the divine beauty of the countryside. Many have found peace here, and it is no surprise that people with nervous disorders and broken hearts have travelled to Italy to be healed.

Nowadays, Italy is most loved by Russian artists, romantics, intellectuals, patriot-Russophiles and President Putin, of course.

It is not just the climate that has curative powers, but the surprising atmosphere of conciliation and happiness that can be compared with no other. The Russian literary critic P V Annenkov wrote the following about Rome in the 19th century: 'The voice of Europe reaches this place weakened and barely audible. However, this is not the Chinese isolation from everyday life but something artistic and higher, like a house in the country, where a great person worked. Sometimes it seems to me that Europe purposely keeps this astonishing city, which is surrounded by dead fields with ruined water channels, graves and theatres, as their villa, whither she sends her sons to recover from distemper, anxiety, political stress and all their troubles.'

Russia and Scandinavia

Norway and Finland are Russia's two northern neighbours, with which they share a border (in Soviet times, these were the only capitalist countries which bordered on the Soviet Union). Russia has ancient but entirely different relations with them. The close links with Norway date back to the time of the Viking raids, and for the most part were founded on mutually beneficial conditions. There was joint trade and Norwegian warriors were invited to Rus to strengthen the country's army.

One of the specific features of the relation between Russia and Norway is the fact that they have lived in peace for a long period of time. There were problems naturally, but they never became serious incidents and were usually resolved by peaceful means. Alexander Nevsky sent an ambassador to Norway to regulate the question about taxing the Danes and the Saami, taxes which were being collected by both the Norwegians and the Russians. The question was decided without any undue delay, though it did not particularly alleviate the sad fate of the Saami as it simply made double levies legal. He was also the first to sign an official agreement with Norway in 1251. The second agreement in 1326 confirmed the land border (which effectively already existed) between the two countries. It is still in place today and has not been altered, nor has it ever been violated by military actions.

Tense moments arose from time to time after the Second World War, when Norway became a member of NATO. Nowadays, people write about the difficulties of 1968, but it was nevertheless possible to avoid open conflict. Finally, although the two countries had different ideological systems, they existed peaceably during the Soviet period, side by side on the cold island of Spitzbergen where the Norwegian and Russian working camps got on together (characteristically, in 1941, 900 Norwegians and 2,000 Russians were evacuated from this Norwegian island), which says a lot in itself. Even now, almost half the population of the island is Russian.

It is impossible to tell when and how the Russians and the Finns started conversing. The tangle of Slavic and Finno-Ugric names on the map of northern Russia is witness to the fact that the two peoples have been living side by side since time immemorial. The Russian historian V O Klyuchevsky had the following to say about the first historically verifiable meeting between the Russians and the Finns: 'How did they meet and how did one side act on the other? In general, the first meeting was a peaceful one. Neither in written history, nor in the folk legends of the Great Russians, has there remained any recollection about persistent or widespread battles between the newcomers and the indigenous peoples.'

This peaceful meeting long acted as a deposit for the continued peaceful co-existence. True, the Finns fell under the power of the Swedes, which was bound to affect their Russian neighbours. However, enmity and hostility appeared in relation to the occupying Swedes, who used the country as a base for military conflict with Russia, rather than with the Finns under their power, for whom the Russians felt sorry.

Pushkin's descriptions are, as usual, full of meaning and easy to remember; 'sad outcasts of nature' and 'wretched Finns' was what he had to say about them. In his famous poem 'The Monument', dreaming about how his name will be spreading throughout 'all great Rus', he recalls a Finn immediately after 'the Slavs' proud grandson', which shows a recognition of their place in Russian history:

'I shall be noised abroad through all great Russia, Her innumerable tongues shall speak my name: The tongue of the Slavs' proud grandson, the Finn, and now The wild Tungus and Kalmyk, the steppes' friend.'

And from 1809, the fates of Russia and Finland were so intertwined that closer links would simply not be possible.

Granted special rights, Finland became part of the Russian empire and the Russian emperor added 'Great Prince of the Finnish Princedom' to his title. This was not a conquest; the countries were joined in accordance with an agreement between Russia and the Swedes, who relinquished their control. Despite the stereotypes which arose, the relations between the Russian and Finnish peoples were quite friendly during the Imperial period (as much as they can be in such a situation). A Finnish textbook even talks about 'unusual success' during the first 60 years of the union. For example, the Finns still remember that the wonderful collection in Helsinki library exists thanks to a Russian *tsar*, who ordered that one copy of each book published in Russia be sent there as a matter of course. Thanks to this, during the years when the Soviet Union was sealed off from the West by the Iron Curtain, many researchers came to Finland in order to work on 'Russian' themes. As for the construction of the Finnish capital, well, every Russian person who has stood in the main square will have felt some sort of solidarity with his northern neighbour, so much is it homely and familiar.

However, the idyll did not last forever, and the history of relations between Russia and Finland was darkened by various difficulties, including insurrection, terror and war. Things were particularly bad during the Second World War when Hitler used Finland as a base for attacking the Soviet Union. But afterwards, the relations between the countries were just as close as before. A neighbour is a neighbour. Russians well remember the dead years, when but scant links remained with the West, and in the Soviet Union they ate Finnish cheese and biscuits, and Finnish sausage on a celebratory table was the sign of a Soviet citizen's well-being.

Nowadays, it is surprising, even incomprehensible, how the Russians would have been able to do without Finnish porridge, buckwheat, jams, butter and milk, to mention only the essential items. Driving past neat and carefully tended Finnish fields, they would know that Russian breakfasts were growing there and thank God that they were not going to end up hungry.

In his book about Russia, Mauno Koivisto (at various times the president and prime minister of Finland) surveyed Russian history in a fairly critical way and came to the single conclusion: 'To live with a kind neighbour provides security. We would also like to be a kind neighbour to our kind neighbour.' That's the way it balances out.

The development of tourism is adding a sense of unity. Russians always enjoy heading north to go on holiday, particularly when you can guarantee a good level of service and comfort. This is particularly good for those who want less of the exotic and more of the comfort.

No other countries were as close as the Russians, Norwegians and Finns. Although we were so close to each other historically and geographically, it didn't prevent us from lacking true and serious knowledge of the characters of Norwegians and Finns. Italian manners or the English way of life happened to be much more interesting to us than national peculiarities of our closest neighbours. Famous Russian writer Karamzin, returning from his famous European expedition, wrote down his impressions of the Norwegians: 'we were met by Norwegian fishermen. The Captain waved his hand and in two minutes the whole deck in front of us was covered with fish… As well as money, the Norwegians, who are great drunks, wanted rum, which they drank like water and then, as a sign of kindness, clapped us on the shoulders.' The impression of drunkenness has gone, and we are left with the fish. All that the ordinary Russian knows about the far-off Norwegians is that over the past few years, there has been an enormous amount of salmon appearing on Russian shelves.

Our knowledge of the Finnish character is not much better. Russian writer Michael Saltykov-Shchedrin wrote in the mid-19th century that 'the Finns have a tendency towards drunkenness, although they have no wine, with the exception of their helmsmen who are strictly prosecuted. But having made their way to Petersburg, the Finns drink themselves into oblivion, lose their money, horses and harnesses, then return home as naked as the day they were born.' For all that, the subject of drunkenness was so close for the Russians that they were pleased to note this weakness in others.

Russia and America

The relations between Russia—or rather the Soviet Union—and the USA were, for a long time, of vital importance in world politics. This was bound to have an effect on the feelings of ordinary Russians. For the Soviets, America was capitalism at its most quintessential, and it was used to frighten children while they were still at kindergarten. It was the 'They' who were in opposition to 'Us'. Because of the political correctness policies of the time, the military departments at the institutes of higher education did not refer directly to the 'potential enemy', but the latter did have all the attributes which allowed us to identify it: a hymn, a flag and a language. The Americans were the exploiters par excellence of the ordinary working class, the oppressors of those with a different skin colour, warmongers and the enemy of the peace, with whom it was necessary to fight in order to create a radiant future for our planet. While the Europeans had, for the most part, their own romantic elements and were more often than not just characters from literature, the Americans, who had never been seen that way by Soviet citizens, were more real and contemporary.

But there was also something else. The USA was the country which could, if it joined with the Soviet Union, help save the world. Inasmuch as the old world was more or less a myth, we looked to the Americans as people like ourselves, with whom it was possible to come to an agreement. Information about America, even when it was negative, was noticeably prevalent in the Soviet mass media, in comparison to other capitalist countries. On top of this, the 'forbidden fruit' is always sweeter. However much we were force-fed with horror stories about the terrible contrasts of American life, where millions of poor lived in destitution and a few rich enjoyed all the blessings of the world, it was the latter that captured our unfailing interest, in particular as the Soviet system collapsed. Many secretly thought of America as some sort of paradise, where every person could have his own yacht and villa, where everybody smoked foreign cigarettes and drank beer from cans (this was thought to be particularly chic).

With the onset of *perestroika* and the dismantling of the Iron Curtain, America became the country to which Russians most wanted to travel. Against the backdrop of the chaos at home, the far-off country became a model, an ideal, a dream. People tried any methods, legal or otherwise, to get there so that they could have a look—even if only briefly—at the miracle. The first information was very comforting. Everything there seemed to be as we had thought, perhaps even better. The first emigrants (some of whom had remained there illegally) were trying particularly hard. They sent photos home to their families, with commentaries like 'Me in front of my house' (which they give to anybody who asks), 'Me and my fantastic new car', 'Me on the golden Californian beach', and 'Me with a can of beer'. Of all of these, the only one that really corresponded to reality was the can of beer.

Then came the disappointment. It turned out that the Americans had their problems and their difficulties as well. They do not actually give out houses and cars to people and you need to work long and hard (very hard, longer and in a more disciplined way than in Russia). New York really was the 'city of contrasts', as they said in the old Soviet films, where luxury and destitution lived side by side.

And the education system was a disappointment too. I have been studying the evolution in the relation of young Russians (university students) to the USA for 15 years. Initially, everybody was trying to go to the States on trainee programmes. But gradually people started asking "Maybe we could go somewhere in Europe?" It was closer, and more understandable.

Russians are still enticed by America. Anybody who needs convincing need only take a look at the queue outside the American embassy. But there are no longer any secrets, no idealisation, no dreams; now there is only reality. And that is always less interesting.

THE NATIONAL CHARACTER

CHAPTER 3

'I do not hesitate to say that, of all the people I ever knew,
the Russians are the most genial and hospitable.
It is true the ranks in Russia are very distinct and marked;
but the humane spirit of Russia thaws all coldness,
breaks all conventional barriers,
and fuses the whole into one national feeling,
as in no other land.'
—Cassius Marcellus Clay, American diplomat

THE RUSSIAN CHARACTER VIEWED FROM OUTSIDE

The Russian character, as any other, has mainly been formed by time and space. History and geographic location have left their indelible mark on it. History explains and justifies much, but unfortunately very few people actually know it. Centuries of constant military danger have made the Russians particularly patriotic and desirous of a strong, centralised power; the difficult climatic conditions have made it necessary to live and work collectively; and the limitless spaces gave birth to the particular Russian characteristic of doing things in a big way. For all the conventionality and relativity of this type of generalisation, a number of regularities and general traits can be distinguished in the Russian character.

What does the Russian character look like when viewed from outside, and from the Western point of view in particular? The following generalisations have been put together on the basis of notes written by 19th and 20th century travellers, and also on the basis of surveys carried by the author over the last ten years.

Western views on Russian politics are amazingly stable. They can be expressed with one word—despotism. The despotic Russia is usually opposed to the democratic West; this helps some to feel the advantages of their own system fuller and better. From time to time within history, there are periods when the West is full of hope and proclaims the coming of freedom to Russia (as it happened in 1861 at the time of Great Reforms, or in 1985 at the time of *perestroika*). However, usually these periods are followed by disappointments. Here is what American president Abraham Lincoln wrote (1855): 'In Russia...despotism can be taken pure, and without the base alloy of hypocrisy.' And here is the opinion of the English journalist (1891): 'In Russia there is no law outside the autocrat's will, as interpreted by his officials; no independence, no self-respect.' At the same time, strong power is supposed to be a must for Russia because it is said to be the condition of peace and order in it: '...Russia of those days wanted nothing more than to be governed with a firm hand, whatever the liberal professors and students, and the intelligensia generally might think or say to the contrary.'

The Western views on Russian economics are, relatively speaking, unanimous. In the opinion of Western observers, the main obstacle of its regular development is in the national character of Russian, i.e. in the lack of individualism, in the social character of their consciousness (which many pre-revolutionary authors called 'communist'), etc. At the same time, many observers admire this feature, for example an American senator: '...Individualism...may be an ineradicable part of the Anglo-Saxon nature...the racial tendency of the Russian (is) to do business on the communistic principle. Where like undertakings by Americans, or Englishmen, or even Germans, would first be interrupted by contentions and then destructed by quarrels, and finally break down by the inability of the various members of the association to agree among themselves, the same number of Russians get along very well together, and practically without antagonism.'

However, most people in the West believe that it is the lack of individualism that interferes with the normal development of Russia. The following opinion is characteristic of the time: 'They are, as a people, incapable of the economic advancement or of the adaptation to modern conditions by which alone they can hope to survive and win ultimate success in the struggle...it is certain that it would take many generations to bring this (economic and industrial progress) about with the Russians under the most favourable conditions, and it certainly will never happen until individualism of effort is encouraged and personal energy rewarded.'

The position of our Western contemporaries is close to the opinion expressed 100 years ago. Almost 90 per cent of those people asked think that individualism is an essential condition for Russia to develop normally, and the lack of individualism in the Russian character is a barrier on the road of the country's economic development.

Talking about the main features of the Russian national character, here are the most frequently mentioned ones: (the quotations in brackets are taken from various travel writings):

- hospitality

  ('The Russians are accustomed to a sort of princely hospitality...')
- religiousness

  ('...religion in Russia...whether believed or not, will always remain a part of patriotism, and since there is a Russian nation there will be a Russian religion at the core of it.')
- sincerity and openness, often concealed by outer reservedness

  ('During travels Russians become very talkative and while they are as curious as Scots—they are sincere and open about their even very intimate affairs to such an extent that we can hardly imagine.')
- kindness and at the same time extreme suspiciousness

  ('A student makes a lamp-shade out of the portrait of the Emperor Nicholas. An Englishman or Frenchmen visiting this student for the first time see merely the Emperor Nicholas' portrait on a light-shade, but a Russian entering the room understands that the young man regards Nicholas as an obstacle to enlightenment.')
- feeling of brotherhood, solidarity, lack of individualism

  (Russian can't 'live apart in detached farms and crafts as in modern England; and the Russian is a social creature and pines for the presence of his fellows.')
- patience, endurance
- dodginess, falsity

('With all his air of simplicity it would hardly be wise to trust the word of a Russian peasant, or indeed of a Russian of any rank…')

- natural laziness
  ('He is lazy, shiftless, apathetic, you say, coming from the busy West…')
- indifference to political freedoms, the conservatism of thinking, fatalism
  ('…in such a country as Russia…given justice at home and a guarantee against foreign aggression, the vast majority of the population would care not a rap for 'liberty'')
- light-mindedness, carelessness
  ('…an important lesson that all Russians have still to learn…is the value of time')
- capacity to give up everything for the sake of an idea or a passion even if it will do nothing but harm
  ('Their unbounded power of losing themselves in a feeling, an idea; their capacity for self sacrifice')

MODERN WESTERN GUIDEBOOKS TO RUSSIA

Generalised images of the Russian character nowadays are given in guidebooks which have been published in the West over the last ten years. The overall picture that they paint does not give cause for joy, which is strange for a guidebook that should join rather than separate people, to help them to converse and not hinder them.

The first thing that attracts your attention while reading Western guides on Russia is an atmosphere of mystery and vagueness that surround it. From this comes the main aim of travelling to Russia. If there is a mystery, it is necessary to solve it: 'Moscow and Saint Petersburg have always offered an intriguing and challenging destination for travellers, and in these times of dramatic change, the challenge and intrigue are perhaps even greater. Cast aside all your preconceptions and bring along an open mind and a sense of adventure—then you can begin to explore the heart of this vast enigma called Russia, and perhaps shed a little light on its mystery.'

What are the ways of demonstrating the 'mysterious Russian soul' to a reader of Western orientation literature?

There are two main extreme and contradictory tendencies in portraying Russia and Russians today. On the one hand, Russia is shown as a backward and crippled country, the former 'Evil Empire', with wretched fate and people. Travel guides on Russia are filled with unpleasant descriptions, frightening scenes and dark sides of city life. The authors use different methods: from overstressing and emphasising real drawbacks to open lies. And these guides usually have just a few illustrations.

'More than 8,5 million people live in Moscow, a strange but fascinating metropolis that lacks the efficiency, comforts and conveniences that are commonplace in nearly every other world capital. Even the most well-informed tourists are taken aback by the city's comparative backwardness. In many shops and restaurants, prices are totaled on abacuses, not machines. Common amenities taken for granted in the West, like taxi cabs, restaurants, mail or travel by air, often involve hassles and disappointments for the business visitor.'

'A housing shortage, shop queues, ecological pollution, an increasing crime rate, speculation, prostitution and racketeering are just some of the problems.'

'Until relatively recently, central Moscow was a scene of shoving shoppers, crowding into dusty, virtually empty stores to fight for the right to buy a piece of meat for the family dinner.'

'Shortages also sapped the flavours of Russian cuisine. Even the famous Russian beetroot soup, *borscht*, appeared in restaurants as cabbage soup without a single beet.'

Here we find everything from exaggeration (there were shop queues for meat in the beginning of 1990s, but I don't remember fights for a piece of meat) to misunderstanding (Russian beetroot soup *borscht* without a single beet is called *schi*, also a very traditional Russian soup).

On the other hand, Russians are very often romanticised. The idea is that inspite of all hardships, hunger, darkness and harshness of life, Russians are very warm-hearted people, that they have 'mysterious souls'. According to the authors of guidebooks, Russian people—all the time they can spare from fighting for a piece of meat—talk philosophy, read intellectual books and recite poetry. They are surprisingly generous, and are ready to share everything with you even if they have nothing.

'Late into the night, educated Russians debate philosophical dilemmas…worrying at each point and fuelling the furious discussion with copious amounts of vodka. They buttress their arguments with lengthy quotations from the world's greatest books. Western visitors are often surprised to find Russians more well read than they are, even in their own language's literature.'

'Guests in a Russian home warrant a feast, even in times of shortages. There is always a spare bed, even when a family of four lives in a single room.'

'…If a Russian associate invites you to his or her home, to a restaurant or to a reception, be aware that Russians are well informed on a vast range of non-business topics—an airline pilot will be able to tell you about Pushkin, for example.'

'…put these same people in a living room, or in any one-to-one situation, and the rude street fighters become generous and welcoming.'

All this is good as an illustration of the mysteriousness of Russian soul, but is also very contradictory and doubtful. It is obvious that a character of any nation is full of contradictions. But in all this conglomeration of mysteries and contradictions while reading about Russia, one idea is lacking—that it is just a country as anywhere else, and the Russians just people as anybody else.

As I have mentioned before, the mysteriousness of Russians in most cases comes from the misunderstanding of their culture and traditions. One of my favourite examples of cultural misunderstanding deals with a smile as part of behaviour. Foreign visitors always complain about strange behaviour of Russians in the streets and public places. They say, "Russians are wonderful people, but they never smile to a stranger, they look so gloomy and serious when they are walking down a street". Travel guides justify this behaviour on the ground that Russians are too overburdened with everyday hardships and sorrows to feel like smiling.

'If crowds on Tverskaya Street or Nevskiy Prospekt look dour and miserable, spare a thought for the hardships they must endure, and remember that their glum faces conceal the true warmth and hospitality of the Russian character.'

My students at the university have a similar opinion about the famous Western smile, "They are so strange, they smile all the time, even to an absolute stranger without any reason or meaning." In Russia, a person who smiles without any reason is considered to be stupid and light-minded.

In this strange and unattractive world of guidebooks live rather strange and unattractive people.

'To Westerners, Muscovites are unusually warm and forthcoming, but with one another they are often churlish. A ride on the subway or bus during rush hours can be bruising, and don't expect to hear an 'excuse me'...from a Russian who accidentally jabs you with an elbow on a crowded bus or train.'

'The inefficiency of the system causes low morale, and Soviet citizens seem to take every opportunity to complain about their lives, jobs, government and fellow countrymen. Many may annoy and depress you with their repeated requests for help in leaving the country. Employees in restaurants and shops may shock you with their blatant dishonesty. Often, they lie because they are too lazy to make an extra effort.'

'Muscovites tend to be rather rude in the streets but this comes from spending a quarter of their lives in shop queues.'

Thus the picture is complete. The people seem to deserve the country they live in. At the same time, the simple premise is lacking. Russian people are neither good nor bad; they are just humans, without any special mysteries, paradoxes, faults or merits.

There are a lot of wrong ideas and misunderstandings between Russia and the Western world. When I was lecturing in the USA, one of my students who was in her fifties once said to me, "When I was a girl I always felt so sorry about your people. I used to cry when I was thinking about your miserable lives." I told her that was exactly how I felt about Americans when I was a girl. I couldn't listen to the terrible stories about racism, poor people sleeping in the streets, unemployment and many other unbelievable things. We both had only one piece from the huge picture of national lives of both countries.

Two Sides of the Story

I was giving an 'orientation course' for foreign students who came to the Faculty of Foreign Languages at Moscow State University. When I told them that I considered my childhood and students years to be the happiest time I had, they did not believe me. I remember happy days, my large and united family (family in the Russian sense of the word including various kinds of relatives), lots of friends, joyful trips to our *dacha* (little summer house) and to the seaside and beautiful bright dresses that my grandmother used to make for me. For my students from different countries, it was the time of Khruschov's voluntarism, Brezsnev's stagnation and the all-embracing KGB rule—a dark and dangerous period. In the recent Russian history, there is no place left for people with their normal ordinary lives with everyday joys and sorrows.

COLLECTIVISM

One of the distinguishing traits of the Russian national character is collectivism or communality. Here is a typically Russian situation to illustrate it. Cars are hurtling down a highway at great speed, significantly in excess of the limit. Suddenly, all the oncoming cars start flashing their headlights. The Russian driver reacts immediately—you need to take your foot off the accelerator as there is a speed check up ahead. With due decorum, he drives past the traffic inspectors and he in turn warns oncoming traffic. Representatives of the law-abiding Western world may well consider this to be hooliganism and potentially dangerous to other road users. For Russians, it is a natural expression of friendly solidarity, a collective guarantee. It is natural for a country in which the feeling of helping each other out of a hole is extremely important, in which laws often contradict common sense and road signs sometimes run counter to simple human logic.

For centuries, Russian peasants, who made up the overwhelming majority of the Russian population until the start of the 20th century, lived in communal groups called peasants' communes. These groups brought the peasants together and were their protection from the outside world,

from foreign invaders, brigands, civil servants and so on. All the important questions were debated together at a general gathering. Together they decided how much land to allot to each person, so as to keep to the principles of fairness, whom the assembly would help, whom to send to war, how to pay taxes, whom to punish for crimes and how, and so on. Even family questions, if there was a conflict, were brought for general discussion. This system did not allow the weak to fail (destitution was unknown in Russian villages), nor did it allow the strong to rise up. Thus, despite the commonly held belief, the system of collectivism, social equality and egalitarianism was widespread in Russian society long before it was set up as a social structure that led to bloodshed. In these conditions, the principle of mutual support becomes even more important than the self-preservation instinct.

Peasants in their commune not only decided problems but also celebrated festivals and worked together. When at the beginning of the 20th century, Prime Minister P A Stolypin's reforms gave legal backing to and financially stimulated leaving the communes, the peasants were in no hurry to change the way of life to which they were accustomed. 'In the *mir*, even death is beautiful' goes the Russian saying. *Mir* was what the serfs themselves called the commune. Actually, *mir* has a number of different meanings: it is the opposite of war (i.e., peace), a collection of peasants, and it is also the world (*Miru mir* or peace to the world). And for the peasants, the commune really was all of the above. It protected them, gave them stability, and was their world.

The communes ceased to exist in the 20th century. The new conditions and the introduction of collective farms in Soviet times made it impossible for this institution—which was so democratic by its nature—to

The work in the collective was a joy and sometimes turned the peasants' tedious tasks into a holiday. For example, everybody took part in pickling cabbage in the autumn. Pickled cabbage was an important product for the peasants as it was the main source of vitamin C during the winter. Each housewife could have done the job in a few days if she worked hard. But it was more fun doing it together. So women gathered at each house in t working together and chatti singing songs

exist. But overall, the Soviet system supported the idea of collective work, personal contact and mutual help. Even at the end of the 1980s, students used to go out 'to pick potato' instead of studying—the students would go off to help collect the harvest in the villages. How much it actually helped productivity in the farms is debatable, but as far as the students were concerned, the advantages were obvious. After a month spent overcoming joint difficulties, joining in collective work and celebrating festivals together, the students came back different people. They had strengthened their ties, deepened their friendships and learned more about one other. In a word, it was the realisation of the concept so beloved in Soviet pedagogy—the collective.

Winning the Prize Together

Nowadays, the innate feeling of solidarity among Russians sometimes confounds certain Western ways of doing business. One particularly clear example: as part of an advertising campaign for Fanta, there was to be a draw held between those who had collected caps from Fanta bottles that made up a certain set of figures that were printed on the inside of the cap. In Moscow, Saint Petersburg and other towns, markets suddenly and naturally sprang up, where the owners of caps joined together in groups, so that they could try their luck at winning the desired prize collectively.

This feeling of collectivism explains the Russians' lack of hesitation in getting involved in the affairs of their friends, neighbours or even passers-by on the street.

Making decisions as a collective is also normal for Russians. An American tourist travelling through Russia with a group of Russians never ceased to be amazed that the group had no leader who was responsible for making decisions. Everybody simply got together, discussed the situation which had arisen, then jointly took a decision and carried it out. And it is precisely in this way that important questions are decided in Russia. Moreover, as in ancient times, this may involve people arguing, discussing or even falling out. But as a rule, a solution is always found, whatever the situation, and nobody will want to 'go against the collective group opinion'.

This foreign tourist was also surprised by the naturalness and spontaneity throughout a long and difficult journey. And this is also an important trait in the Russian character. In the morning when they were getting ready to leave, nobody knew where they would stop in the evening. Wherever they got to, that would be the place, and who knew what could happen on the way, argued his Russian companions. At first he thought it crazy that nothing was planned in advance; their night-stop had not yet been decided and river crossings had not been booked. Towards evening, the group would simply stop in a village and ask the locals where the best place was to spend the night. Soon it became clear that this was the only system that unfailingly works in Russia. It was simply not possible to book crossings in advance; in some places it did not even exist. And when it came to accommodation, nobody knew better than the locals, and trying to find out from Moscow any information about the situation in such places was very difficult, even impossible. Most importantly, this naturalness completely suited his co-travellers.

Foreigners living in Moscow with their families never cease to be surprised by a certain situation. If they have taken their child out for a walk on a cold morning without a hat, a hail of advice and reproaches about their flippant attitude towards their own child will rain down upon them. Getting advice from strangers on the street is fairly normal in Moscow.

Russians love to ask for and give advice. In Soviet times, there was even a pun about a man who was trying to get help, but everywhere he only received advice. "We are, you see, a country of councils". Like all puns, this joke is difficult to translate accurately. However, if read aloud, this version comes close. The word 'Soviet' has a number of meanings. The one which is usually meant in English is a group or council (as in Security Council). However, it also means advice or counsel. Hence the translation could be misinterpreted if read out loud, as 'We are, you see, a country of councils/counsels'. This is also, in its way, a result of communal living: before starting something, get the advice of your neighbours.

Russian collectivism should never be understood in a simple, or worse, in an idealised way. Of course, collective work or play, friendship or help are good things. But it is collectivism that gives rise to upstarts. Remember the well-organised queues of English individuals. Bypassing a queue in Russia is tantamount to heroism.

And collective responsibility sometimes results in a lack of responsibility: why should I tidy away, maybe somebody else will do it?

One of the interesting results of the Russians' collective consciousness is the system of connections that is usually called *blat* (getting things through your influence, or because you know the righ people). 'You scratch my back and I'll scratch yours' is a very simple principle. This system was particularly widespread in the last decades of the Soviet era, when there were shortages and deficit of goods. At that time, it was impossible to buy anything, but anything could be obtained. And 'anything' could be a ticket to the Bolshoi Theatres, a pair of evening shoes, Finnish sausage, a place at a good school, medicine, in short, anything that could be supplied.

Sometimes, 'chains' were formed. For example, you need a trip to a good sanatorium, but do not know the right people. So you manage to get hold of, for example, some good coffee for somebody, and they then manage to find a new tape recorder, and at the end of a long series of exchanges, you have your trip. The system was complicated, but there were those who were masters at the game. Even in Soviet times, people railed against the system and it was ridiculed in the press and films. But despite this, it was alive and very effective.

Nowadays, the situation is sometimes absurd. On the one hand, it is possible to buy anything at high international prices. On the other hand, the old system of *blat* still works, and it will guarantee you quality. And so if you are going away for the weekend and ready to pay 4,000 rubles for a room, you will still end up doing it through an acquaintance.

The problem is that nowadays even if you pay for something, it is not a guarantee of quality.

There are still many things that the Russians like to do collectively, for example to visit friends or to go for a walk. Foreigners frequently complain that if they invite a girl on a date, she would turn up with a load of friends. But it is also interesting for them, she would say, and why should I prevent my friends from getting pleasure.

An expensive school or hospital may turn out to be staffed by doctors and teachers who have got into a good place by *blat*. So in order to avoid making a mistake, you are better off asking your friends' advice.

THE ATTITUDE TO MONEY AND RICHES

The attitude to wealth and money is extremely complicated in Russia. Russian culture and literature have always taught that wealth does not imply happiness. The idea that happiness cannot be bought for money is deeply rooted in the Russian mentality. Russian history gives striking examples illustrating this.

By the second half of the 19th century, some Russian merchants had become very rich. Their entrepreneurial and business talents were widely acknowledged. However, some inexplicable feeling of guilt for the abundance of wealth made them spend a lot of money on building churches, schools and hospitals (not for their workers or personnel but for the local poor) and financially support various charity organisations. Their children and grandchildren spent their means on the development of arts and culture; they bought the richest collections of works of art, financed folk crafts, opened new theatres and supported young talented artists. For example, the world-famous Tretyakov Gallery was opened in Moscow due to the money, enthusiasm and exquisite artistic taste of Pavel Tretyakov, a representative of a famous merchant dynasty. Moscow Arts Theatre was founded by the legendary theatre director Stanislavsky (whose actual name was Alexeev and who also was a representative of a merchant dynasty) with the money of another Moscow merchant, Savva Morozov. Many of the merchants (for example both Savvas—Morozov and Mamontov) were brought to bankruptcy by their patronage of arts and charity activities. However, saving money for its own sake was pointless and a burden on the heart.

Despite the widespread idea that bribery is quite common in Russia, we would strongly recommend you to refrain from giving bribes before you consult some Russians. It is no secret that bribery is a way to solve many problems in Russia, but a wrong time, a wrong way (too open) or the right people may spoil the matter, hurt the people, or make them angry. You may be surprised when you discover how often the popular Russian principle 'poor but proud' will turn out to be more important than the offered money.

This attitude to riches, in conjunction with economic instability, meant that it became senseless for Russians to save money. Why should we save money, which is in itself evil, and which could also lose its value at any moment? It would be better to spend it. This is where the now famous (and sometimes sad) Russian squandering is from. The same merchants, famous for their patronage of the arts, give us examples of spending money on the grandest scale. They laid on sumptuous banquets, to which they invited crowds of people, showered their mistresses with expensive presents and sent their shirts to be laundered in Paris.

Nowadays, you quite often come up against the same situation. Who is buying the most expensive houses in Europe, who stays in the most luxurious rooms, and who pays over the top for a bottle of exclusive wine (although in their hearts, they sometimes dream about good old vodka)? "We love the Russians," the manager of a large real estate company in London recently said in an interview for Russian television, "they buy the most expensive property and never bargain."

But spending money is not only a trait of rich people (very rich people, in fact, never fling their money around, even in Russia). Having earned a sum of money through hard toil, a Russian will probably spend it on a trip abroad, or on new clothes (even if they are not needed), in other words on something it would be perfectly possible to do without.

We are not talking about squandering and flippancy peculiar to Russians. Simply that the attitude to money is completely different from that in the West. One friend exclaimed, "Can you imagine, that Englishman is not that poor, lives decently and has his own house. He says to me, all my life I have dreamt about trying some special type of champagne, but it's expensive, costs 25 pounds. Can you imagine? Well, I went and bought it for him, let him fulfil his life's dream." And it hardly needs saying that this was somebody who did not have his own house, and his salary could not even be compared with that of the Englishman he had decided to make happy.

The Experience of a Lifetime

Not so long ago, a Russian émigré who had gone to live in America was talking about his first attempt to live in his new homeland. Before leaving Russia, he had somehow managed to earn a tidy sum of money. He came to New York, rented an expensive flat in a prestigious area, decked it out with wonderful furniture and bought an expensive car. Then he joined an expensive sports club, bought himself good clothes and started to go to expensive restaurants with his friends, who had come from all over America for the occasion.

It hardly needs saying that this happiness did not last for long. The money ran out and he was forced to move out of the flat and sell the furniture and the car. But having ended up in some loft in New York, the émigré did not regret a thing and looked back on his short happiness with pleasure. There is even a saying in Russia: 'But then, there will be something to remember'. That is when you have spent your last penny on pleasure.

Alongside this flippant attitude to money, there is the precise opposite in Russia. The hard, hungry years during the war and the post-war period have left an indelible mark on the Russian people. There are still old people who, hidden from the younger members of their family, will dry out bread for, as they say, 'a rainy day' (in Russian 'for a black day'). And interestingly, they are not incompatible. Those people who deny themselves everything, who save up the pennies, can suddenly spend it all on something which is not needed and totally unexpected. The fear of hunger and the ability to save money are two entirely separate things.

THE ATTITUDE TO THE LAW

The attitude of Russians to all kinds of law, rules and instructions is very complicated. For instance, walking in a Moscow park located in a heavily populated district, we noticed many signs saying 'No dogs. Penalty...'. Under these signs, dozens and even hundreds of dogs were enjoying themselves. It looked natural: they had to be out for a walk,

НА ТЕРРИТОРИИ
Пушкинского
МУЗЕЯ–
ЗАПОВЕДНИКА
ЗАПРЕЩАЕТСЯ

ВЪЕЗД
МАШИН

ЕЗДА
НА ВЕЛОСИПЕДАХ

ВЫГУЛ
СОБАК

Signs like this are not always obeyed in Russia.

and that was the only patch of greenery in the area. The prohibiting signs under the circumstances were obviously absurd and could not be obeyed. As children in the park were not less numerous than dogs, it became clear that children were having their lesson of attitude to rules and instructions: some of them may be neglected.

If you are aware of this kind of Russian attitude to laws and rules, you will not be shocked seeing students smoking happily under strict sign saying 'No smoking!' or hearing people asking about prices for alcohol in a kiosk with a sign 'Not licensed'. This kind of knowledge is vitally important for visitors in Moscow. For instance, zebra crossings do not work in Moscow in spite of the rule. Cross with care!

THE ATTITUDE TO TIME

Time doesn't matter. It is hard to say what played the deciding role in the formation of the attitude the Russians now have to time. Maybe it is the limitless space, in which it is hard to say at what time you will arrive. Maybe it is the climate, when a sudden blizzard can spoil all your plans. Or it may be that the peasant past of the Russian people, who were accustomed to living within their own village, meant that the world was extremely limited. It is no accident that a journey to the neighbouring province was considered to be a journey 'into a foreign land'.

The Russians have a very relaxed attitude to time. Having popped in to see you for five minutes, a Russian friend can easily stay three hours. And being 15 minutes late is not considered to be late at all. Nowadays, in addition to the climatic, natural and geographical difficulties, you also have traffic jams in big cities, and working out how long you are going to be really is very difficult.

Russian Time and American Time

A friend of mine was extremely surprised by an official meeting in America. On her invitation, it said that the meeting was from 5:00 pm to 8:00 pm in the evening. For the Russian heroine of this story, it was only important that the guests would start arriving at 5:00 pm. Imagine her surprise when she noticed that at 8:00 pm, when she thought the evening would just be getting going and everybody would switch out of 'high society' mode, all the Americans started to leave. In Russia, if you invite people, you do not imagine that there are such things as time limits. The party will continue for as long as there are people who want to carry on.

SPOKEN AND WRITTEN WORD

There are two sayings in Russian which, better than anything else, reflect the importance of the spoken and the written word in Russian life: 'paper won't blush' and 'a word is not a sparrow, if it flies away you won't catch it'. The spoken word has always carried more weight than the written word.

Russian merchants were proud of their 'precise merchant's word'. Anybody who broke their word could not count on being a business success, although a lie was not in itself considered to be shameful. In questions of trade and relations with the state, merchants not infrequently had recourse to different sorts of ruses. But once they had given their word, they had to stick to it.

Even now, many people still have more faith in the spoken word than the written word. They often even feel uncomfortable signing a contract or an agreement. If somebody has given their promise, why insult him with your mistrust?

The attitude to pieces of paper is generally sceptical. Maybe it is that they are required too often and lose their meaning. Or there may be a more serious reason. For many centuries, the written word could only be the word of God (as it was for the peasants till the 20th century), written in the Holy Book and which was their main reading. Everything else was simply not worthy of being written down.

In general, Russians do not take papers very seriously. If asked, people will get any document for you and will not feel the slightest pangs of conscience about this lie. After all, it is only a piece of paper. If some strange people have a reason for asking for it, well, I ought to give it to them. That is the way many document are obtained in Russia—through connections. Medical documents, licences and certificates can all be either bought or otherwise obtained.

And this is why Russian people are often bewildered when various embassies increase the number of documents that are needed for a visa application, in the hope of keeping some sort of control over those applying. It is always possible to get hold of a document, and often the shadier somebody is, the easier it is for him to get the necessary certificate. It is only honest and law-abiding citizens that have problems. And that is why the British embassy is particularly respected. It requires a reasonable number

In the education system, oral exams have traditionally held sway. Nowadays, when Russian education institutions are following the Western system, many have expressed their doubts and dissatisfaction. Teachers consider that they can always spot whether a student is ready or not during an oral exam. And written exams are nothing; you can copy things, or get the answer right by chance.

of documents and after that they can make other checks if necessary. Endless papers in Russia do not prove anything.

MAIN FEATURES OF THE RUSSIAN CHARACTER
Patriotism and Self-Criticism
A distinctive feature of a Russian is patriotism. It may take different forms; it may be quiet, hidden and shy. Russians are inclined to self-criticism and self-reproach. One should not forget that it is the other side of pride and self-esteem. Do not be deceived by statements like 'It is impossible to live in this country!' Russians often complain about their own way of life (indeed, there are enough grounds for it) but they will hardly appreciate the same kind of criticism from strangers.

Understanding Freedom
A distinctive idea of the concept of freedom has developed in Russia. In itself, it has never much interested the people. Protected by the commune, lost out in the endless spaces of the country, the Russian peasants did not really feel their personal dependency. They paid their taxes as had their forebears, worked on the land, and the commune decided any questions that arose. Of course, there were cases when the peasants were treated badly, but this mainly concerned those who were directly in the service of a landlord or court servants. As long as a peasant was providing the means of income, it would have been stupid to squeeze him further without reason. Both the landowners and the state understood this.

The whole world welcomed Alexander II's reforms to free the serfs from their obligations. And why should they not have? In a single day, millions of serfs gained their freedom. They turned from slaves into people. Only the serfs themselves were unhappy and they all looked for another authentic law. What is freedom for a serf? An abstract idea. You cannot spread it on bread. But now, instead of paying the usual taxes, they had to buy their own land. More importantly, with money that was beyond the reach of the serfs. That much they did understand.

The people were attracted to the revolution not by promises of freedom, but of peace (in the First World War) and land. After *perestroika*, the outside world again rejoiced that freedom had come to Russia. But many people missed the stability and order, the clean streets and the affordable prices. And this is why many sections of society feel nostalgia for the old times. And what of freedom? It was the writers, political figures, intelligentsia and dissidents who felt the lack of freedom and the eye of the KGB. For most people, all this was just empty words.

Compassion and Patience

Compassion is a characteristic trait of Russians. And it sometimes co-exists happily with a kind of childish brutality. In some cases, it is a waste of time trying to argue or insist on one's rights. This will not have the slightest effect on the other person. But if they pity you, this is already a guarantee of success.

Politicians frequently play on this characteristic of the Russian soul. Successful heroes do not inspire much empathy, while the poor and unfortunate inspire compassion and the desire to help.

Patience is also one of the Russian people's favourite and valued qualities, 'A love comes with habit' or 'Be patient and love will come', as the saying has it (in Russian, it sounds more compact and thus interesting 'Sterpitsya—slubitsya').

In Europe, Cinderella pretends to be a beautiful princess, the prince falls in love and then marries her, even though she is actually something else. In the Russian fairy tale, the situation is reversed: the prince loves a frog and then it turns into a beautiful princess. First compassion for an unhappy creature, then patience and finally a beautiful wife, and with a guaranteed dowry. Well, in the fairy tale at least… But many believe, and wait patiently.

Suspicion and Trust

The spirit of collectivism and brotherhood has given rise to many national Russians features. Relations among people are informal and friendship is appreciated very highly. You must be prepared for a long and detailed answer to a habitual question: 'How are you?' The usual formal reply of foreigners may hurt Russians. A well-know director of a Moscow theatre, Galina Volchek, told a story about a peculiar linguistic experiment she carried out in America. She answered the question of 'How are you?' with a hasty 'My husband has drowned himself'. In reply, she heard the conventional 'Glad to hear it'. Even if the story is not quite true, it is quite interesting because it illustrates the reaction of a prominent, much-travelled, educated and well-read Russian woman who defied the foreign formality of communication because of Russian traditions.

Foreigners are invariably astonished or even shocked by the openness of Russians about their private affairs. Russians are not good at impersonal small talk. Consequently, do not be surprised if during one night's train journey from Moscow to Saint Petersburg, complete strangers who happen to be in the same compartment with you will manage to let you know all the minute details of their private life.

Communication in Russia, even if it is business, is always a very personal matter. Questions concerning your private affairs, private emotions, the state of your heart and soul are as customary as life stories. Probably this is a reason why the famous Western 'weather talks' are not common in Russia. Russians are often hurt by the widely-spread Western custom of sending 'ready-made' postcards.

More than Words

A friend of ours told us how she had received a letter from her American acquaintances after a long silence. She was overjoyed, anticipated reading it but was deeply hurt when she read the printed 'Happy New Year' and a signature 'Anne and John'. A Russian regards it not as a sign of attention but rather as a sign of neglect. It means that these people had no time to write even a few words about their life, work and family. That is just what a Russian expects from correspondence.

However, Russian openness lives side by side with suspiciousness and secrecy. A simple but illustrative example. Picking wild mushrooms is a national hobby and a kind of national sport in Russia. Mushrooms are considered to be a favourite and delicious dish. Returning from the woods, mushroom pickers usually try to cover their baskets with leaves and twigs. The idea behind it is: 'Other people should not know how much we have gathered. If we have many mushrooms, they will run to the woods and discover our mushroom places or they will envy and dislike us. If we have few mushrooms, they will laugh at us that we do not know how to do it.' Being too cautious and secretive may lead a Russian to an involuntary deception or to an unnecessary complication of simple things and situations.

Superstition

The Russians are superstitious, both the educated Russians and young people and businessmen. There is a certain set of rules which, to be on the safe side, everyone tries to observe. For instance, when you are invited into someone's home, you should observe the following omens: don't greet anyone or bid them farewell across a threshold, it means a quarrel; don't sit 13 people round a table, it means a death; don't whistle in the house, or there won't be any money; and if you have spilt the salt, you must throw a little over your left shoulder and spit three times, or otherwise there will be a scandal. There are a great number of such omens, so don't be surprised at what might seem to you to be strange behaviour on the part of your Russian friends.

TRADITIONS OF SOCIAL INTERCOURSE

CHAPTER 4

'There is character in them—Russian character—which is
politeness itself, and the genuine article. The French are
polite, but it is often mere ceremonious politeness. A
Russian imbues his polite things with a heartiness, both of
phrase and expression, that compels belief in his sincerity.'
—Mark Twain

IN THE PREVIOUS CHAPTER, we talked about the peasant commune as a determining factor in Russian life. Its influence on communal life is obvious in contemporary life, including its effect on the traditions of social intercourse. In the commune, your entire life was lived out in full view of everybody else. Therefore, your way of life and living conditions were constructed taking into consideration how it would look to your neighbours. Two contradictory feelings clashed and for many Russians, they are still important today. The first is not to stand out, to live as everybody does, so as not to make your neighbours jealous. According to Russian superstitions which exist unchanged to this day, the jealousy of those around you will undoubtedly lead to loss and unhappiness. This is why people prefer not to put their wealth, their happiness or their purchases on display, and this has always been the case. Because you never know. Russians are extremely worried about 'the evil eye'. And one of the favourite sayings in Russia is 'God looks after those who look after themselves'.

One French specialist working in a Russian company sent joyous messages round to his companions after the birth of his child, with details about the child's weight, length and medical condition, including a photograph. For him, it was the natural thing to do. He had happy news and he wanted to share it with the whole world. His Russian colleagues, including those from the new generation of Russians, were surprised and criticised him. Was he not afraid? You should

hide whatever is most important to you and not show it to anybody, to protect it from something unfortunate happening. In particular your child, and in particular just after birth!

On the other hand, the fact that you were always on full view meant that other people's opinion was extremely important and naturally you wanted to look your best. Shortly before the 1917 revolution, there were reforms to grant people the possibility to divide up their land and become private entrepreneurs. Very few people actually took this up and many of them later asked to go back to the commune, even though an individual enterprise was obviously more productive than the commune and brought a sizeable profit to its owner. Wealth lost its meaning if there was nobody to whom you could boast about it. The opinion of neighbours, work colleagues, distant friends and so on is still very important for Russians. Many are irritated by this and ask, "What difference does it make to you what that neighbour from downstairs, whom you do not even know, says (or thinks) about you?" But it is important and for many, it is a deciding factor in the way that they behave.

As a result, two extremes rule over Russian life. In your day-in, day-out ordinary life, you need to be the same as everybody else and not stand out. You can walk around in whatever comes to hand, however you like, eat from ordinary plates, whatever there is. But on a special day, everything must be the very best: clothes, food, tableware, etc. Even if the guests who are coming are not particularly pleasant and do not inspire your respect, you must nevertheless make sure that everything is the best.

INTERACTION WITH FRIENDS AND COLLEAGUES

Relations within the social structure are not less complex. On the one hand, there exists the strict hierarchy of Russian society, respect for those who are superior and the social dependence of positions.

On the other hand, it is not all so simple as it looks. For example, the relations between the boss and the subordinate do imply that the former takes all responsibility on himself/herself, but this does not mean that they cannot communicate on equal terms. Generally, these relations in Russia seem to be less formal and more human than in many Western countries.

Besides, there exist some specific pride of 'a little person', described in many works of Russian literature. Even a tiny screw in a big mechanism may stop its functioning. People do not forgive neglect or disrespect, even if you are a big boss or have a lot of money, etc.

On such occasions, a polite request instead of an order may perform miracles. Very often, attention and respect are more important to people than money and career. No wonder that a common person describes the boss he/she likes with words like 'respectful', 'attentive' or 'nice'.

Friendship is highly valued in Russia and occupies an extremely important place in life. Quite often, friends perform the same functions that in Western culture

It is recommendable to bring some little souvenirs to Russia: for a person on duty in the hotel, a secretary at work, a nurse in hospital, a neighbour, etc. But do not regard them as bribes or good deeds on your side. There is a Russian proverb: 'It is not your present but your love that is dear to me'. Attention and human kindness are appreciated here (not the financial value of souvenirs).

Friendship and group activities are important to the Russians. Here, families and friends enjoy some winter games together.

would be entrusted to psychoanalysts. Friends are needed, above all, so that there is somebody to talk to about your problems. They are the people with whom you can share your innermost thoughts, your desires, and sometimes even your intimate secrets. They are needed when you are happy so that you do not celebrate the numerous festivals on your own: invite them to a birthday party, for New Year, or simply because there is good (or bad) weather.

Close relations with friends often last a lifetime. It is not uncommon that those who first sat together at school when they were seven years old are still friends on their deathbeds. They attend each others' weddings, bring up their children together, go to the seaside together, or the cinema or theatre, bury their loved ones, in short, live out their lives side by side. When it is not possible to meet up, they speak by phone or write letters. They suffer when there are arguments or conflicts, and betrayal or a break in relations are taken as seriously as a divorce.

THE ATTITUDE TO WOMEN

The attitude to women in Russia may also cause some problems. On the one hand, it is more traditional and conservative than in most Western countries. On the other hand, one must not forget that the Russian woman was proclaimed 'free' immediately after the Revolution of 1917. The first constitution of the Soviet state declared equal rights for men and women. Up to now, the following situation is typical: the wife has a more prestigious and better-paid job, but it is the husband who is the head of the family and has the last word. The most interesting thing about it is that a situation of this kind often corresponds with the woman's ideal of family life, according to which it is the man who is the master of the household; he earns the money and takes decisions. Interviews with modern Russian businesswomen occupying high positions in various firms, banks, ministries, state institutions, etc. can be easily summed up by a simple motto: a career is good but family happiness is better.

The specific attitude to women and their place in the family is reflected in the Russian language. A man '*zhenitsa*',

which means 'takes wife', a woman '*vykhodit zamuzh*', which means literally 'goes behind her husband like behind a stone wall'. The Russian woman's striving for a strong man (a stone wall) is very far from being inactive, in fact just the opposite. Nowadays in Russia, you will hardly come across a housewife, and usually only among certain layers of society. For example, it may happen in military men's families as they move frequently and suddenly from place to place, or among 'new Russians' for whom a non-working wife at home is a social mark of their prosperity. The absolute majority of women work full-time and not only for financial reasons, but because they are eager to put into practice their skills and talents, to do something useful and important.

At the same time, family values are still very significant in Russia. That is why unmarried men and women arouse suspicion; something must be wrong about them. Lonely women often suffer from an inferiority complex. A colleague of mine, a career woman and an academic earning a decent sum of money, refused to go to a meeting of her former fellow students because 'they will ask questions about my husband and children and I have nothing to say'.

The relations between 'a strong man' and 'a weak woman' is rather a game in modern Russia society, but both sides play this game very thoroughly.

In the streets and at public places, it is manifested (alas! more and more seldom nowadays) with showing respect and support: men open and hold the door, give up a seat in public transport, let a woman pass first, help a woman on with her coat, etc.

The game goes on in business relations. Western books on doing business in Russia often describe some specific difficulties that women in Russia are confronted with because 'they are not treated seriously'. Here it is important not to confuse form with content. As has been mentioned above, businesswomen are common in Russia. In some spheres such as education and trade, they even prevail. However, certain customs are still kept. If you are a woman who has come to Russia on business, remember, please, that your 'gentle sex' will draw a special attention of Russian men. They may kiss your hand at the moment of introduction, or, particularly, at departure. They will let you pass, often with the words in English, 'Ladies first'. At a party where a woman is present, there will be an inevitable toast 'To fair ladies'. Signs of special attention to women, hints of courting and flirting are acceptable at business meetings in Russia. Please do not take this sort of playful behaviour for condescension. If you are a serious businesswoman, it will be noticed and highly appreciated, though it may only increase men's gallantry.

FASHION AND THE ATTITUDE TOWARDS IT

A distinctive attitude towards fashion has developed in Russia over the centuries. For a long time, the idea of fashion simply did not exist. Europeans had long since been carried away on the new waves of clothes, interior design and behaviour, but Russia still lived mainly by the old traditions, from year to year, from century to century, wearing similar clothes and living in the same conditions. And this was true in poor as well as rich homes. The difference was not in style but in the degree of luxury: dresses were of one and the same design, but could be adorned with bits of glass or precious stones.

The revolution occurred under Peter I, who propagated new customs (sometimes forcefully) based on the European model. But there is a saying which became popular under Mikhail Gorbachev and which tersely sums up the specific nature of Russian life: 'we wanted for the best but it turned out as usual'. Thus, Peter decided to change the magnificent clothes of the Russian *boyars* for practical suits in the Dutch fashion. And as a result, not long after the death of the *tsar-reformer*, Russia swung wildly to another extreme, splendid and exaggerated European clothing. From that moment in the mid-18th century, the concept of fashion appeared in Russian culture and was firmly associated with the West.

In general, across the country (if one excludes a small fashionable group in the major cities), Russians still prefer austere, conservative clothes. In the villages, people still pay very little attention to them. They go out in grey, colourless clothes, which are very practical and easy to clean.

Older people prefer dark colours. The bright clothes worn by European pensioners puzzle Russians, who consider that people should dress according to their age: bright and even provocative when you are young, austere when you are an adult, and sombre when you are old. However, when there is a holiday or festival, people dress up; indeed it's a must. A white blouse or shirt is still seen in Russia as the main component of being dressed up.

The Russian Style

A Russian woman married into a large American family. She always stood out when the whole clan gathered once a year. All the daughters and American wives went to their parents' place in the country in practical, everyday wear: jeans, T-shirt and trainers. Our Russian wife always dressed up and surprised everybody with her high heels, fur collar on her best coat, jewellery and manicure. For her, she was being invited out and that meant she had to look her best. And her husband was always very proud of her.

Nowadays, Russian markets are filled with foreign goods. But most of them are cheap, synthetic items produced in

China. Many recall with sadness the old days when you could buy cheap, simple, plain clothes produced in Russia from natural fibres. Cotton and wool were, for a long time, cheaper than artificial fabrics.

Quite often, Russian women are said to lack a sense of style. Simple, dark clothes were standard and easy to understand. Now, with the enormous selection, many women buy clothes on the basis of price, availability or brightness. The combinations that result are various and sometimes ridiculous. At the same time, there are also stylish Russian women, who when dressed in their most fashionable and up-to-the-minute outfits are ahead of their European counterparts.

THE ATTITUDE TO FOREIGNERS

Perceptions of other people are always contradictory and generalising. Of course in a large multinational company in Moscow and Saint Petersburg, the attitude to foreigners is calm, neutral and well balanced. In this short period since the Iron Curtain had been removed, Russians and foreigners have been learning how to deal with each other. In big cities all over the world, they are also getting used to Russian visitors and treat them like any other tourists. London, Paris and New York are overflowing with Russians going there for all possible reasons: business, shopping, anxiety for knowledge, interest in culture, desire to spend or earn money, etc. They dissolve into one huge faceless and nationless crowd of foreigners who are drawn to these famous world magnets.

Generally speaking, the attitude to foreigners for the rest of Russia (with the exception of big cities) is a combination of curiosity and mistrust, of goodwill and jealousy, of hospitality and apprehension (The famous Russian hospitality sometimes takes exaggerated forms with foreign visitors). Misunderstandings and lack of knowledge keep some old ideas and stereotypes deeply rooted. These views are formed by old Soviet ideology that was very efficient, refreshed nowadays by television news, foreign films and especially American and Latin American soap operas.

The collective portrait of a foreigner viewed through Russian eyes may be represented as follows: rich, polite, artificially smiling, well bred, demanding, possibly a spy or a potential spy.

Surprisingly, it is all true vice versa. Foreigners' attitude to Russians is also often a mixture of curiosity and mistrust. There is a great amount of fear in it, the fear of Mafia, of strange, unpredictable behaviour and of cheating. In Italy, a Russian family was going to rent an apartment. Everything went smooth as long as the Italian side thought that they were dealing with the British (the conversation was held in English). But when the truth came out, the Russian family was almost immediately rejected and nothing could prove that they were not hidden terrorists.

The collective portrait of a Russian viewed through foreigners' eyes: gloomy, unsmiling, hospitable, drinking vodka, wearing fur hat, unpredictable, emotional, passionate, possibly a member of Mafia.

WHAT SHALL WE TALK ABOUT?

There are any amount of themes suitable for discussion during receptions. Russians love to talk about the family—this is a theme that is always popular—the problems of everyday life (it is pleasant to hear that they exist in other places too and that people, when it comes down to it, are the same everywhere); they will be interested to hear about the country you come from, about your company, your impressions of Moscow and Russia, etc. In a word, Russians like candid conversations—about themselves, about you. Unexpectedly frank conversations about illness, family and other everyday troubles are quite usual. In Russia, to share woes and problems means to become friends. Incidentally, if you are asked for your impressions of Russia, I don't advise you to launch out with criticism, even if your Russian partners themselves make scathing remarks about their own country. And, of course, be ready to discuss business in any situation. If your Russian partners are intrigued by a project, they will discuss it all the time, everywhere and whatever their condition.

Such informal contact over a glass of vodka will on the one hand enable you to pick up new information about your partners, and on the other to establish personal contact which is so important for the conduct of successful business in Russia.

The Russians don't go in for formal 'social' chat. Be prepared for the fact that someone who is entirely unknown to you may, during an official function, tell you about his life in intimate detail, in which case he will expect the same from you. Many Russians find the formal meetings that Europeans or Americans are used to puzzling: what is the point of it all if one can't relax and have a heart to heart?

Finally, politics in Russia is a very complicated problem. Nowadays, Russians do not like to talk politics to strangers. Political views are utterly confused, and the habitual terms of social life like democracy, capitalism, freedom, etc. are just empty shells which may be filled in Russia with a different meaning. Forget politics if you are interested in establishing good contacts in Russia.

SOCIAL TRADITIONS AND ETIQUETTE

The love of sitting down to eat and the inclination for a communal life have inevitably led to the fact that Russians love celebrating all sorts of various events. Everything personal becomes general property, for example your birthday. It may become less important as you get older, but in Russia it is always celebrated. Firstly at home with your relatives and friends; on occasions, if there are a lot of guests, the celebrations are split over two days. And sometimes, after two days of celebrating (and particularly if the heroine is a woman), she will need a good holiday, since she has to take care of all the preparations, entertainment and tidying up. Men help, of course. They carry all the food home, open the bottles, set the table and do the washing up. But the women themselves will not allow them to take on any of the more responsible tasks.

So the table is set and people celebrate, dance and indulge in one of their favourite pastime—singing songs. This surprising tradition is still very much alive. After a certain

Russians love to get together for celebrations, and singing is very much a part of the occasion.

number of drinks, when the conversation starts to flag, the guests start singing. Often it is the older generation that sings, but the younger guests join in and will often know the words and melodies of the old songs. They sing all sorts of songs, from old romances to traditional Russian songs to Soviet ballads. Songs from the time of the civil war are very popular as they are both rhythmic and melodious, and even the youngest generation sings heartily, although they do not even remember what happened when the Red Army fought and 'from the taiga to the British Seas was the strongest of all'. But the most popular songs are those about love, particularly unrequited, and there are many in the repertoire.

You would also celebrate your birthday separately at work. If it is a jubilee, you need to ensure a large table covered with food and drink. Everybody gathers to celebrate, usually in the second half of the day (but in working hours). If it is just an ordinary birthday, you can get away with a few bottles of wine, a cake and some sandwiches (in Russia they are always opened, without the top slice). This is important as many people will bring presents and it would be a simple lack of respect not to offer them something.

Other events are also celebrated at work, such as weddings, being promoted, starting work or leaving the company, a large bonus, in short anything that has the slightest significance should be celebrated with friends, relatives and colleagues at work. There is even the superstition that if you do not celebrate some event, then it will not bring success. All the main holidays are also celebrated at work. Which means that as of about ten days before the New Year, getting anything done is very difficult, as the workers celebrate the forthcoming New Year in most organisations. So you should not be surprised if doctors in hospitals, teachers at schools, postal workers and shopkeepers are occupied during this time and do not react to your requests and comments.

Weddings are celebrated in great style. Magnificent white dresses and a long veil for the bride have come back into fashion in the last few years. As many people as possible are invited (it is important not to insult anybody), including distant relatives who only see each other at weddings and funerals. Tradition has it that the richer the wedding and the greater the number of guests, the longer the happy couple will live together. Sometimes, the scale of such celebrations surprises, and people will give their last pennies so that their child celebrates the wedding day 'no worse than other people'. The tendency to show off really comes to the fore in this instance.

There are many traditions to be observed: the happy couple are showered with seed, the bride's shoe is stolen and everybody looks for it, the couple is met with bread and salt and so on. It is usual to bring a good present that will be useful in the house during their married life. Nowadays, many people give money, but that is the privilege of close relatives only.

In the last few years, people have 'remembered' a new tradition: the groom must carry his bride over seven bridges. So the lively group goes from bridge to bridge, carries the bride, and at each place has a drink, getting livelier all the time. There is even a joke that if nobody got drunk and started fighting at the wedding, then the wedding was not a success.

Weddings are registered at a registry office called ZAGS (Otedel Zapisi Aktov Grazhdanskogo Sostoyaniya—the Department of Registering Certificates of Civil Status). Weddings involving foreigners can only take places at certain ZAGS (in Moscow, for example, there is only one for

A joyous couple registering their marriage at the registry office.

the whole city). Those who want a religious ceremony must take their marriage certificate and passports to a church. And they must, of course, be baptised in the Russian Orthodox Church. Nowadays, getting married in church is very popular, and not only amongst believers. The ceremony is beautiful, ceremonial and, it is considered, gives an extra guarantee that the union will last.

After registering the marriage and before sitting down at the banquet, it is traditional to go to pay respects at some important historical or cultural place. In Moscow, people usually go to the Kremlin, where there is the memorial of the Great Patriotic War (the Russian name for the Second World War) and the Tomb of the Unknown Soldier to lay flowers. This tradition was very popular in Soviet times. Other favourite places are Sparrow Hills, from which you get a great view over Moscow. The happy group opens champagne, takes photographs, chats, and generally makes a lot of noise.

Each region has its own places where people go. Moreover, they are spread across all sorts of times, ideas and beliefs, and can be religious or historical monuments, or something from Soviet times (quite often war memorials), or something

It is traditional to start wedding celebrations at Sparrow Hills in Moscow. Here, the bride is surrounded by friends and family.

cultural. In Petersburg, people go to the statue of Peter I, in Kaluga to the St Tikhon's Hermitage, in Tula to the Lev Tolstoy Country Estate-Museum.

Funerals also have their own rituals. It is traditional to invite as many people as possible, so as not to offend anybody, and also to show respect to the departed. After the official ceremony at the crematorium or cemetery (many people, especially believers, do not recognise cremation), everybody is invited to the home of a close relative of the departed for a funeral banquet.

Funeral banquets are a very old custom. It is possible that they date back to pre-Christian times, when the sumptuous funeral feasts ensured that dead warriors would have a successful life in the next world. The tradition of laying a large feast for a funeral is still alive in Russia. Even the atheist years could not destroy this custom. There will be a well-stocked table, people drink a lot of vodka, and on this day, you cannot turn anybody away. An empty place is set for the departed with a glass of vodka and a piece of black bread, and when remembering and toasting the dead, you never touch glasses.

Foreigners are often surprised by this Russian 'barbarism', throwing a party for a funeral. But the tradition has its own deep reasoning. Firstly, it is a way to have final remembrances about the departed. Secondly, it helps to distract the relatives' attention from the sad event and to calm them, as they have to prepare the meal. And finally, a banquet with alcohol, as they say nowadays, will reduce stress in a natural way, without taking medication. Smaller, but nonetheless obligatory, funeral banquets are held on the 9th and 40th days after death.

When you are dealing with Russians, you need to remember that celebrations are an important part of their everyday life. Not only the state holidays, but many personal moments which may at first glance seem unimportant turn into a grand event. Lack of money and being tired after work are not good reasons for cancelling these small pleasures.

ALTERNATIVE LIFESTYLE

In Moscow and Saint Petersburg, you can find the same sort of alternative lifestyle as in any large Western city, sometimes even more. In major Russian cities and regional centres, there will be some traces of it. In the rest of Russia, it does not seem to exist.

SETTLING IN

CHAPTER 5

'The traveller in Russia will hear '*Si chass*' pronounced
a good many times daily while he is in the Empire...
The literal translation of '*Si chass*' is 'This hour';
and perhaps this will account for the fact that it is
often an hour before a simple demand can be met.'
—Thomas Knox

FORMALITIES

Writing about the formal requirements on foreigners who come to Russia is not just difficult, but almost impossible. Firstly, they change—sometimes radically—very quickly, so any information included in a reference or guidebook is instantly out of date and does not reflect reality. Before coming to Russia, you must check and recheck all details, preferably at the Russian embassy, as not all companies will have the most up-to-date information.

The second difficulty is that the requirements and formalities are so tangled and indeterminate that it is sometimes difficult to get at the truth.

The Right Rules

Not so long ago, a foreigner who works in Russia and has a Russian wife and children was held on the border at Sheremetyevo Airport, as although he had a residency permit, he did not have a visa in his passport. They kept him for seven hours, threatening him with deportation.

The Russian relatives of this luckless foreigner got in touch with all the people they knew, right up to high-ranking officials in the Ministry for Foreign Affairs and the Ministry for Internal Affairs. In the end, the foreigner was fined and released, but the most surprising thing about the story is that nobody could say whether or not the border guards' requirements were legal or not. There is supposedly a statute which says that if you have a residency permit, you do not need a visa, but nobody could be 100 per cent sure.

Finally, one more difficulty in Russia is the all-important human factor. If the border guard does not like you, if you act provocatively or rudely, they can find fault with anything. They may not deport you, of course, but it will still give your nerves a good shakedown.

But it is precisely this human factor which is the way out of most situations. The main things to do when talking with Russian representatives of the state is not to swear, not to claim your rights by making reference to the law and do not tell them that they live in a barbaric country and that you cannot imagine the same thing happening anywhere else. Which actually is unjust. It is just that foreigners rarely come into contact with that side of life, while Russians know what it is like to get a visa, or a work permit or a residency permit abroad.

You simply need to be polite, remain calm and try to come to an agreement. The best thing is to try phrases such as "Well, what can we do?" or "What to do now?", which give people the opportunity to help you and be of use. An unhappy and downcast appearance will create a better effect than an aggressive and purposeful one. Word has it that money can also help on occasions, but it is important not to make a mistake that could worsen the situation. The opinion that all problems in Russia can be solved with a bribe is wrong. It is possible to ask something like "Maybe there is a fine to pay?" and not just to slip somebody some notes.

It is not all that bad. The vast majority of foreigners in Russia live and work successfully. Tourists and those visiting the country for a short time just need to remember one important fact: your visa is not only stamped when you cross the border, but it must also be registered. If you have been invited by a company, that company will handle the registration. If you have a private invitation, then registration is done at the same place where the invitation was issued. The easiest option is hotels, which register you automatically, even if you only stay for one night. Word has it that for a small sum, hotels will sometimes stamp your passport even if you are not a guest at the hotel, but I would not advise placing too much trust in such information.

If you have come for a long stay, to work or to study, then your documents, and the documents for your family, must be arranged by the organisation that is inviting you, and it is better to discuss this early. Trying to do everything yourself is a difficult and intricate process.

Foreigners who come to Russia usually ask what to bring. Not so long ago, the list was long and included toilet paper and golf balls. These balls, which will fit any outlet for flushing away water, were particularly popular among British authors who complained that in Russia, there are no plugs for baths and sinks, from which inhabitants of the British Isles so love to splash themselves with water. In Russia, it is not usual to take a bath in public places, and people only take baths in their own home—in their own bathroom. The reason for this is personal hygiene. A word of advice: if the bath in your hotel does not have a plug, you would be better off taking a shower. In expensive hotels where the bathrooms are clean, there will always be a plug.

In Russia, you can now buy practically everything that you can buy in other countries. The main problem is that these items are often more expensive in Russia than they are elsewhere. So it is a question of which is better, to pay over the odds in Russia or to pay for extra luggage, and people have to decide for themselves.

Fake Goods

Alcoholic drinks, tea, coffee, expensive perfumes and medicines often come without any guarantee of quality (even the price you pay is no guarantee). So if you are a big coffee lover or it is important for you to have a particular medicine, it is better to bring it with you.

HOME AND FAMILY

The home plays a very important role in Russians' lives. Its meaning in Russian is very wide and does not distinguish between the place where you live, the family and the building itself (for comparison, think about the difference between 'house' and 'home' in English). Everything is rolled into one all-inclusive word, '*dom*'.

Moreover, the building itself is not so important. Of course people in Russia, as everywhere, are proud of their 'family nest'. However, very few people can now say 'This house was built by my great-grandfather'. And this is not just to do with the cataclysms of the 20th century (first the Revolution, then the Civil War and Second World War) which literally wiped many houses from the face of the earth, and sometimes whole villages or settlements. Traditional Russian houses have been made of wood since time immemorial. And not just in the villages, but in the towns as well. Wood was the most widely available, cheapest and most practical material for those living surrounded by the endless Russian forests. On top of this, it was considered to be better for your health. People thought that a wooden home 'breathes' and lets those who live in it breathe better too. Stone, on the other hand, is a cold, alien material that does not let air through. It is interesting that when stone houses came into fashion and became a symbol of prestige and well-being in the 19th century, the rich preferred to build a house with a stone first floor (to keep household items) and a wooden second floor (to live in). Some went even further and built a

Old wooden houses still line the streets of Russian towns.

traditional wooden country house and then decorated it in such a way as to look like stone. This decoration was so well done that from a distance you could not tell the difference. And you can still find examples of such houses in provincial Russian towns.

Wood, although convenient and practical, has one important characteristic: it burns easily. Therefore, it is not surprising that over the centuries, fire was the main disaster in Russian towns and villages. Sometimes, a whole block, or even a small village, would be completely destroyed in a single night. But life continued. And Russians learned to build things again quickly. Together with the commune, they helped one another and built new houses. In the middle ages, there was even a house market in Moscow. Any house you bought there was like a child's construction set Lego: all the pieces were pre-fabricated and you just slotted them one into another.

So Russians have not developed any great attachment to property or to a house as a building. People know that it can all be destroyed in just a few minutes. English novels in which the hero or heroine fights for the family home are alien to the Russian soul. Just build a new house, it is not that important.

Russians love the fairy-tale bird, the phoenix. From time to time it burns, so that renewed and even more beautiful, it can rise again from the ashes. And just like the fairy-tale phoenix, Russian houses were born again after the fires. And so, life was constantly renewed.

Much more important, from the Russian point of view, was the land on which they live and on which their ancestors toiled. Everything changes, but the land remained the standard for permanent value. Russian peasants have considered the land to be theirs since ancient times, even if in reality it belonged legally to their master.

Nowadays, the peasant roots that most Russians have are making themselves felt again. As mentioned briefly in Chapter Two, at the beginning of *perestroika*, as part of fulfilling the production programme set out by the government, city-dwellers all over the country were given plots of land. It was a sort of 'feed yourself' programme: here's some land, grow what you want on it. These plots were small, usually four *sotkas*, but demand for them was huge. A sort of farming madness gripped the country. Doctors, teachers, engineers, people who had been born and grown up in cities and who had only ever seen fruit and vegetables on shop shelves, started growing all sorts of plants on their tiny plots of land with an enthusiasm hard to capture in words. Packing themselves into already packed local trains on the weekends, they heroically carried seedlings and planting stock in one direction, and their harvest in the opposite one. A professor that I know, who is a famous microbiologist, grew remarkable tomatoes in his vegetable beds. For some reason, they were multi-coloured, but all winter he demanded that his wife feed him only the results of his own efforts, considering all other produce to be of a low quality.

Some ancient, centuries-old passion for the land, for their land, awoke in these people, who had been torn from their roots a long time ago. Interestingly, the houses that were built on these plots were extremely primitive: a little barn with a table and a bed was entirely sufficient. At this time (the second half of the 1980s), the winds of change brought Brazilian and Mexican television serials to Russia, and Russians fell in love with them instantly. The burning passions of these Latin-American heroes found their echo in cold Russia, which was standing on the threshold of great changes and looking with uncertainty to the future. For some reason, the word *'fasenda'* (which meant the country estate of a rich land owner) entered the Russian language from these serials. Anybody who had even the tiniest plot of land—on which there was a cabin for two with toilet in the nearby woods—would on getting onto the local bus announce joyfully to the others, "I'm off to my *fasenda*". In the winter, proud 'landowners' would tell their guests, "We grew this out at the *fasenda*." And for many Russians, these tiny plots of land with their primitive shacks, answering the centuries old yearning that each person has for the land, still remains a *fasenda*.

The concept of home is closely tied in the Russian consciousness with the concept of motherland. In Russian, the word 'motherland' (*Rodina*) has the same linguistic roots as the word 'birth', and it is the place where you were born and grew up (and, in olden times, lived out your entire

Country houses of the Russian nobility are very beautiful. This one is now called Gorki Leninskie, as this was the house where the founder of the Soviet state died.

life). A character in the popular Soviet film *Garage* says at a meeting "I sold my motherland for a car!" Everybody looks at him in open shock, imagining some sort of passionate spy, and then he announces that he is talking about the house in which he was born.

Sometimes, people talk about their 'small' motherland, so as not to get mixed up with the large motherland, Russia. This link to a house and the territory which immediately surrounds it is particularly noticeable nowadays in large towns. For example in Moscow, a number of former villagers live within a limited space. Their 'Moscow' is two or three streets around their house, they know a few shops and the local market, hospital and school. For them, everything else, including the centre of Moscow, is the back of beyond, a place they will visit a few times in their life.

So the concept of a home is extremely wide for Russians. It is the actual space, and the family that lives there, the land that surrounds it and the so-called 'little' motherland where one was born and grew up. The home, in all its multifariousness, plays an extremely important role in Russian life. Russian folk tales are good examples of this. Most of their characters leave their home at the beginning and then return, having completed their heroic deeds and brought back a beautiful wife. Or at the very worst, they build a new home.

Returning Home

Grigory Melikhov, the hero of Mikhail Sholokov's novel *Quiet Flows the Don* (which is far from being a fairy tale), is caught up in the Civil War, which rolls through the places he considers to be home. First he joins the Whites, like most of the Cossacks, and later switches over to the Reds, and finally he ends up on his own. Suffering, blood, political swings and passionate love, all this it would seem will be never-ending. There is only one thing left for him to do. At the end of the novel, he returns home to his land, as that is the only place where he can find peace and truth. Readers—with the benefit of hindsight about subsequent history—suspect, of course, that after such an unstable life, Melikhov is unlikely to be allowed to find peace in his home over the coming years, but as far as the general idea is concerned, that is not important.

LIVING IN RUSSIA

Nowadays, hotels are divided—as they are all round the world—into good but expensive, and cheap but not so good. The only thing is that the price-quality gap may be more noticeable in Russia than in other countries. Hotel prices in Russia are higher than in other places, and even if you pay a large sum, you may still only get a mediocre room. We shall talk more about Russian hotels in Chapter Seven.

If you are planning to live in Russia for a while, and in particular if you have a family, it is better to rent a flat. Again, prices are quite high. A three-room flat (this means kitchen, bathroom, corridor plus three rooms) in Moscow will cost at least US$ 1,000 a month, and depending on the size and its location, prices can go up to astronomical. Prices round the country are lower, but then the choice of quality accommodation is very limited.

As with visas, it is better if your accommodation can be sorted out by the organisation which invited you. If that is not possible, there are two other options. The first and most popular in Russia is to find a flat through your friends. This is the way it is usually done. The second is to rent accommodation through an agent. It is most important not to make a mistake and end up in the hands of swindlers. Therefore, if your friends can recommend which real estate agent to use, that is also preferable. You are better off going to a large company, even if the rates of commission are higher. There is a well-known saying in Russia: 'Misers pay twice', so any attempt to save money may turn into trouble.

Finding a Place to Stay

Notices about flats to rent can be found in all sorts of papers with advertising space. One of the more popular is *Iz ruk v ruki* ('from hands to hands'), for which there is also an Internet version, but all the adverts are of course in Russian.

If you have come to study, the institution will usually put you in a student hostel. Some of them are in a miserable state.

Cheap student accommodation is mainly a leftover from the old times, when they were basically paid for by the State and students had to make some symbolic payment to live in them. This accommodation, which used to be practically free, has in many cases not been redecorated since the fall of the Soviet Union. But most educational institutions now have reasonable accommodation 'on a commercial basis', in other words you have to pay for it.

Buying furniture, moving house or renting any kind of vehicles (including those with removers) is not a problem nowadays, it is just a question of money. Unfortunately, those companies that work with foreigners have a tendency to up the price of their services, so you are better off contacting an

Tips for Settling In

As for the problems of settling in, one has to keep in mind the following recommendations:

- Don't try to find out the juridical truth about all formalities. You will waste your time and come to nothing. The legal system in Russia is complicated and tangled, differs from region to region, from district to district, and is sometimes unknown even to the officials. Rules and regulations may change every month, so it is tricky to follow them directly. Even the highest authorities may give you the most contradictory and confusing information.
- Rely upon the company you have been invited by. Normally, they can manage all the questions concerning your housing, financial matters, health and transport.
- If the company refuses to solve your problems, look for a Russian friend or foreigner who has lived long enough in Russia to have Russian friends.
- And finally, remember that all the formalities may be solved through establishing personal contacts with the officials.

ordinary company. True, you may have difficulty explaining yourself, so it would be better to enlist the support of somebody who speaks Russian.

When bringing your own possessions, it is important to remember that you must declare all valuables in written form. Otherwise, it will be difficult to take them out on the way home. These include jewellery with precious stones, antique objects and works of art. Formally speaking, you must declare all possessions that exceed in value approximately € 2,000 per person. But nobody really follows this rule.

SPECIFIC FEATURES OF EVERYDAY LIFE

Everyday life in Russia is different, depending on whether you are talking about town or village life. Those who live in the towns usually have modern conveniences such as a toilet, hot water and electricity. Living in a village, you will only have the third. The Bolsheviks considered the electrification of Russia as one of their important achievements. There was even a slogan that read 'Communism is Soviet power plus the electrification of the whole country'. Unfortunately, similar slogans regarding water supply and sewage networks were not put forward, so out of all these conveniences, villages only have light.

Even in the cities, there are certain specific features to bear in mind. For the most part, Russians live in quite crowded conditions, which leaves its mark on the way that they live. If possible, they try to have a separate room for chatting and watching television, which is grandly named the 'living room'. But the living room, bedroom and office are frequently one and the same room. We are not talking about the richer sections of society, whose flats and houses are built and fitted out in the best European traditions and whose way of life is similar to that in Europe.

Contemporary Russians spend a lot of time at home. The toilet and bathroom are usually separate; if they are together, it is a sign of poverty. Carpets are very popular, either on the floor or hanging on the walls. They are partly a sign of wealth, and partly help to keep the heat in. Expensive items are kept for guests and brought out on special occasions. People are usually not demanding. They eat from simple, old crockery, not willing to use the good stuff for themselves.

Many Russians, particularly the older generation, have a prejudice against chemical cleaning agents. They consider them harmful to one's health and not necessary. In general, people have their own idea of what is cleanliness at home. Some think that washing the floors is sufficient. And there is another strange phenomenon: many housewives will spend the whole day flitting about with a duster, but nothing actually gets cleaner as a result.

Storing up stocks of food in the autumn to eat over the winter is also very popular. Many families will pack their balconies and cupboards with jars of pickled cucumbers and tomatoes, vegetable marrow preserve, mushrooms and jams from various berries. Some housewives show an unrestrained imagination and make, for example, jam out of vegetable marrow or watermelon rind. The better the housewife, the more stores she will have.

The situation with rubbish in the country is not, in general, a happy one. Everything is thrown out together, without any

attempt to sort out different types of rubbish. As a rule, the attitude to rubbish is fairly flippant, and it is usually thrown out by men hurrying to work or children when they come home from school. Sometimes, spontaneous rubbish dumps appear: somebody throws their rubbish out in the wrong place and then slowly everybody starts throwing theirs there too. Unfortunately, this is a serious problem in Russia, and one which is far from having a solution.

Water, heating and electricity are still reasonably cheap. You pay for water and heating by the month, and not by amount used. And Russians have grown used to using them lavishly. They even get irritated sometimes when travelling abroad about the 'miserliness' of foreigners who keep an eye on the use of light, water and heat.

Cities now have the whole range of services such as laundrettes and dry cleaning, sometimes with home delivery. Self-service laundrettes are not widely available, and trying to find one is virtually impossible.

Once a year, your hot water supply is turned off for up to one month. This is supposedly for repair work to be done on the pipes. This old tradition is a hindrance and irritates people as it is usually done in the summer when it is hot and you need to wash more often than usual. But there is nothing you can do about it. You just need to grin and bear it. And count on your friends who may allow you to come round and wash, since the water is turned off at different times in different areas of the city.

Overall, all the services you need for daily life are available, but with one problem: either they are expensive or of poor quality. However, this problem is not national but worldwide.

EDUCATION
Kindergartens and Schools
During the Soviet times, the country was very proud of its facilities for children. At that time, there was a popular slogan which read 'All the best is for the children'. And in reality, much was done for them and was available to all. They were not particularly luxurious, but the kindergartens and day nurseries were high quality and cheap, and available to practically everybody.

Nowadays, there is a marked contrast between the state children's institutions of the old system, which are slowly living out their last days in poverty, and the new type of private institutions. The former receive miserable state subsidies and survive on the enthusiasm of the old school of teachers, but getting a place at one of them is very hard since they are affordable and demand is high. The latter are opening in ever greater numbers in the big towns. The conditions in them are good and it is easy to get a place, but the prices, as a rule, remind one of the elite educational institutions around the world. The golden mean, unfortunately, does not exist. As with other situations, when choosing a place for your child, it is best to rely on the advice of friends or neighbours.

There is a similar situation with schools. The free schools are often in a sad state, and you can clearly feel the lack of money and people. The paying schools cost a lot of money, which is no guarantee of a decent education.

Concerning ways of entertaining children, the situation is now a lot better, although only in the large cities. There you can find the old traditional zoos, circuses and children's theatres, as well as the newer, Western-style entertainment centres, which are opening all the time.

Only private and very expensive day care (or kindergartens) for younger children is available for foreigners in Russia. Much

A geography classroom in a secondary school in a Siberian village.

more accessible and reasonable is babysitting. It is better to look for a babysitter through your friends (that is how it is done by Russians) or through special companies which can be found on the Internet. In this last case, it may be much more expensive.

Institutes of Higher Education

In Russia, September is the month of knowledge. The academic year in all educational institutions and schools starts on 1 September. For 250 years (Moscow University, the first and the main university in Russia, was founded in 1755), higher education has played a significant role in determining how people live in Russia. Moscow State University now has some 26,000 students and 7,000 research students, as well as about 2,000 foreign students who have come from all over the world to study. Times, governments and even state systems have changed, but somebody with a higher education (particularly from a university) has always occupied a special, respected place in society. So what is the modern Russian student like?

In order to get into, say, Moscow State University, students have to undergo a rigorous selection process. The most popular faculties at the moment are foreign languages, law, economics and psychology. These are the subjects that are considered to be the most advantageous from the financial point of view, since they give you the chance to find a well-paid job. One of the new tendencies of modern life in Russia is that students have a more practical attitude to higher education. If in the old days simply having a university education was sufficient to start a good career, young people now look at everything when choosing an institute or faculty: the set of subjects to be studied, whether there are hands-on practicals, whether it is possible to go on a placement abroad, and even the way that the degree subject will be written on their diploma.

This sort of practical approach to study is linked with another new tendency in modern Russian education: the desire for courses to be more practical and close to life. Previously, the education programme was mainly aimed at students gaining wide, fundamental knowledge in one or another field, whereas now, in accordance with the spirit of the times and the demands of students, it is increasingly narrow and concentrates on specific, highly-specialised areas of knowledge. New subjects are being introduced, with the aim of bringing science and life closer together, and of giving students the knowledge that they will need in the future when they get a job. There are a number of new subjects in the humanities, such as Public Relations, Intercultural Communication and Management in Different Spheres. At the same time, certain subjects are disappearing from the list being offered by the faculties—those of a narrow, scientific and academic nature such as Theory of Science and Methodology of Science. This coming together of education and life, sometimes at the expense of fundamental academic knowledge, is the result of changes in the requirements and ideals of Russian society over the last ten years.

It is not surprising, therefore, that the words written on your diploma did not previously have any particular meaning, as the most important fact was that you had a higher education, whereas now they will determine whether or not you can get a specific job. And the choice is wider. In the Soviet Union, institutes of higher education, and in particular universities, numbered in single figures. After the start of *perestroika*, this increased a hundredfold, although the level of education varied wildly. Only a few, with Moscow University at the head, kept their exclusive place in the state and public system.

For many Russian families, a higher education is still an object of special prestige. Even if the parents were unable to finish their education (for whatever reason), they consider it a necessary condition for their child to succeed. Many families will deny themselves everything in order to give their child the opportunity to study at university. Despite the fact that education in Russia is still basically free, you still need a fair amount of money to study. This helps to pay for tutors who prepare you for the exams and your daily expenses while you are studying. State stipends are still paid to those studying on day-time courses, but they are so small that without parental support, it is unlikely anybody could survive on them.

Currently, the main reasons for wanting to study at a university are a desire to occupy a respected place in society and the wish to find a good, highly-paid job. These goals have become more individualised than they were before, when more abstract ideas like doing something for the social good and developing science were the main stimuli for studying.

Russians and Higher Education

At the start of *perestroika* in the 1990s, there was a marked drop in the number of those interested in higher education. It turned out that any cunning young person could make a tidy capital on speculation or in politics, without any diplomas or knowledge. However, time returned everything to its rightful place and the traditional values have started to come back into Russian society. One of them is a respect for higher education. This tendency has become especially noticeable at the university. In 2001, about 20,000 school leavers competed for the right to enter Moscow State University, and of those about 4,000 got in. For example, the competition for the foreign languages faculty was about ten hopefuls for each place. Nowadays, with the whole world open for Russia, and contacts with both the West and the East, there has been a great effect on society. A knowledge of foreign languages has now become a determining factor in a good career.

On average, Russian students study for five years, though there are some exceptions such as medical students who study for longer. At the end of their studies, they have to take two or three so-called state examinations on set disciplines in their chosen speciality and also defend their diploma. For those specialising in the humanities, this means a small, independent piece of research on a selected topic which the potential graduate must present to a state commission at an open public meeting. As a result, the student receives a so-called Specialist-Diploma. Over the last few years, there have been attempts to introduce a two-stage education system as in the West, with a Bachelor's degree awarded after four years and a Master's after another two. At Moscow State University, this system is already running successfully in the economics faculty. However, both the students themselves and their parents are more familiar with (and understand better) the traditional five-year diploma. Additionally, because of the frequent changes to the education system over the last ten years, a certain suspicion of all things new has grown in Russian society, and people fear that what has been introduced today will be cancelled tomorrow and they will be left without any diploma. The instability and constant reforms (which sometimes contradict one another) are another trait of modern Russian education.

One of the new introductions at Russian universities is paid education. The financial difficulties in the state inevitably led to a reduction in the state allocation for the education system. But the necessary expenses have grown. Technical progress, the appearance of new teaching technologies, the possibility to develop international research connections and the emergence of new areas of knowledge have all required significant funding. At the same time, a group of people has appeared in Russia over the last decade who have significant financial means and are prepared to invest them in the education of their children. Paying students are accepted into Moscow State University in accordance with its traditions, on the basis of strict competition. Those who successfully passed the entrance examinations study for free, irrespective of their parents' financial situation. Those who did not get the right number of points but still did well in the exams and got positive marks have the possibility to enter into an agreement with the university and pay for their education. The overall cost of the course depends on the popularity of the various subjects. In Moscow State University, the greatest number of paying students are to be found studying economics, law, foreign languages, government administration and international relations.

The introduction of a paid tuition programme led to new social problems. In the first instance, teachers and students underwent noticeable difficulties trying to get used to the new conditions. Education in Russia has always been noted for its

The main building of Moscow State University—one of the architectural landmarks of Stalin's epoch.

democratic nature, and during the Soviet years, the principle of equality was at the fore. Free education gave no grounds for inequality to arise in the relations between the students, and meant that the teachers' authority was unshakable and the principles of teaching beyond reproach. These students (and their parents), having paid for their studies, often consider the education process as some sort of item which they have purchased, and complain to the teachers and administrators, thinking that they have the right to get involved in the faculty's teaching plans. At the same time, there arises an opposing tendency: paying students are afraid of their situation, thinking it to be a sign that they are lagging behind and intellectually inferior to those students who had been accepted through the competition to free places. In the last few years, the situation has calmed down, and society's opinion about paid education is changing. More and more people are saying that it is necessary and that it has value at the government level, although it has to be said that the issue is far from being resolved.

The set of disciplines in the education plan for the faculties (in Russia, these are equivalent to the various colleges or departments that make up a university) is fixed. This set is identical for all students of the same faculty, and the student only chooses the subjects for specialisation in the final years. Thus, historians have to listen to a full set of lectures about all periods in the history of the development of humanity and about all areas across the globe, as well as a series of additional historical disciplines. The students go through these issues during the first three years of seminars. In the fourth and fifth years, they have the chance to select a more specialised region and time, for example the history of England in the Middle Ages, and study specific problems in more depth.

As before, the university is not only a centre for education, but also for research. The students take an active part in the research life in a wide range of forums. Every spring, there is a pan-university research conference called 'Lomonosov Readings', at which the students and the teachers have the possibility to present the results of their research and discuss different types of research questions. The best are rewarded and published.

Moscow University

Moscow University has practically everything that a student needs to study: a wonderful library (which is one of the oldest in Moscow), its own publishing house, sport complexes, accommodation for those students not from Moscow (the cost of which is minimal and affordable to everybody), a cheap canteen and a café. Many faculties have computer classes, language-learning rooms, video classes and copy centres. Unfortunately, it has to be said that a lack of funds means that it is only rarely that a student can actually make use of these facilities. The main teaching aids still remain the blackboard and chalk (for teachers) and notebook and pen (for students).

Student Life

At the university, classes usually start at 9:00 am and last until about 3:00–5:00 pm for the first years (the older the students, the more time is given over to independent study). Each class lasts one hour and 20 minutes, without a break, and classes come in two main types. The first is lectures, where between 100–400 students (depending on the faculty) listen to their teacher, occasionally asking questions in written form. The second type is seminars, with a much smaller group of students (10–25 people) and the main form of teaching is joint discussion of various course-related topics. The culmination of both lectures and seminars is an examination, which in the Russian education system is traditionally done orally.

At each seminar, the students receive homework. The second half of the day, and sometimes the weekends, is set aside for this homework (on average students study 5–6 days a week in the lower years and 3–4 days a week in the upper years, when more time is spent on individual research). Nowadays, Russian students in general have a more serious attitude to homework, preparing for examinations and the process of studying in general. They are more purposeful and more conscientiously fulfil their teachers' requirements as they can see more clearly the final goal of their education: a prestigious job, good salary and the possibility of travel abroad. For their recent predecessors, student life often became more important than the academic process. Not infrequently, their time at university became a way of filling up their reserve of knowledge, of having an interesting and constructive time, when it was possible to do what you enjoy doing and then simply pass exams in most of the subjects so that you can then forget about them.

To Party or Study?

During the Soviet period, there was a system of mandatory state assignment for graduates and so some sort of job (better or worse but all with roughly the same salary) was guaranteed to them by the state. Now Russian students have to think about their future on their own. In order to find a good job, you must study well. There was an interesting result to a survey carried out at one of the evening events at the university. As part of an advertising campaign, the students were offered the chance to take part in a draw for free entrance tickets to popular Moscow clubs. At the same time, each of them was asked which of the clubs they would prefer to go to if they won, straight after the end of the evening. Only 25 per cent of those asked made a definite choice, 35 per cent answered that they would rather go home and go to bed, and 40 per cent said that they had to prepare for their examinations and did not have the time to go out partying.

However, some traits of the 'Russian student' have remained unchanged and often force the foreign teachers working with them into a dead end. Very few of them give their work in on time, and as a rule the Russian teachers do not expect them to. They know that the deadline given is an ideal and acceptable only to the most organised students. Another problem is the so-called 'copying', which particularly shocks American teachers. This topic opens up both a particular feature of Russian mentality and, to a certain extent, shows the character of the relations between the students in the group. In Russian educational institutions, copying and plagiarism are banned, as they are in other countries. Many teachers take this issue very seriously. They make frequent demands that the students bring nothing with them to examinations except a pen and a piece of paper, and that they sit well apart from each other. At the same time, there really are serious differences of opinion over this issue, caused, above all, by the historical, cultural and educational peculiarities of the development of Russian society.

Traditionally in Russia (in fact, ever since Moscow State University has been teaching), progress in studies has mainly been assessed by oral examination. In this case, copying loses the meaning that it has when taking a written exam. Even if the student succeeds in writing something down when preparing the answer, experienced teachers can spot this immediately while the student is answering. Furthermore, an oral exam supposes a wide-ranging discussion of topics covered by the course. Written work is usually given to the students with so many different variants and in such an amount that copying off each other is practically impossible. As a result of this, copying (even if it does take place) has no practical effect on the outcome of the exam. Students do not denounce those who have been copying. If somebody has been sufficiently subtle to do it, fellow students will never tell the teacher about it. The collective feeling is still very strong in Russian society. It should also be remembered that Russian students enter university in a specific faculty and they will be formed into groups from the start of their studies and will remain in them for five years. Naturally during that time, reasonably tight and close bonds are formed and each group is its own sort of collective society and family. Under such circumstances, informing about the minor sin of one of your colleagues is considered to be improper. On the other hand, the students well know that one single chance success does not give them any significant result. Finally, for Russians (students and teachers alike), informing about an offence committed by a colleague is closely tied with the concept of 'denunciation', which, because of certain historical and political reasons, evokes an extremely negative association.

Teachers in Russian education institutions are well respected. There is always a certain distance between student and teacher, irrespective of the age of the latter. This comes through in the way they address each other: always using the polite form and by name-patronymic, and unless there are familiar relations, this continues in everyday conversation too. It is true that over the last few years, some of the signs of respect have been imperceptibly disappearing from university life. These were

Students in an English-language class at the Moscow State University.

mandatory until not so long ago, such as standing up when a teacher comes into the auditorium, raising your hand if you want to ask a question or answer one, and a number of others. Students have become more demanding; they write complaints more frequently if they do not like something about the quality of teaching. However, on the whole, the internal form of the relations between students and teachers has for the most part remained at its former level of respect and trust.

Nowadays, the students, particularly in the upper years, not infrequently find themselves a job. This may be purely for financial reasons, to support themselves and sometimes their family, or in order to find and occupy in advance a good position, thereby assuring their future. Students usually work in various companies as secretaries, assistants, managers or translators. In Russia, students only very rarely, in cases of extreme need, try to earn a bit on the side as a waiter or shopkeeper, as they usually do in other countries. These professions are considered to be service industry jobs and not compatible with the great 'title' of university student. Students are not particularly encouraged by their teachers and the university administration to find employment, since it is rarely possible to fit it in with their study, and the latter usually suffers as a result.

Social life, which a mere 20 years ago was a significant part of student life, has now noticeably declined. A multitude of youth and social organisations, the purpose of which was to educate in a variety of ways (ideological, moral, patriotic, working and social), have been left in the past. Students are now more individualistic. However, we can see a tendency to revive the best traditions of the past. Students readily participate in various pan-university sporting events, come together in student amateur dramatic groups, and organise theme evenings. The Moscow student body is fairly passive politically; the heavy workload, search for a job and the political reshuffling which has become standard in contemporary Russia have all meant that today's students do not take an active part in the political life of the country, indeed are little interested in it.

Tatianin Day

One of the most popular social events at Moscow State University is Tatianin Day, a student festival which is held every year on 25 January and marks the start of the winter holidays. It was on this day (which is the feast day of Saint Tatiana in the Russian Orthodox Church) in 1755 that the Russian Empress Elisaveta Petrovna signed the order to open Moscow State University. From that day on, it has been considered to be the university's birthday and Saint Tatiana the patron saint of all students and teachers. And this has always been the students' favourite holiday. This is how the famous Russian writer A P Chekhov jokingly described it at the end of the 19th century: 'This year we drank everything except the Moscow river, and that was only because it was frozen … Pianos and grand pianos trembled, orchestras played Gaudeamus without stopping, voices were strained and croaky. It was so much of a jolly caper that one student, overcome by emotions, bathed in the reservoir where sterlets swim.'

Nowadays, it has become less noisy and more of a festival. On this day, the university holds a general meeting, the students meet the rector, there is a festival, concerts and dancing. New traditions have appeared: at the height of the celebrations, the rector personally pours *medovukha* (an old Russian drink made from honey), there is a competition between all the students called Tatiana at the university and so on. The festivities are rounded off with fireworks outside the main building on Sparrow (Lenin) Hills, the highest point in Moscow.

The students are now more independent than they used to be. In Soviet times, educating the soul in collectivism was part of the general teaching process, but now there are fewer events which bring the students together. And their personal problems (material difficulties, the ever increasing workload with the new knowledge being added on to the old, and sometimes the necessity to work) are all the greater. However, the relations between the student body in general have remained fairly close. They meet regularly in their free time, go to the cinema and theatre or do their homework together. It is common for them to pay visits to one another, go out of town, visit the country, or to go on excursions and tourist trips.

FINANCIAL MATTERS

Here are some hints about money matters. Credit cards have been successfully introduced in larger cities, department stores and supermarkets. However, after the financial crisis

We witnessed an incident in a Sberbank (the state bank of the Russian Federation) affiliate when ten-dollar bank notes were scrupulously examined, rubbed with an eraser, scrubbed by the nail, tested in a special electronic device, and finally rejected. The frightened owner's question: "Are they forged?" was given a firm answer: "No. But they cannot be accepted as it is a flaw of the American Mint."

of August 1998 caused by the default of Russian rouble, they are no longer fully reliable. Therefore a certain amount of cash is highly recommendable for your trip to Russia.

The most widely spread kind of hard currency is undoubtedly the American dollar. Then comes the Euro. Other kinds of hard currency, including British pounds, are exchanged rarely and reluctantly. Dollars must preferably be new, clean and in mint condition ideally.

The banking system of Russia is still radically different from the Western one, especially as far as personal accounts are concerned. Money for a Russian, first and foremost, means cash. The personal accounts, which are considered to be unreliable especially under the circumstances of a crisis, are regarded only as a place to keep cash; one can put the money in and take it out from the account in an affiliate of the bank.

Prices in Russia are very unstable. Generally, everything is quite expensive; Moscow is sometimes called the most expensive capital in Europe. On the other hand, some Russian products are still sold by 'old' prices, which, when they are converted into dollars, are next to nothing.

If you are staying with a Russian family, it is useful to know that the cost of accommodation in this country includes cold and hot water supply, heating, gas and local (within the city) telephone calls, while electricity and long-distance calls are paid separately. The latter are particularly expensive.

Many companies now pay their salaries through banks, so it may be necessary for a foreign employee to open a local bank account. To do this, you will need your migration card, your registration in Russia and your passport.

HEALTH

The situation in the major cities today is in general similar to all over the world. There are the remains of the old free health system, which have gone into decline over the last few years, and the modern and super well-equipped clinics and hospitals, where you have to pay for treatment. Many large firms and companies pay for their employees' health care. Emergency medical services—even in the larger cities—are far from being at the cutting edge, and so it is best to have a contract with some private clinic, including one that covers emergency services.

By dialling 03, anybody can call for an ambulance to come to any location at any time of day, but unfortunately you have no guarantee that it will arrive quickly, or that you will receive professional medical help. Furthermore, the ambulance doctors like to take their patients to hospital, as this relieves them of the responsibility for any consequences, and the hospital to which they take you may not be one of the best.

There is a paradoxical situation in Russia today with regard to medicine. The country has wonderful doctors who are able to perform miracles, undertaking unique operations and developing new forms of treatment. At the same time, the general health system is in a state of complete decay. This is particularly true not of the higher echelons but the middle and lower levels, the regional general practitioners, medical nurses and dry nurses. Somebody who has had a unique operation carried out may then die because of insufficient attention from the general medical staff.

Unfortunately, medical help across the country leaves much to be desired. There is a lack of money, salaries are not paid and equipment is not bought. In many of the outlying regions, there is just a heroic and enthusiastic doctor's assistant, faithfully sticking to his belief in the Hippocratic Oath, selflessly treating several villages. But that situation can be found anywhere.

You can't get your visa to Russia without medical insurance. And you don't need anything else in case of emergency. For regular problems, you can go to any medical institution and get what you want for your money.

SHOPS AND PURCHASES
As with many other questions concerning life in Russia, shops vary widely depending on what exactly it is you are talking

about. The major cities are now replicas of their Western and American counterparts. Supermarkets are enormous, and there are shopping centres with shops from international chains such as Ikea, Auchan and Stockmann. The whole feel of shopping and the range of products is very similar to those abroad. The difference between supermarkets in Russia and those worldwide is not in their size or scale or structure, but just in being open 24 hours a day, and weekends are no exception.

Traditional Soviet-style shops still remain and can be found everywhere. The selection they carry is more limited, but usually includes the basic foodstuffs and commodities, and the relation between seller and buyer is more personal. If you have established some sort of contact, you will be given advice on what to buy, or more often what not to buy, if a product is not fresh. These shops are usually open from 9:00 am until 9:00 pm, with a break for lunch from 1:00 pm to 2:00 pm, or from 2:00 pm to 3:00 pm.

In the small villages in the provinces, the selection of products will be very limited, with only the bare necessities (if there is a shop at all).

A Shop with Nothing

An amusing and enlightening episode occurred with some friends of mine. Having got carried away mushroom picking, they realised that they were hungry. But they were a long way from home, and in any case did not want to go back. So they decided to go to the nearest village. The shop door was invitingly open, and the seller was standing on the doorstep. You can imagine their surprise when she suddenly blocked the door saying, "We don't have any food, only bread." Having decided that this was all right, my friends agreed to buy bread. But still she would not let them in. "They haven't brought it yet." That's the sort of shop it was.

After *perestroika*, kiosks became a very popular form of sales point. They usually carry the same range of items: something sweet (chocolate, cakes, biscuits), tinned foods, nuts, crisps, cigarettes and a lot of alcoholic drinks. A few years ago, a law was adopted banning the sale of strong alcoholic drinks in such open kiosks. The owners quickly found their feet, added a bit on to their kiosks and carried on selling as before. They are usually open all day, without any lunch break, but do not always sell quality products.

The markets (food markets and general markets) have now become an important part of trading in Russia. Their prices are usually lower than in the shops, but there is no guarantee that the item or piece of food you buy will be any good. It's down to luck. As a rule, the prices in such markets are fixed and there is no point in bargaining.

However, the agricultural markets where they sell food produced by individuals and organisations is another question. Here you can bargain, all the more so because when the traders see a foreigner, they often up the prices. Produce is considered to be of better quality than in the shops, fresher and with less artificial additives. The markets carry a lot of vegetables from the south of Russia and also early season local produce. Visiting such markets is interesting from the cultural point of view. They are noisy, colourful, the traders are often interesting characters, and some products can only be found here, for example fresh forest mushrooms, berries and so on.

You can buy fresh fruits and vegetables at the agricultural markets in Russia.

Modern shops and crowds of shoppers can be found at GUM, the state department store in Moscow.

TRANSPORTATION

It is safer to call a taxi by telephone, even though it is a little more expensive and may take longer. Nowadays in Moscow, there are many private taxi services; you may look up their telephones in telephone directories or just ask somebody you know or the hotel people.

It is a popular custom to stop taxis in the street. It is still more popular to use private cars that will give you a lift readily; for many people, it is a common way to earn money now. There are more chances to get a *chastnik* (the owner of a private car) than a taxi, and it may be much cheaper (sometimes three times as cheap). Some people do this sort of job only on their way somewhere, so do not be disappointed or hurt if they refuse to give you a lift; it has nothing to do with you, only with your route. Do not forget to agree on the price before the trip. Of course, there is a certain risk about this kind of transport, but not much and it is very popular with Muscovites as it is much cheaper and quicker than official taxis called by telephone. In spite of the idea spread among foreigners that a car having a passenger or passengers may stop for you, this hardly ever happens in Moscow.

A guide to Moscow says that a packet of foreign cigarettes is enough to cover Moscow from end to end. Indeed, it was true for a short period of time some time ago. However, now a packet of cigarettes will not be of any help, only money must be paid, and rubles are better (for you) than hard currency.

Hiring a car in Moscow is easy now as all the largest foreign firms have opened their affiliates. But driving a car in Moscow is difficult. Not all the rules, though they are the same as in the rest of the world, are always obeyed, especially those concerning speed limits. It is not customary to give way to other cars or to let them pass. If you add bad traffic jams and occasional shortages of petrol, it will become clear that you have to think twice before you hire a car in Moscow. However, those who are used to driving in Naples or standing in traffic jams in London or New York are convinced that driving in Moscow corresponds to Western standards.

It is rather difficult for foreigners to buy cars in Russia. You are allowed to have your car registration only for the same period as your own registration, which is a maximum of one year. This means that every year you'll need to go through the same procedure, which is very time-consuming and expensive.

It is very easy now to rent a car in Russia. There are major international renting companies as well as local ones in all central cities. All you need to have is your passport and driving licence.

A foreign driving licence is valid in Russia during the first six months of one's stay, generally speaking. There are special rules and regulations for different countries, depending on separate agreements. It is possible to get a Russian driving licence after the first six months and going through a special examination on the knowledge of Russian traffic regulations. It is not as easy as it sounds, especially taking into consideration that the exam is in Russian.

There are many different types of public transport in the cities. Firstly, the Metro, which can be found in Moscow, Saint Petersburg, Samara, Yekaterinburg, Nizhniy Novgorod, Novosibirsk and other cities. The Metro is considered to be a very reliable form of transport, with trains running regularly and only short intervals between them. Once upon a time, the Russians were proud of their Metro, the beauty of its stations and its cleanliness. The beauty remains, each station is a work of art with mosaics, statues or marble, or all of them together. The best architects and artists in the country took part in designing them. This is particularly the case for stations built from the 1930s to the 1960s. But the more modern stations have also continued this tradition.

But the stations are not so tidy now. They are cleaned less often, less care is taken and there is more rubbish. Previously if somebody had had a drink, he would approach the Metro with caution, even if he was well dressed and only slightly tipsy. The watchful police made sure that only sober, tidy and well-behaved people entered the Metro, as though it were a palace. Nowadays, you can find down and outs, drunks and homeless people, so although the former wonders are still there, they are mainly in the surroundings. But on the whole, the Metro is a good and reliable form of transport.

Apart from the Metro, there are buses, trolleybuses and, in some cities, trams. Their main problems are that they are irregular (snow in the winter and rain in the autumn means that you can wait a very long time, as they seem to react to bad weather too) and overcrowded (frightening crushes and flying elbows are not uncommon and you need to be prepared to battle in order to get into and then put up with the squash).

Increasingly popular are the *marshrutkas*, or minivan taxis, that run along bus routes. They are more expensive than the buses, quicker and more comfortable (there is no standing), but they are also not that reliable.

MEANS OF COMMUNICATION

The Russian post, which is the main means of communication in the country as a whole, is slowly losing its position. It has become unreliable: letters take a long time, and there is no guarantee that they will actually be delivered at all. Economic problems have meant that the low-paid job of a postman has become extremely unpopular in the country, and nowadays, there are some regions in which there are simply no postmen at all and letters are simply piling up somewhere or other.

On the other hand, the Internet is actively spreading throughout the country. The capitals and other cities are already well covered, although it will not reach certain

villages for some time yet. Internet cafés are, for the most part, located in Moscow and Saint Petersburg.

It is hard, almost impossible, to get a city telephone landline number in Russia. There has always been a lack of numbers, and reason for speculation. The out-of-date phone switchboards in Moscow are now being updated, and so we have been promised that this problem will soon be solved, even if only in Moscow.

Cell phones became a passion for the Russians soon after they appeared here. Everybody in the cities now tries to make sure that they have one, including small children. People talk on cell phones at every opportunity and wherever they like. Many organisations have already introduced a ban on telephone conversations during particularly important meetings. While in theory talking on the phone during a business meeting is considered to be extremely impolite, in practice many people break this unwritten law.

Here is a typical situation from a trip abroad. A group of Russian tourists is on an excursion, let's say in Pompeii. The women and the children are listening and looking round in wonder, walking in an orderly group. A man, looking like a businessman, has stepped a short distance to the side. He is undoubtedly trying to sort out on his cell phone why the aluminium has not been unloaded, or why the covers have not been put on in time.

If a group of people comes into a restaurant or café and sits down at a table, they will all pull out their cell phones and place them on the table, so as not to miss a call. Sometimes, you will even see that a group of people sitting together are all talking separately, each on their cell phone.

By the way, Russia, unlike other countries, does not have a system of free incoming calls to mobiles (except from another number served by the same provider). So remember, if you are making a call, the person you are calling also has to pay.

TIPS FOR FOREIGNERS IN RUSSIA

Nowadays, there are a lot of foreigners in Russia. Some come to work in the many international companies, others bring up Russian families, while others still simply love this strange but very pleasing (if you love it and do not notice its daily drawbacks) world. Foreigners who work in Moscow, Saint Petersburg or other large city frequently like to get together in certain places and chat, creating their own special Russo-foreign world. And life in Russia has its own specific features.

First a word about crime in the city and safety measures. Usually, Western travellers come to Russia full of apprehension, having heard numerous stories about the Russian Mafia, crimes and the free-for-all that reigns in the city. Of course if we compare the situation in Moscow of 20 years ago and that which exists in the city today, there are far more infringements of law and order and less safety. If, however, we compare Moscow to any other major city in the world, the situation will be found to be very similar; any densely populated city is dangerous.

The precautionary measures you should observe derive first and foremost from common sense and are no different from those necessary in New York, Los Angeles, Paris and so on. It is not wise to take chance acquaintances you meet on the street back to your hotel room, to wander about the city if you've had one too many, to wave large packets of money around and so forth. On my first trip abroad—to London in 1990—I was robbed in a market and lost all my meager resources. Moreover, it was done in an extremely cunning and brazen way. This did not prevent me liking London, but convinced me that life is life everywhere.

Yes, in Russia we have thieves, criminals, a great many problems and complex situations, but this is the case in many other places as well. Life continues and many problems which are new for Russians are well known to representatives of the Western world—unemployment, homeless people on the streets, medical care and education that you have to pay for and so on. Try to walk round Moscow without negative feelings. In Russia, there is a saying: 'Whatever you are frightened of will happen to you.'

Among problems specific to Moscow, the following should be listed:

- Take care on the streets. As distinct to European and American drivers, Russians consider that the driver has right of way over the pedestrian. Remember that in Russia, drivers don't stop at zebra crossings. Even the green light of a traffic lights is not necessarily a guarantee that you are safe; a car may come hurtling out of a side turn following a green arrow and is unlikely to give way to you.

- Don't change money on the streets. Even if the exchange rate is exceptionally favourable, the chances of being cheated are very great. Do this at hotels, banks and official exchange offices. Be careful altogether on the streets. There is a lot of street trading at attractive prices now in Moscow, but it is best not to go for it. Be particularly cautious about buying foodstuffs and alcohol. It is better to buy all this at a more expensive price in big stores.

- In Moscow, it is not easy to find public toilets; they are virtually non-existent. The toilets in restaurants, cafes, museums, theatres and other public places are only for visitors to these venues. Remember this before leaving them.

- One should not always believe public signs. A 'No Smoking' sign does not necessarily mean that this activity is forbidden, while 'Open Round the Clock' is by no means a guarantee that the doors will be open at any time of day or night. It is always better to ask or check up, so as not to find yourself in a tricky situation.

THE RUSSIAN FEAST

CHAPTER 6

'Their table is always open to friends and acquaintances,
and a friend may bring to five or six persons to dinner,
and even at the end of the meals you will never hear a
Russian say, "We have had dinner; you have come too late."
Their souls are not black enough for them to pronounce
such words as this. Notice is given to the cook,
and the dinner begins over again.'
—Casanova, Italian adventurer

THE TRADITIONS OF RUSSIAN HOSPITALITY

Traditionally, hospitality is considered to be the distinguishing trait of the Russian character. For a Russian to entertain someone well—whoever he may be—means first and foremost to feed him well. I remember how astonished some Russian young people were at an American student's account of her meetings with her grandmother: "I go to visit her at her home and we have coffee and biscuits and chat." Not one self-respecting Russian grandmother would start on a discussion of problems, however serious, until she had fed her grandson or granddaughter to bursting point. The first and overriding instinct of a Russian housewife is to feed her guest, even if you have dropped in unexpectedly. To refuse to eat, more often than not, will be taken as a slight.

For the Russian in general, any informal contact will usually lead to eating and drinking while sitting round the table.

However straightforward and mundane the issue of food may seem, it is often the cause of a great many problems and intercultural conflicts. For though one may speak a foreign

If we turn to history, we will find that Russian merchants concluded most of their major deals over a meal at inns. In the second half of the 19th century, a Muscovite described one of the well-known Moscow inns: 'Bubnov's Traktir plays a major role in the life of the Gostinny dvor traders. Every day, excepting Sundays and holidays, it is packed from early morning to late at night with merchants, bailiffs, buyers and workmen. Here, after prolonged tea-drinking, deals were done and large sums of money changed hands.'

language to perfection, make an exhaustive study of foreign traditions, remember all the rules of conduct, it is often very difficult to force oneself to like foreign food. One only has to think of such foreign delicacies as Korean dogs, Chinese caterpillars, African roast grasshoppers and, for good measure, French frogs.

Foreigners and Russian Food

Shortly after the start of *perestroika*, people who were interested in Russia and learning Russian were drawn to the country. At that time (the late 1980s and early 1990s), there were few hotels, and many people stayed with Russian families. For the latter, it was a way of earning a bit of money and, more importantly, the possibility to chat with foreigners, which at that time was both new and interesting. Interestingly, most of the complaints were about food. The Russian hosts tried hard, but their ideas about when and what to eat differed from those of their guests.

The favourite Russian dishes of buckwheat porridge, sausage, potato, and fatty, meaty food were not always suited to people who were used to a more vegetarian diet. Some popular Russian dishes aroused foreigners to horror and even refusal, for example *holodets* or cold jellied meat, which is eaten as a delicacy on festivals. It is made by boiling pigs or cows trotters for about six or seven hours, then the bones are removed and the remaining meat covered with the stock. When it has cooled down, it looks something like meat in jelly, but not entirely transparent, and with a specific taste. Many people find it 'unusual' and given the ingredients, it looks simply barbaric.

In addition, many people in Russia eat a full breakfast, then take their main meal at lunchtime, and in the evening prefer tea or a light supper, which does not really correspond to the eating habits of Europeans and Americans. Nor will the hosts leave you in peace until you have tried everything, and will be offended if you refuse to eat one of the dishes. In short, there were many complaints.

The Russians ran up against a similar sad culture clash when they started travelling abroad. They just could not understand how in rich countries where the shops had so much food, for lunch they served you a thin cut of meat (and there were exactly as many pieces of meat as there were guests), a light salad, and then moved straight to dessert. According to Russian traditions, if guests come round, your table should be so covered with food that after everybody has eaten their fill, there is still food left over.

In many cultures, Russian included, you can create serious offence by refusing something that is offered to you. And so I recommend treating this question seriously and responsibly.

Those who have invited you and prepared a banquet do not expect anything in return. If you nevertheless want to thank them for their hospitality straightaway, you can invite them to a restaurant. But choose carefully, as restaurants in Russia belong to different social strata and can say much about the status of the person inviting. You would be best to get advice from friends, partners or simply the staff at your hotel. Russians do not like formal invitations, so however strange it may seem, it may be best not to do anything, and limit yourself to some indeterminate future wish such as 'when you come to England…' rather than make a mistake or be too formal.

EATING HABITS

So what are people's eating habits in Russia? In the morning, Russians have breakfast, and a full breakfast at that. In the middle of the day, they take dinner. In other words, their main meal. In the evening, they have supper, which is lighter. The concept of 'lunch' remains faithful to the traditional Russian meaning, although the English word has now entered the Russian lexicon (in particular the phrase 'business lunch', which is now offered by most restaurants in big cities). Nowadays, with most members of the family working and only coming together at home in the evening, there are many people who take dinner after work. Nevertheless, people prefer the traditional eating habits when possible (on weekends and public holidays, for example).

In Russia, it is traditional to have a family evening meal, when everybody sits at the table. If somebody comes home early and somebody later, it is usual to wait until everybody has gathered before starting to eat. Food is, above all, about company, conversation and telling the day's news. Nowadays, the role of 'conversation' is often played by the television, but even watching television while you are eating is a joint activity, and so there is still company nevertheless.

The main problem is that any foreigner in Russia faces the threat of overeating. In line with Russian traditions, supper is not so plentiful. There is even a Russian saying about healthy eating habits: 'Eat breakfast yourself, share lunch with a friend, and give supper to your enemy.' But if guests are coming round, the evening meal is turned into a veritable banquet. So you need to be prepared for the fact that in a single day, you may have to have two dinners (during the day and in the evening), not to mention a whole load of snacks in between.

Meals in Russia start with *zakuskas* (pre-meal snacks), which are brought to the table at the start (or, if you are entertaining at home, are already on the table). It is not usual to have an initial aperitif. Foreigners are always surprised by the abundance and variety of these *zakuskas*. It is usual to serve a number of different salads, cheese, cold cuts of meat, herring and other fish delicacies, caviar, salted mushrooms, cucumbers, tomatoes and other vegetables, fresh vegetables and herbs, cooked potato, pies with savoury fillings and much more besides. What you may consider to be a sumptuous spread usually turns out to be just a prelude. You would be well advised to make sure of this right at the start by saying something careful like "What a wonderful spread! I assume that there won't be anything else?!" If you are then told that this is only the start, I advise you not to get too carried away with the *zakuskas*.

After the *zakuskas*, people eat soup. Nowadays, soup is often missed out at such evening events, but during the day it is an integral part of the Russian table. Many Russians consider that dinner without soup is not dinner at all. It can stand on its own as a food, and in Russia is called the 'first course'.

For the hot dish, the 'second course' in Russia, there are a number of things you could be offered: fried meat, chicken

Typical *zakuskas* to go with vodka.

(by the way, the Russians love chicken and do not consider it to be a 'second-class' meat), a Russian national dish such as *pelmeni* (minced meat in pastry pillows), or traditional Russian meat in pots. People also like patties made from minced meat, but they are considered to be an everyday dish not to be served on special occasions.

Russians have historically eaten a lot of meat and a meal without meat is considered incomplete. They also love fish, but eat it less. Over the last few years, fish has become much more expensive, even low-quality frozen fish. Markets are the place to buy fresh fish. The main fish served to guests on special occasions is usually sturgeon or salmon. Vegetables are not considered to be a dish in themselves and are only served as a garnish. So in most cases, you will be served meat for dinner.

Given this, it is not easy for vegetarians. In addition, because of the climatic and economic conditions, during the winter fruits and vegetables come in limited variety and are expensive. Those which nowadays are brought in from abroad in large quantities year round are not a big favourite with the Russians (even if they can afford to buy them). People think that they have no taste and no smell, and call them 'plastic'. The frost and economic difficulties have taught people to

Kilka (salted small fish) is a deli favourite in Russia.

eat filling food, which would give their body a large energy reserve. People who refuse to eat animal products are often looked upon in Russia as rich eccentrics.

Finally, after all of this, there will be tea. The Russians love tea no less than the English. Coffee, usually instant, is generally drunk in the mornings. Tea is always accompanied by dessert: cakes, biscuits, sweets, jam, honey and so on.

Eating Against Your Will
In Russia, there is a popular fable: A man by the name of Demyan invites his neighbour to partake of his fish soup. The latter declines the offer, explaining that he is stuffed to the gills. Demyan continues to insist, describing the delights of his soup. The fable ends on a sad note: the two friends fall out. In Russia, this sort of situation, when you are forced to eat against your will, is known as 'Demyan's *uha*' (fish soup). It is a situation, alas, you have to be prepared for when visiting Russians.

In Russia, this fable surprises no one. Refusal of food, whatever the reason given—that you are full, slimming, not used to eating at this time of day—is taken as a slight. The only exception made is for illness. Here you will always be understood. Only remember that virtually every Russian is a medical expert of a sort, so don't try to pull a fast one; you will be found out immediately. If you are really ill, have no qualms about refusing, but be ready for a host of questions and advice, for there is nothing the Russians like better than to discuss medically-related topics.

In Russia, as everywhere, it is now fashionable to be on a diet. Young and not so young women, having watched American films and read European fashion magazines, try to conform to the fashionable idea of being slim. This imitation of Western culture is a characteristic phenomenon in Russia, particularly in its educated regions. But overall, society for the most part still lives to national traditions.

BANQUETS AND BUSINESS RECEPTIONS
Meeting guests is always a happy occasion for Russians, and so receptions, including business meetings, quite often turn into a full-blown banquet. Buffets are still not very common in Russia, although some leading companies and organisations are trying to introduce them into Russian life. However, the

Russians' favourite way of gathering, including for business purposes, is still to sit down in the traditional way and eat food together, where you can relax, make yourself comfortable on a chair and eat and drink properly.

It is usual to remain at the table throughout the whole meal. Unless there is space to dance, which is the only good reason for leaving the table, the guests will sit for a number of hours without moving from their places. The whole time, they eat, drink, converse and pronounce toasts. Of course, we are talking here about traditions. Nowadays in the big cities, such receptions are very similar to their Western counterparts, but this concerns a very limited circle of people.

AN INVITATION TO A RUSSIAN HOME

Inviting somebody to your home is common in Russia. You may be invited by the most unlikely of people for the most unlikely of reasons, for example by the friends or relatives of a not-so-close Russian acquaintance. And they will invite you just like that, to do something pleasant. Foreigners sometimes eye such invitations with suspicion, trying to guess what these unknown people want, and why they have laid a table and spent so much time to entertain their guests.

The reason is simple. In Russian culture, the concept of guests is still very important. To take somebody in and feed them, to show them respect simply because they are a guest, is entirely normal in Russia. And foreigners are an additional source of entertainment. Even nowadays, not everybody has the chance to travel (for many it is financially impossible), but the surrounding world is of interest to many.

Invitations come in all shapes and sizes. You are usually invited in advance, always verbally (with the exception of weddings and particularly important jubilees), either by telephone or in person. But there are also sudden, spontaneous invitations.

Spontaneity and unpredictability are characteristic of all forms of business meeting in Russia.

Unexpected visitors in Russia are fairly common. While in America, for instance, you are required to fix the time and place of meeting in advance, in Russia, they like spontaneity.

You've gathered together, you are in a good mood, you feel like company—excellent, we'll go visiting, even if no one is expecting us. In such a situation, it is best to 'float with the tide' and rely on your Russian partners and common sense (should your companion be drunk, for instance, it is best to stay at home).

If you are invited to a private home, it is customary to take presents. What is more important is the thought rather than the present, thus any small thing will do. Tea (good quality), original sweets, calendars, towels and bottles of alcohol are always appreciated. Be careful when buying drink in Russia for there is a lot of fake stuff around; do not buy from the kiosks and small shops on the street.

If your relations with your hosts are informal, a teapot, a mug or something useful around the home makes a good present.

It is the custom to give the children of the house small presents. To have at least a sweet for a child is more important than a present for the grown-ups.

Finally, if you have nothing else to give, a bunch of flowers for your hostess is always appreciated. In Russia, it is customary to give women flowers, even without a particular reason. It's essential you give an uneven number of flowers, for even numbers are for funerals only.

If you have just been invited round for a meal and not for a special occasion or evening, you may be fed in the kitchen. Don't take this adversely. Far from indicating contempt, this is a compliment in a way. In Russia, only close friends are received in the kitchen; in many families, it is considered the cosiest place and it is certainly the best loved.

More often than not, a reception in a Russian home will consist of sitting at length round the table. If everyone gets up, it is probably a signal that the evening has come to an end.

Apart from business lunches and suppers, the Russians like organising what they refer to as 'cultural programmes'. This will include, for instance, outings to the theatre. Russian ballet is just as superlative as it ever was! In Russia, it is customary to dress up for the theatre; it is considered to be a special occasion. Foreigners are also often taken to the circus. Don't be offended by this and think that they have a poor opinion of your mental capacities. The Russian circus is considered to be one of the best in the world, and Russians have the right to be proud of it. It is a very colourful spectacle and you will almost certainly enjoy it (added to which you will have something to tell your kids about at home).

You may be taken to other somewhat unexpected places where the Russians like to relax. So if you are invited to the bath-house, don't take it as a hint that it is time you had a wash, but as your partners' wish to give you pleasure.

Invitations involving a trip to the countryside are very common, especially in the summer—to *dachas*, excursions, or simply to get out of the city. From the Caucasians, the Russians have borrowed the tradition of *shashliks*, i.e., barbecues. They like to roast meat, fish, chicken or vegetables over hot charcoal in the open air. Trips to the countryside are considered to be one of the best ways of entertaining and establishing contact with one's foreign partners.

In Moscow, an immediate reply to the hospitality you have been shown is not expected of you. For your Russian partners, you are a visitor to their country, which means that

Shashliks are very popular in Russia and enjoyed in many other countries as well.

it is their job to receive and entertain you. It will be quite a different matter if, in the future, they should go to your country. There they will expect the same sort of reception as they organised for you.

The Lures of Moscow

Life in Moscow can be fun. An amusing story is told about a leading Italian tenor who came to Russia on tour in the mid-19th century. It is said that he 'gave himself up' to the temptations of life, and Moscow and the Moscow ladies were his ruin. By the end of his first season, he had learnt to drink vodka and nibble at the traditional fare of salted cucumber and ham, while he knocked back cold champagne as if it were water. He went for rides on sleighs and was an adept hand at driving *troikas* himself, he 'loved to excess' and was loved even more, carrying off from Moscow, it appears, two ladies at once. He was happy, but he spoilt his voice and soon disappeared from the Moscow opera scene. All those who are in danger of getting too carried away by the entertainments Moscow offers to the foreign businessman would do well to remember this tale.

RESTAURANTS AND OTHER PUBLIC EATING PLACES

In Russia, it is not traditional to go to restaurants, at least not simply to eat, although people will go if there is a special reason. Of course, the tradition of dining in restaurants has taken root in the major cities over the last few years, but mainly in certain fairly small circles, and in general it is not usual. Even for special occasions, it is traditional to invite guests to your home, and many consider an invitation to a restaurant as a sign of a lack of respect, that people are 'too lazy to organise it at home'.

There is a huge divide across the country concerning the number and quality of restaurants and eating establishments as a whole. In Moscow, Saint Petersburg and other big cities, a large number of varied places have opened and continue to open. In medium and small towns, there will be a limited choice. And in villages, nothing at all.

If you live in a big city, as most foreigners do, you won't have problems with dining out. In recent years, a great number of Western-style restaurants has opened in Moscow,

Russians enjoy a good meal together, and the best place to have it is usually at home.

and here you will doubtless be taken for appearances' sake. If you are given the chance of choosing where to go yourself, I would suggest you opt for the more traditionally Russian restaurants, of which there are quite a number now too in the city. Of course, they are stylised and not truly authentic, and more likely than not geared to the entertainment of foreigners. However, you may find yourself feeling somewhat lost in such places, so it is best if you go with a Russian.

In Russia, it is not the done thing to split the bill. In the overwhelming majority of cases, the person who has invited you pays. Bear in mind that an invitation to a restaurant means that all expenses involved are taken care of, unless the conditions are otherwise agreed at the outset. As before, going to a restaurant for a Russian is considered to be a special occasion, a social outing. Food in cafeterias or in office canteens is another matter altogether. In such places, each usually pays for himself.

If as a businesswoman you find yourself in a male collective, it will be rare that you pay for yourself. Even if the invitation originates from you, the men—particularly the elder and middle-aged generation—will probably not allow you to pay, and if you insist, they may take it as a personal offence. In such a situation, you might try saying that it is your firm who is paying the bill and not you personally, though this fact is not always understood by Russians. The situation may be different if you are in female company or that of young people.

In Russia, it is not usual to go into a restaurant just to have a cup of tea. If you have sat down at a table, you will be expected to make a proper order. And if you just order a salad, the irritated waiter will look at you askance.

Apart from Western-style restaurants, which do not differ in any significant way from their foreign counterparts, there are various types of national restaurants. In smaller towns and working regions, you often come across canteens. The food is simple, the selection small, but the prices are considerably lower than in restaurants. In such places, you usually take the food from the counter and clear up yourself. Sometimes, the food can be better than in restaurants (and in Russia, the highest compliment is to say that food is 'just like home cooking'), but it is easy to be mistaken and end up in some cheap, semi-clean establishment with poor quality food. You have to take your luck. And there are no rules for telling a good canteen from a bad one. Eating in restaurants is more reliable, although there are exceptions here too.

It is usual to leave a tip in restaurants, regardless of whether service is included in the bill or not. You should leave about 10 per cent of the total, often rounding up to the nearest appropriate figure. By the way, many very expensive restaurants have now opened up in Moscow and Petersburg, so you are advised to study the prices on the menu well before sitting down.

Many international restaurants and cafés have opened in Russia over the last few years. The ever-present McDonald's and Kentucky Fried Chicken have filled all the more or less big cities. There are also networks of Japanese (very popular in Moscow), Italian, some Chinese and other restaurants. Of course, you can always go in if you are overcome with a bout of nostalgia. But with the exception of the very expensive ones, they are only a poor reflection of the national cuisines.

TRADITIONAL RUSSIAN CUISINE

The main features of Russian cuisine are simplicity and traditional recipes. Its advantage is not its refinement or intricacy, but its abundance. Good food is, above all, fresh and not spoiled by various types of culinary refinement. Foreigners often find it too simple and insipid. And in truth, spices, which do not grow in Russia, are rarely used when cooking. The main ones are laurel and black pepper, the latter usually whole, so the food is not that spicy. On top of this, food is usually well fried or boiled, and often it is braised or baked for a long time.

The main ingredient of Russian cooking, if not life, is bread. Interestingly, historically if the grain crop failed, this often led to a lack of bread in Russia and famine, from which whole villages were sometimes wiped out. You would have thought that Russia is not like an uninhabited island, that there are fowl in the woods and fish in the rivers, but a lack of bread was a much more frightening and demoralising factor, and people simply gave up.

Traditional Russian bread is very different from most Western counterparts. It is spongier, heavier and always made of a yeast-based dough. Only black or rye bread is considered to be real bread. White bread or wheat bread is called a roll in most places (except Moscow). Bread is served with every meal, for breakfast, dinner and supper. And many people will still not eat anything unless they have bread. When travelling abroad, many Russians complain that they always have to ask for bread.

The craving for black bread is so strong that in Soviet times, when travel abroad was limited, Soviet diplomats living in various countries used to ask the few countrymen who were travelling to the countries where they were stationed to bring some black bread with them. So it was that people, many of whom were travelling abroad for the first time, would take bags containing black bread.

Russians particularly like items made of groats and flour. Porridges made from various grasses (rice, buckwheat, wheat, oats and others) are eaten by adults and children alike. And not just for breakfast with something sweet, but as a garnish to a main course at lunch, or as a meal in its own right.

One of the oldest dishes, which is still popular today, is *bliny* (or pancakes). A ritual dish since the time when Russia was a pagan country, they are round and golden and symbolise the sun. They are always eaten at Shrovetide and at funerals, and this ancient tradition has survived both the Christian Rus and the atheist Soviet periods. They can also be eaten without a special reason, with jam, sour cream, butter and condensed milk. *Blinies* with savoury toppings such as caviar (if available), herring or salmon are particularly popular. Nowadays, most restaurants that serve Russian cuisine will have *blinies* with various toppings. They are usually tasty, and you need a special ferment, which is hard to produce at home.

The Russian Appetite

The famous Russian author Anton Chekhov wrote a tale which is remarkable from the point of view of the problem of the national character. Chekhov is world-renowned for such plays as *Uncle Vanya*, *The Three Sisters* and *The Seagull*, which still play in theatres all over the world. But in his youth, he was famous for his short humoristic tales. One of them, called *The Stupid Frenchman*, describes the French clown Henri Pourquoi who is on tour in Moscow. Before the show, he goes into an inn for a bite to eat. There he sees a gentleman eating *bliny* with caviar (it was Shrovetide period). The Frenchman was surprised how the man could be eating that much dough. And the story goes on. More *blinies* were brought, with caviar, with fish, with onion. Then they served soup, followed by more *blinies*. In the end, the Frenchman realised that the man had decided to end his life committing suicide in the most unusual way, by overeating. He went up to the man with an appeal to think about how wonderful life is, and that everything would be all right. The man was very surprised, as he had eaten no more than everybody around him. It was just a quick bite before the real banquet for which he was invited. "Oh, country of miracles," thought Pourquoi, leaving the restaurant, "not only the climate but even the stomachs here perform miracles! Oh magical country!"

Soups also hold an honoured place in Russia. They are always served as a first course at dinner. For many families, a day without soup is simply impossible. They may lack the more expensive foods, but they have to have bread and soup. There are many types of soup. The most well known amongst foreigners, and the most traditional in Russia, is *schshi*, which is made from cabbage and vegetables in a meat stock. The classic recipe uses sauerkraut. Russians have become so used to their soups that, if we are to believe the legends, they fermented vine leaves while in France during the war with Napoleon in 1812 just so they could make soup. The famous French author Alexandre Dumas wrote a recipe book amongst other things, and included the recipe for *schshi* as one of the achievements of Russian culinary thought. A southern version of *schshi*, with added beetroot, is known as *borschsh*.

The multi-national nature of the Russian empire, and then the Soviet Union, has had a great effect on the traditions of contemporary Russian cooking. Georgian *shashliks* (marinated meat cooked over coals), Uzbek *plov* (braised meat, vegetables and rice), Armenian *dolma* (minced meat wrapped up in vine leaves), Ukrainian *vareniki* (cottage cheese or berries in pastry) and many others have now become an important part of the Russian table. Restaurants serving the local food of the various nations in the former Soviet Union can easily be found in all the large cities. And they are extremely popular.

DRINKS

The most famous of the non-alcoholic drinks in Russia is undoubtedly *kvas*. In olden times, it was called 'liquid bread'. Made by fermenting wheat, it was not only the main drink but also a very important addition to food. It was used to make cold soups, and meat and vegetables were stewed in it. A peasant's lunch would quite often consist of *tyurya*: bread was crumbled into a pot and *kvas* was poured in, which meant that they could eat a satisfying lunch out in the fields.

The *kvas* which is sold in cities nowadays differs from its historical version. It is more liquid, sweet and aerated. In fact, you are extremely unlikely to find good *kvas* in bottles (it is more likely to be some sort of lemonade with brown colouring). Some restaurants prepare their own *kvas*, and in the summer it is still sometimes sold in cities on tap from large round portable barrels. That sort of *kvas* is considered better.

Of all the many dishes that were made using *kvas*, only one is still made, and it is very popular in the summer. It is a cold soup called *okroshka*, and is prepared from various vegetables (boiled potatoes, spring onion and cucumbers) with hard-boiled eggs and sausage added. Just

In the villages, they still sometimes make the old village *kvas*, and in fact the further east you go, the more chance you have of finding it. It is not sweet and is thick and cloudy, and any modern town-dweller, including Russian, would think twice before trying it. It looks very off-putting, but the taste does refresh you and it is natural.

before eating, and sometimes straight into the soup bowl itself, you pour the *kvas*, then add sour cream and eat it. On a hot summer's day, it is very refreshing.

Kvas is a reasonably unusual taste to the foreign tongue. This is how an old guidebook, published in London in 1849, described the process of making this strange Russian drink: 'Quass, kvass (national drink) is made of a pound of salt, two pounds of barley meal, and a pound and a half of honey.'

And then the soup, made using it: '*Batvinia* (national soup) is not only composed of raw herbs, berries, chopped cucumbers, black bread, lumps of ice, and cold fish, but

that the whole of these ingredients swim in cold *quass*.' Hardly appetising!

However, many of the foreigners who were horrified by the description of *botvinya* in the guidebook undoubtedly wanted to try it once they had read the following phrase from S T Aksakov's *Family Chronicles*: 'After the cabbage soup there followed *botvinya* with ice, with transparent *balyk* (cured fillet of sturgeon), yellow as the wax of salted sturgeon and with shelled crayfish.'

There are other non-alcoholic drinks in Russia, including a wide range of mineral water, with the favourite still being Borjomi, from Georgia. Of course, all sorts of Western drinks such as Coca-Cola, Fanta, Pepsi and so on have become popular amongst Russia's youth (like everywhere else), although many do not encourage this tendency, considering Russian-produced drinks to be more healthy.

Alcoholic drinks are a separate question. Everybody knows that Russians drink a lot, and that is by no means a groundless stereotype. Whatever the reason may be, the cold climate, the desire to create a cosy atmosphere, historical traditions, etc., the Russians are good at drinking and love to do so. Food must be accompanied by plentiful libation. In addition, if people in Western cultures can drink small amounts throughout the day, Russians prefer to drink lots all at once.

Alcohol has traditionally been considered to be the best way to relieve tension, create an atmosphere of trust and help people to relax. As long ago as the 16th century, a German diplomat wrote, 'They are great masters of drinking... Anybody who wants to avoid the next toast must pretend to be drunk or asleep.'

Nowadays this situation is reflected in jokes. Extract from the Moscow diary of an American businessman:

'Spent the whole evening yesterday drinking with Russians. I almost died.

Today, I spent the whole day taking the hair of the dog with them. It would have been better to have died yesterday.'

Russians drink a lot, and with great pleasure. If your physical health allows, drink with the Russians; if it does

In most shops, you usually have a good choice of alcoholic drinks.

not, pretend. Lift the shot glass to your lips and take a small sip, otherwise you will be plagued with demands to drink immediately. Even if you refuse using the reasonable excuse of physical incapacity, your refusal can destroy the atmosphere of trust and goodwill. The traditional question asked by a drunk Russian who wants you to drink with him is very characteristic: "Do you respect me?" A refusal under such circumstances means a lack of trust. It is better to pretend that you are drinking, and even better to drink a little, to create an atmosphere of mutual understanding.

In Russia, it is traditional to drink only after a toast. While eating, unless a general 'command' has been given (by way of a toast), people only drink juice or mineral water. The most flowery and the longest toasts are of course made in the south of Russia, and in particular in the Caucasus, but even in Moscow the ritual is strictly followed. While people are sitting round the table talking, it is usual for somebody to stand and say a toast. The most traditional and the simplest are 'for peace and friendship' or 'thanks to the hosts' or 'to your wonderful city', and these are sure to win a Russian's heart.

There are many traditions associated with the drinking of alcohol. After a toast, you must touch glasses (the

Russians usually start their drinking and celebrations with a toast.

only time you do not touch glasses in Russia is if you are remembering the dead) and then drink (alas, you are often required to down it in one!). Once you have touched glasses, you are not allowed to put yours down until you have drunk from it as this is considered a bad sign. Empty bottles should never be put on the table. They must be put under the table if they cannot be taken out immediately. And there are many such 'rules'.

Of all the alcoholic drinks in the country, the favourite is vodka. It is drunk neat, without ice (but chilled) and is always followed by a *zakuska*. There is a whole range of *zakuskas* specially to be eaten after drinking vodka. One of those at the top of the list is salted cucumbers, prepared in a specific Russian way. Small cucumbers are covered with a special salt solution, allowed to ferment slightly, and then ideally placed in barrels (in the city, they are usually stored in glass jars) with spices and garlic. In a few days, they are ready. Other *zakuskas* for when drinking vodka include herring, salted mushrooms, sauerkraut and, in more refined circumstances, red or black caviar.

Apart from vodka, Russians drink wine (mainly the women), champagne (the so-called Sovietskoye, produced in

Russia, which is sweet and fizzy), cognac and other drinks. However, even if you buy wine with a recognisable label and pay good money in a proper shop, you may get home and discover that it is a fake, and moreover that the bottle not only does not contain bad wine instead of good, it may not even contain wine at all.

Over the last few years, the production of different sorts of beer has taken off in Russia. Beer is also a popular drink, but although there are many different types and competing companies, they all taste the same, a middling lager, though they are not bad.

RUSSIAN TEA DRINKING

The history of the spread of tea in Russia is surprising and paradoxical. It is not known for certain when it first appeared in the country, but before the 17th century, it was not widespread among the people. According to the legend, the Chinese drink was brought to Moscow in 1642 by the Russian ambassador to Mongolia and presented to Tsar Mikhail Fyodorovich, who liked it instantly. Surprisingly, within the span of 150 years, this rare and expensive drink became the national beverage. Although apparently an expensive drink that required much effort and a number of gadgets (and on top of this, seemed to have no visible effects on the drinker), it was to become an important part of Russian culture.

By the middle of the 19th century, the consumption per head in Russia was second in the world only to England. Tea was drunk at home and in inns, in the cities and the villages, by the rich and the poor. It became an integral part of Russian culture, as did the gadgets for preparing and drinking it: *samovars* for boiling the water, porcelain teapots for brewing the tea and cups and glasses with holders for drinking it.

There are a number of traditions linked with tea drinking in Russia that are different from elsewhere in the world. The tea is brewed in a small pot, then a small quantity is poured and the cup topped up with boiling water. Tea is drunk with various different accompaniments such as rolls, *barankas* (a dry, ring-shaped roll) or *pryaniks* (spice cakes), which are specially produced to be taken with tea. Honey and jam are also served with tea, and they are eaten from little dishes using a small spoon, usually without spreading them on bread. This usually surprises foreigners, who are familiar with spreading jams and preserves on bread or toast.

Russians also like sweet tea. If you are out eating somewhere and ask for tea, unless you say otherwise, you are likely to be given sweet (sometimes sickly) tea. Some people still like to drink their tea *vprikusku*, taking a bite out of a lump of sugar after each mouthful of tea. Contrary to popular opinion, in Russian villages, tea was drunk and quite often is drunk with milk, and this is called 'whitening'. But this tradition is rare in cities. As for lemon, which the rest of the world seems to think is an obligatory part of tea drinking in Russia, it is actually much less common than most people think. Lemon is quite often put in tea if the tea is of poor quality, as it improves the taste.

Teabags, although widespread because of their ease of use, are nevertheless considered to be 'not right'. At work, many of course drink such tea, but at home they prefer to brew real tea from leaves. If you were to offer your guests tea made from teabags, it would often be considered to be a lack of respect.

For a long time, the Russians drank only Chinese tea. It was brought many thousands of kilometres over land from China. It was thought that this had an effect on its taste and made it different from English tea, which was delivered by boat. In the 20th century, the situation changed. During the Soviet period, attempts were made to grow 'our own' tea, mainly in Georgia and the Krasnodar Krai. The attempt was successful. The tea was not as good quality, but it was cheaper than Chinese tea. From the 1960s onwards, imported Chinese tea was replaced by tea from India and Ceylon, which is sold alongside Georgian and Krasnodar tea but is rated more highly.

The final changes occurred not long ago after the collapse of the Soviet Union. With the development of a market economy, which changed the conditions for importing tea into Russia, the production of Russian tea was stopped completely. There is now a paradoxical situation in the country. On the one hand, the choice of teas in Russia is now enormous. You can buy all the most famous sorts and brands in shops in any major city. Special tea shops and departments are opening, where you can purchase different sorts of flavoured tea. On the other hand, because of the huge demand in Russia, there is also a huge amount of fake tea, and so buying good tea in Russia with any certainty is as difficult now as it ever was. It is no accident, then, that the planes flying from England are loaded up with tea, which people are bringing back as presents and for their own use.

CULTURE AND TRAVEL

'In spite of all the discomforts and deprivations to which travellers must submit, I think Russia so interesting that all these things make but a momentary impression.'
—George Buckham, American tourist

THE RUSSIAN CULTURE

Russia has always been proud of its culture. Not as old as Greek, or as influential as Italian, or as chic as French, it undoubtedly has its own magic and flavour. Subject to external influence as any other culture, Russian culture manages to retain its own unique features.

The beginning of Russian culture coincided with the baptism of Russia in 988. The rich and slightly mysterious pagan culture that preceded Christianity laid a good and long-lasting basis for it. Even today, we find some traces of paganism in Russian folk art, fairy tales, rural traditions and even in some orthodox rituals. Nevertheless, it was the conversion of Russia to Christianity by Grand Prince Vladimir that started the development of various traditional forms of art—painting, architecture, music and literature.

As Byzantium was the source of the new Russian religion, it greatly influenced Russian culture at the first stage. At the same time, this influence must not be exaggerated. It often happens in Russia that foreign arts or ideas or political institutions getting into the Russian soil take absolutely new national forms. They are often so specific and so 'national' that it is often impossible to recognise the foreign original.

The main features of this first rather long period of development of Russian culture (9th–early 18th century) were strong ties with, even dependence on, the Orthodox religion, mostly Greek influence (with Italian influence in the sphere of architecture from the end of the 15th century), a tendency to preserve traditional form and content, cultural uniformity and the absence of social differences in the cultural sphere.

One of the greatest results of the penetration of Christianity to Russia was the spread of written language and literature in the country. Holy books were first brought from Byzantium and later translated into Russian. Soon, additions were written telling about native Russian saints and their deeds. For many centuries, written literature existed in Russia mainly in the form of sacred books and education was in the hands of the clergy. Literacy and education in Russia meant mostly an ability to read 'God's words'. Probably this is the main reason why book reading has become so important for Russians and a general attitude to books in the country has always been so respectful, even venerable.

A rich oral tradition must also be mentioned. Fairy tales, bylines, legends and songs reflect not only the main events of Russian life but also national ideals, beliefs and a way of life. Unfortunately, Russian folklore drew the serious attention of scholars only as late as in the middle of the 19th century. That was the time when its collection and publication started.

Russian icons are now famous all over the world. They were the predominant form of painting till the middle of the 18th century when secular arts began to spread in Russia. Based on the Byzantium canon, they nevertheless acquired a specific Russian character. It is rather symbolic that the beauty of holy images in Russian icons is not external but rather internal. It is not earthly loveliness but heavenly beauty. Nobody can call the Russian Mother of God handsome or pretty, as is Madonna in Italian paintings. Her image is mysterious and spiritual.

Icons were never signed; there couldn't be personal vanity in the sacred art. That is the reason why we don't know the names of Russian icon painters. Only a few of them were kept by history. Andrei Rublev is the most famous and best known among them. His famous *Holy Trinity* painted for Trinity-St Sergius Monastery outside Moscow in the early 15th century became a symbol of old Russia. The Russian Church later canonised Andrei Rublev. Famous Russian

Russia's beautiful churches and historical buildings reminds one of its rich and glorious history in art and architecture. Here is a monastery called 'A New Jerulsalem' near Moscow.

film director Andrei Tarkovsky who made a film about the painter's life reinforced his fame in the 20th century.

Churches with golden onion-like domes became a universal symbol of Russia. Religion played an important role in the Russian life of that period, and it is the religious buildings that constitute the national glory in architecture. Not much is left of Russian civil architecture. An overwhelming majority of buildings in Russia was built from wood till the beginning of the 20th century. Wood was cheap, could be found everywhere and was considered to be healthy for life. It was easy to build a new wooden house whenever there was any need. In case of a fire, the new houses were sometimes made as soon as in a week's time. Only religious buildings—churches and monasteries—were supposed to last long and to stay for centuries. That is why such precious and laborious material as stone was used mostly for them.

The main exception were stone fortresses (in Russia they were called Kremlins) that protected major Russian towns. The most famous of them is the Moscow Kremlin. Wooden

The Moscow Kremlin is the heart of Russia.

walls were erected in 1156 soon after Moscow became known as a town. In the middle of the 14th century, they were replaced by white stone walls (interestingly, even now Moscow is sometimes called 'white-stone town'). A hundred years later, Italian masters built a new Kremlin wall from red brick—the one that remains today. No wonder that externally, the Moscow Kremlin reminds one of castles in Verona and Milan. Italian architects were also involved in the construction of several churches in Moscow, and since that period, the Italian influence is vivid in Russian architecture.

The new period in Russian culture started at the beginning of the 18th century and lasted for two centuries. Peter the Great started the process of the Westernisation of Russia, introducing new ideas and arts that were not as closely connected with the Russian Church as those that were already established. The main features of this period were the expansion of secular culture—with religion still playing an important role—the penetration of ideas and influences from Western Europe, the fast development of state education, new national forms of culture, the consequent social stratification of culture (it became different for peasants and nobility), and finally the flourishing of various arts—which was especially noticeable in the spheres of literature, music, ballet and theatre.

Although religious books kept their importance for Russian people (especially for peasants for whom they remained the main reading until the Russian Revolution in 1917 when they were banned), a new kind of literature penetrated Russian society in the 18th century. First they were primarily French and English novels or German philosophical treatises, read in translation or in the original language (that became an important stimulus for foreign language learning). From the second half of the 18th century, Russian literature emerged.

The first half of the 19th century is called (and justly so) the golden age of Russian literature. Alexander Pushkin, Alexander Griboedov, Nikolai Gogol and Mikhail Lermontov laid the basis of Russian national literary fame. In the second half of the 19th century, Ivan Turgenev, Fyodor Dostoevsky, Leo Tolstoy and Anton Chekhov (to name just a few) brought this fame to the international level. Their influence on Russian society cannot be exaggerated. It can be said that in Russia, literature was as important as life itself.

Starting from the 18th century, Russian painters turned more to secular themes. Educated by the best examples of European art (from the beginning of 19th century, more and more of them were sent to study arts in Italy), they used national motifs in their paintings. Alexei Venetsianov, Karl Briullov, Vasily Perov, Ilya Repin, Vasily Surikov, Boris Kustodiev and many others created their masterpieces that are now kept in various Russian museums. Although interesting and noticeable, Russian painting of this period remained mainly a national achievement.

A search for new forms in the beginning of 20th century brought to life a new generation of Russian painters. Kazimir Malevich (with his *Black Square*), Marc Chagall and Kuzma Petrov-Vodkin overturned all conceptions of artistic form, colour and meaning. It was a kind of revolution that spread all over the world.

Civil architecture was on the rise. Noble estates flourished with the construction of beautiful palaces and glorious gardens. Italian architecture in its best forms, as well as the best French and English architecture, were undoubtedly of great influence. But the result was predominantly Russian: European forms filled in with a Russian content and character brought to life something new and truly wonderful.

Before the 19th century, Russian music was known only in two main forms—church singing and folk songs and dances. Professional composers appeared in Russia rather late. It is customary to consider Mikhail Glinka to be the first (although there were a number of less-known composers before him). He is best known for his operas such as *A Life for the Tsar* and *Ruslan and Ludmila*. As in many other spheres, the rise of Russian music was rapid and glorious. Peter Tchaikovsky and his music is known all over the world. Modest Mussorgsky is known more in Russia, but he was a composer of great and distinctive talent. The beginning of the 20th century brought to life more names of international importance and their work and musical tradition continued during the Soviet period: Igor Stravinsky, Sergei Prokofiev, Sergei Rachmaninov, Dmitri Shostakovich, Feodor Chaliapin and many others.

The 'Ballets Russes' seasons, introduced in Europe by Sergei Diaghilev, opened a new and important page in Russian culture. Russian ballet became known all over the world. Its fame continued through all the 20th century. In times of Cold War in the Soviet Union, there was a popular poem comparing the achievements of capitalist and socialist worlds (guess in whose favour?). There were lines that became part of the Russian language and culture: '…we make rockets and curb river Enisei and even in the field of ballet we are ahead of the whole planet…' In this case, it was true.

Russian folk songs and dances must be mentioned. Not very well known to the world, they are numerous and varying—sad and poetic, funny and passionate. The best thing about them is that they are still sung and danced in Russia, and are now becoming even more popular.

A new epoch started after the Revolution of 1917. The main aim was to introduce completely new forms of culture in a new state, to destroy old *tsarist* heritage and to begin a new life from scratch. But gradually after the first years of searches, trials and mistakes, lots of traditional forms came

A Russian folk dancing group.

back to cultural life. In literature, music and ballet, the best of 'old' Russia was taken into 'new' life.

The main features of this period were the search for new forms, dependence on and control by the state, democratisation of education and culture, and development of old traditions despite ideological pressure. It must be mentioned that the state not only controlled culture but spent lots of money to support artists and the arts. The greatest results were achieved during the first years of the new Soviet state in the field of mass education: universal literacy was introduced in the country.

Russian and Soviet theatre in the 20th century reached great results. The Stanislavsky 'system' influenced theatres in different countries. Moscow Conservatory was

Works of art can be admired at the State Hermitage Museum at Saint Petersburg.

Russian cinema became famous for the names of Sergei Eisenstein, Mikhail Romm, Andrei Tarkovsky, etc. But there is much more than that. The problem is that Soviet and Russian films are based on national concepts and ideas and are not always understandable to a foreign audience. Another problem is that they lose a lot in translation.

a place where many excellent musicians who gained world fame were educated.

Russian culture is rich, diverse and influential. Part of it is well known to foreigners: Leo Tolstoy, Peter Tchaikovsky, Anna Pavlova—these names are an integral part of the global cultural heritage. Golden domes, sober icons, *balalaikas* and ballerinas in white from the *Swan Lake* are the most widespread stereotypes of Russian art. Part of it is hidden from the world: treasures of literature, beautiful estates of nobility, folk songs, masterpieces of decorative art, tragic and comic films, etc. It is a great pity because they are worth being revealed worldwide.

THE RUSSIAN HOLIDAYS

Russians love holidays. And it is not that they, like everybody else, love to be free from work under a well-grounded pretext. Russians are very good at celebrating holidays. Very often, they are celebrated several times: first before the date, at one's workplace with colleagues, then with family, and sometimes later, say on weekend with friends.

Holidays are often called 'red days' in Russian, because during the Soviet times, free days were coloured red in all calendars. 'Red' in old Russian meant beautiful, festive and grand. Probably that is one of the reasons why ceremonial and festive dates are so dear to the Russian heart.

There are many special customs, traditions and superstitions connected with different days. Let's mention the most important of them.

New Year is probably the Russian's favourite. It is always celebrated at work. About two weeks before 1 January, the endless feast begins. All Russia is preparing to meet a new year. The best way to do it is to sit with friends and to have a drink. Champagne is considered to be the main drink for this occasion. Most people still prefer the so-called 'Soviet Champagne'—a sort of sparkling wine produced mostly in

the Crimea. It is sweet, unpretentious, reminds one of bygone days and is rather inexpensive.

A Christmas tree is traditionally decorated, especially in families with small children. Some still prefer to make decorations themselves with the help of the young ones, as it was customary in Pre-Revolutionary and Soviet Russia. In the morning on 1 January, there are presents to be found under the tree.

New Year is always celebrated in the middle of the night between 31 December and 1 January. It is customary to have your glasses full of champagne at midnight and thus to greet the new year. Before that time, people drink for the passing year, talk about its main events and sum up its results. They remember the deceased and drink for the health and well-being of members of their family and their friends.

Later, many people like to come out to continue their celebration. In small towns and villages, after midnight, there are often crowds of people singing songs, playing accordions (older generation) or guitars (younger people), dancing and again drinking. In larger cities, such festivities are sometimes organised by local authorities and are more crowded and less informal. Today, all such late night New Year celebrations are inevitably accompanied by fireworks, petards and rockets.

The tradition to celebrate Christmas was revived not very long ago. During the Soviet atheist times, all Christmas traditions had merged with the New Year holidays. Now it just marks the end of winter festivities.

1 January is a quieter day. Everybody sleeps longer, eats up the night food, watches television and visits old relatives.

International Women's Day is on 8 March. It was one of the most popular holidays during the Soviet times. It marked the beginning of spring and was associated with love, motherhood and family. In schools and kindergartens, children prepared presents for their mothers and grandmothers. The flower of this day was mimosa, brought from the south of the Soviet Union. In Post-Soviet times, this holiday started being criticised for its 'communist past'. But it is still here, is still popular and keeps its traditions.

International Women's Day is always celebrated at work. A day or two before the holiday, the men buys presents and/ or flowers for their female colleagues. Women try to dress up for this occasion and tables are laid with food and drinks. There are no special ways to celebrate the date itself. There is a notion that on this day, men are supposed to do all women's housework—cook food, clean the house and wash the dishes. But this idea is now mostly part of Women's Day jokes.

In 2006, the Russian government introduced a new state holiday, the Protector of Motherland Day, on 23 February. It used to be called the Soviet Army Day and was never a free day. People consider it to be some kind of counterbalance to Women's Day and call it Men's Day.

Easter is the most important holiday for the Russian Orthodox Church. That is probably why this holiday was celebrated even during Soviet times. Ardent atheists had coloured red eggs and baked Easter cakes (they were then called Spring cakes) in their homes for Easter.

Today, the preparations for this day start long before the actual date. To begin with, everybody celebrates Shrovetide (or Pancake week) that precedes the Lent. People invite each other for pancakes and every family tries to outdo others in the way they are cooked and served. After this, more and more people fast or at least try to fast seven weeks before

Easter. Then on the Thursday preceding Easter, eggs are coloured, cakes are baked (or bought) and a special dish called 'easter' (*paskha*) is prepared from cottage cheese. All this is taken to the church on Saturday morning, where it is consecrated with holy water by a priest. It is usually a very colourful picture: people with burning candles, cakes and bright eggs gather outside a church and wait for a priest to come out. Finally on Saturday evening, there is a service which reaches its culmination by midnight. On Sunday, people eat cakes, *paskha* and eggs. They greet each other with a phrase "Christ has arisen!". The response is "(He has) truly arisen!". After that, they kiss each other three times.

May days are exceptionally loved by those who have *dachas* (summer houses), as this is a very good time to go to the country—already warm, usually sunny and the right time to work in one's kitchen garden. It was traditional to have peoples' demonstrations and parades everywhere around the Soviet Union on 1 May, which was at that time called the International Workers' Solidarity Day. People marched with slogans and huge paper flowers in hands, together with their colleagues, friends, families and always children. Many still miss this feeling of unity and universal joy. Now it is transformed into the unintelligible Spring and Labour Day, and has no special traditions except to work on one's kitchen garden.

Victory Day on 9 May is a different thing. It was solemnly celebrated in the Soviet period and is still a very special holiday for the Russian people. It is the day that is almost universally accepted and praised by everybody in this country—the young and the old, the rich and the poor, communists and democrats. Veterans of the war put on their decorations and orders. People drink for victory, for their living and deceased relatives who participated in the war (almost every Soviet family have at least one) and for the times of pride and glory.

1 September is called the Day of Knowledge. This is the beginning of the academic year. There are special solemn ceremonies in all schools, colleges, institutes and universities. Young people wear smart dresses (often white shirts) and give flowers to their teachers. Children who are going to school

for the first time are specially well dressed, have beautiful bouquets and are accompanied by various relatives who attend the ceremony. Later, families try to get together to celebrate the occasion with tea and cakes.

Everybody Has One!

Professional days are very popular in Russia. There are various days, mostly introduced during Soviet times, like the 'Miner's Day', the 'Railway Worker's Day', the 'Doctor's Day', the 'Cosmonaut's Day' and many others. Nobody is left behind; almost everybody has his/her own professional holiday. There may be solemn ceremonies and festive concerts on the most important days.

People in Russia now celebrate various religious holidays as well. Orthodox believers go to church, attend services and light candles in front of holy icons. There are lots of particular ways to mark different days: on Palm Sunday, people bring home branches of pussy-willow; on Whitsunday, they decorate churches with birch trees. More and more people in Russia celebrate their own confessional holidays—the Muslims, Jews, Buddhists, etc.

There are some new traditions appearing in a New Russia borrowed from other countries. The most popular among them is Saint Valentine's Day. Young couples exchange presents and go to cafés and restaurants. Saint Patrick's Day, surprisingly, has also become quite popular with young people in Moscow and Saint Petersburg. There are Saint Patrick's Parades in these cities, and people drink a lot of Irish beer. Nobody knows (or cares) about Saint Patrick, but it is just another pretext to have fun.

Such holidays are usually greeted by young people eager to have a new occasion for celebration, and are criticised by others. Traditionalists consider them to be alien to the Russian way of life, communists call them 'capitalist influence', and all agree that they are commercially oriented. Believers also underline that the above-mentioned saints are not recognised by the Russian Orthodox Church.

TRAVELLING IN RUSSIA

Most foreigners concentrate on the two capitals, Moscow and Saint Petersburg. It is here that most foreign companies are located, and it is here that you will find the best living conditions, Western types of entertainment and many restaurants and theatres. In other words, an exciting life. There are centres in other places like the Urals, Siberia and the Russian Far East. Some regions retain traditional ties, most of which are due to their geographical location. Archangelsk and Murmansk have ties with Norway, Vladivostok with China, and so on. Sometimes, a particular town will suddenly become popular with a specific type of traveller. For example at one time, Voronezh became an extremely popular place to study Russian, for no apparent or logical reason. But most foreigners nevertheless remain in the capital cities.

Furthermore, actually travelling around Russia was considered to be superfluous and unnecessary. Here are some descriptions of small Russian towns (which, by the way, are very lovely) as taken from a mid-19th century guidebook:

'Bogorodsk...This is a district town, but dull, and the streets in many places grass-grown...not even a pig will be there to to greet the traveller, nor a dog to bark at him.

Mtsensk...Road horrible, with ravines. Post-house passable.

Zaraisk...The Kremlin is in ruins, the Gostinnoi Dvor is gloomy, and, in the wooden suburbs, the grass grows in the streets.'

After this, the reader is unlikely to want to rush off to visit these places. But there have always been enthusiasts who are not frightened by the very real difficulties and the gloomy descriptions in guidebooks. And their bravery is usually rewarded.

However beautiful and interesting Moscow and Saint Petersburg may be, they are, like all capital cities, cosmopolitan. Here you have the possibility to hide yourself away in a known world and avoid any contact with that other world of national culture. It is only by travelling round the country that you can understand and feel it, penetrate its history and see the strengths and weaknesses of its people, of those who inhabit it.

Travel, if it is not organised by a tour operator, can be difficult, but if you do not pay attention to the everyday material problems, you can see a lot of interesting things: the wonderful open spaces that formed the Russian character, the long lazy rivers grandly flowing across the plains, the old monasteries scattered in out of the way places, and cosy, quiet little towns with their relaxed pace of life. And most importantly, the people, who are so different from those constantly in a hurry in the large cities, but with whom they share an important cultural unity.

One of the main problems when travelling around Russia is the poor state of the roads. This is a permanent problem in an enormous country with difficult climatic conditions. In the early 19th century, the great Russian poet Alexander Pushkin wrote that bad roads were the great misfortune of Russia. And the situation has not really gotten any better. A number of decent highways have been constructed around Moscow, but this does not change the overall picture. Even the road from Moscow to Saint Petersburg, the main road in the country, is difficult travelling in places. Travelling by car over such roads requires special skill.

Bad roads do not prevent Russians from travelling.

Railways about the country are in a much better state. The main work to build the railways was undertaken from the mid-19th century under Emperor Nikolai I. The Soviet government also paid a lot of attention to railways. As a result, there is a widespread railway network. It is possible to travel about Russia by train, just make sure that you do not make the wrong choice. Trains come in different categories, and the best of them are called *firmenniye*. They try to run on time and are warm and clean. The restaurant car serves Russian dishes and the carriage attendant always brings tea. Traditionally, tea in trains is strong and tasty. Nowadays, it is brewed from a tea bag, but the glass still comes in a traditional glass holder.

Getting Help

People in the Russian provinces are usually more open and benevolent than in fussy Moscow. In most cases, you can be sure that if you get yourself into a difficult situation, they will help out. The desire in Russians to help somebody in trouble, particularly one so helpless as a foreigner in a strange land, is very much alive. But it is essential that you know the language if you are going to travel independently. Without the advice and recommendations of the local people, it is often simply impossible to get by.

Finally, there are well-developed air connections between various Russian towns. Service on internal flights is as a rule worse than on international flights. But in general, it is a reasonably convenient way to travel and, given the size of the country, sometime the only way.

Hotels

At present in Moscow, there are hotels of various kinds. On the one hand, there are top-class hotels of Western style, identical to their chain-variants in Europe and the USA. They may be a little more expensive in Moscow, for example Balchug-Kempinski, Radisson Slavyanskaya, etc.

At the other extreme, there are very cheap hotels of the lowest type, which are bound to cause a cultural shock. Living in this kind of hotels requires some special preliminary training, and they may be recommended to those who are anthropologically interested in every aspect of culturally different ways of life. If you are very short of money and must stay in a US$ 20 room (the minimum hotel price in Moscow), you must be prepared for cockroaches, dirt, a cracked glass, a broken table, a drunk neighbour next door, a bathroom in the corridor and no hint of comfort except for a roof above your head.

In Moscow and Saint Petersburg, such hotels are only among the cheapest, while in provincial towns, they may sometimes be the only choice. You must be ready for quite poor conditions in the very beautiful but poor Russian towns, and please remember that a roof above you is much better than nothing. In this section, we shall describe middle-class hotels where Russians usually stay.

Preferably, a hotel must be booked by your Russian partners on the terms which you specify beforehand, especially if it is you who is paying for the hotel. The situation is more delicate if your accommodation expenses are covered by your hosts, for imposing your demands on your partners may be financially unacceptable to them. In the Russian language, like in English, one shouldn't look a gift horse in the mouth.

It is important to realise that in Russia, prices do not always correspond to quality. Russian hotel prices are usually higher than in Europe and particularly in the USA, while living conditions are worse. An occasional exception only proves the rule. Judging by the price, you may expect a decent hotel room, but a shower may not work or furniture may have been bought as early as the 1970s when the Soviet government, concerned about developing tourism in the USSR, spent some money on furnishing hotels. Since then, the furniture may have not been improved for lack of money.

Do not be surprised or shocked by a broken handle or a leaking tap. The reason for it is not carelessness but a desperate attempt to survive under new social and economic conditions.

On checking in, you are given a so-called 'guest card', which is your official pass to the hotel. If you leave it behind in your room, you may have problems at the entrance, but a conspicuous foreign language may help. Remember, please, that the idea behind this 'guest card' regime is for your safety and to limit the admittance of prostitutes, thieves and black marketers into the hotel, so please go easy on the system.

Legally Married?

Some traditions of the strict Soviet hotel regime are still alive, especially in provinces. While checking in, your passport will be asked for and sometimes payment in advance. If you mean to stay in the same room with a person of the opposite sex, it may cause problems in provincial hotels if the person's name differs from yours. Although night inspections of militia checking your 'moral (or, rather, immoral) behaviour' are gone, some elderly *babushka* (an old woman or grandmother) on duty may still be interested in your marital status as she approves only of legally registered marriages.

On leaving the hotel, you have to 'return' your room to a chambermaid. The tradition is now getting a bit less popular but still there are many places where the chambermaid will thoroughly check every glass and used towels and linen. This procedure may seem strange and humiliating to you, but first, this is a custom (and you are in Rome…), and second, the wages of the woman on duty is very low, which explains why she is so particular about checking every object: she will have to pay for whatever is missing. Do not take umbrage but rather try and understand the woman's feelings.

In most middle-class hotels, room service is very limited. Usually, it is confined to providing you with boiling water, sometimes accompanied with a kettle. Ironing may be a problem, so a travel iron is recommended. In most Moscow hotels, washing clothes yourself is out of the question. Your choice is either to give your laundry to the hotel's or a nearby launderette, but it will take 2–7 days. You may also call the service people to your room or flat. It may be a little more expensive and—what is much worse—you have to be stuck in because the people are usually quite vague about the time of their arrival: 'working hours', which means in actual fact from 10:00 am to 6:00 pm.

Eating in such hotels is also very average. If you want to eat cheaper and better, you must go downtown. If you prefer comfort to prices and quality, you may eat in the hotel. In small provincial towns, a hotel restaurant is often the very best in town.

It is not recommendable to use tap water for drinking. Mineral water is now sold everywhere, as well as bottled natural water. However, do not panic if you drink some water from the tap; diseases that you can catch from water are extremely rare.

Hotel administrators are worth mentioning. They require a special handling. If you manage to be on good terms with them, they will provide you with all imaginable comfort.

Do not expect any assistance from them which seems natural to you. The woman on duty on your floor may be absent when you need her, or she may have tea with a colleague or talk on the phone with such an important air as if she was solving the world's problems, though in actual fact she may be speaking to her grandson about his home assignment. Her lack of attention to you may hurt you, but this kind of 'independent' behaviour from service people is often a way to compensate the faults of their social position, to overcome an inferiority complex. Their wages are low and they can hardly be dismissed because it is difficult to find volunteers for this kind of underpaid work. Sometimes, the women are graduates from universities who had to take this 'unprestigious job' under some unfortunate circumstances. Also, people of the older generation were brought up by a popular poem by Vladimir Mayakovsky saying: 'Soviet people have their own pride: we look down on bourgeoisie.'

An American who visited Russia in the early 1990s later wrote a book about this visit. He described an example of his communication with a woman administrator of this kind. First she completely ignored him, but after a nice heart to heart talk, she not only brought him some fresh tea but also gave up her supper for him and provided him with a little alcohol 'to keep him warm'.

In such cases, a small sign of attention or respect or a little souvenir may help and melt the ice. If you speak a little Russian, spare some time and talk to the administrator. Complaining at something may be of great help. Pity and sympathy are great qualities of the Russian heart, and the result may surpass all expectations.

Thus, a hotel should preferably be chosen either by recommendations of the people you know who stayed in the hotel or by the advice of your Russian partners. Do not expect too much. Average hotels, as a rule, lack the comfort and conveniences of similar hotels in Europe and America. Try not to get upset by the absence of some services you are used to. Remember, please, that the country is facing serious economic problems, and that the idea of comfort in Russia is different from that in the West. If it is warm, dry and clean, a Russian traveller will be happy. Before you get angry and start to reprimand somebody or demand something, try to understand calmly what is happening. For instance in summer in Moscow, hot water is always switched off for a month, and no scandal can help (only largest hotels may have their own system of water supply). Finally, if you are coming for a longer period of time (a month and more), it is highly recommendable to rent a flat: it is cheaper, more convenient and gives more freedom. It is not customary in Russia to invite people to a hotel room, while a flat permits you to meet both business partners and friends more easily.

PLACES OF INTEREST
Moscow

There is an infinite variety of sights to be seen in Moscow. We will confine ourselves to naming the most important of them.

If Moscow is the heart of Russia, then the Kremlin is without doubt the heart of Moscow. The first reference to Moscow is in 1147, and this is the year which is considered to be the foundation date of the city. The ancient Russian chronicle informs us that in 1147, Grand Prince Yuri Dolgoruki, the founder of Moscow, 'gave a most sumptuous banquet'. The first settlement here was on the site of the present day Kremlin, where wooden walls were erected by 1156. Those walls which we see today were built later—in the l5th–17th centuries—by Italian masters who were working in Russia.

We will just mention the most important of the sights in the Kremlin. Firstly, there is the Cathedral of the Assumption (1479), where the Russian *tsars* and *tsarinas* were crowned and the metropolitans and patriarchs buried. Also in the Kremlin are the Armoury Palace and Diamond

Fund, collections which are often compared to the Jewels in the Tower. However, in terms of their variety, value and range, the Kremlin treasures obviously surpass those in the Tower. A visit to these collections is a must for visitors to the Russian capital.

Also in the Kremlin is the Palace of Congresses, which holds 6,000 people and was built in 1961 as a venue for the Communist party congresses. Concerts, especially performances of ballet, are held in the palace almost daily.

There are many other sights to be seen in the Moscow Kremlin: the Tsar Cannon, cast in 1586, which has never been fired, the six-metre-high Tsar Bell (recast in 1735 from the older one) which has never been rung, and much else.

All foreigners visiting Moscow know that they have to visit Red Square (Krasnaya ploshchad) which adjoins the Kremlin. The name 'red', which is often associated with the Communist era, is in fact of much older derivation. In translation from the Old Russian, *krasnyi* (red) means *krasivyi* (beautiful). The most striking sight in the square is Saint Basil's Cathedral, which for many people epitomises Russia. The cathedral was built in 1555–1560 to commemorate Ivan the Terrible's conquest of Kazan. According to legend, Ivan was so enchanted with the cathedral that he had the architects blinded so that they might never again create a church of such magnificence. For all that is said about the eclecticism of this building, it never fails to work its magic on the viewer and remains a place of pilgrimage for all tourists, Russians and foreigners.

Leading public figures of the Soviet era are buried behind the mausoleum in (or by) the Kremlin wall. Here one may find the names of the heads of state, including Stalin, of army commanders of the rank of Marshal Zhukov, of the first man in space, Yuri Gagarin, and even of an American—the journalist John Reed, author of the book *Ten Days that Shook the World*.

Another famous sight on Red Square is the Lenin Mausoleum. Not so long ago a place of mass pilgrimage, the mausoleum today is the subject of lively debate: should Lenin's embalmed body remain where it is, or should the leader of the world proletariat be buried according to Russian Orthodox tradition?

The Saviour Tower with its clock (Moscow's Big Ben), whose chimes are relayed over state television and radio, is also on Red Square. Bordering on the square opposite the Kremlin is the long facade of the state department store, better known as GUM, built at the end of the last century. Today it contains largely Western shops, but the interior of the building is of interest in its own right to lovers of architecture.

The Old Rebuilt

In recent years, buildings demolished in the 1930s have been rebuilt on Red Square, such as the Kazan Cathedral and the Iversk Gates, which guard the chapel that contains the icon of the Virgin of Iversk (or rather its replica), one of Moscow's most sacred objects of worship.

Running along the north-west side of the Kremlin walls is the Alexander Gardens, laid out at the beginning of the 19th century on the spot where the Neglinnaya River—which flowed into the River Moskva—was buried in a conduit. There is always a lively throng in the gardens as this is a favourite walking place with both tourists and Muscovites. By the entrance (closest to Red Square) at the north-east end of the gardens is the Tomb of the Unknown Soldier, in commemoration of the soldiers who lost their lives in the Second World War (1941–45). It is traditional for newly-weds to come here straight from the registry office and lay flowers at the tomb. The brides dressed in white, grooms in dark suits and their smartly-attired guests provide a colourful spectacle for onlookers.

Those interested in history and architecture will find a visit to the Novodevichy Convent (1 Novodevichy proezd). most rewarding. Founded in 1524 in a picturesque location on the river bank not far from the city centre, the convent became very prosperous over the centuries due to the donations it received from its distinguished recluses: the widows of tsars and their unmarried daughters would go into retreat here from the bustle of the world. The delicate tracery and harmony of the convent's architecture is most

A visit to the beautiful Saint Basil's Cathedral is a must for all travellers to Moscow.

striking. Adjoining the convent is a cemetery where many outstanding Russian and Soviet public figures are buried (the cemetery is second in terms of importance after that of the Kremlin walls). Among them are the writers Nikolai Gogol, Anton Chekhov and Mikhail Bulgakov, the composer Sergei Prokofiev, the founder of modern Russian theatre, Konstantin Stanislavsky, the head of the Soviet state, Nikita Khrushchev and many others.

Visiting Kuskovo

The Kuskovo museum-estate (2 Yunost Street), which once belonged to the distinguished aristocratic family of the Sheremetievs, provides a fine evocation of time gone by. The well-preserved—both externally and internally—palace and other buildings, a romantic aureole (Count Sheremetiev married his serf actress, an action which could only have been motivated by strong passion), the marvelous park surrounding the palace where one can walk in fine weather, all this makes a visit to Kuskovo an unforgettable experience.

Of the museums, one must mention above all the Tretyakov Gallery (12 Lavrushinsky pereulok), with its collections of Russian icons, paintings and Soviet art. Lovers of the French Impressionists and Post-Impressionists should visit the Pushkin Fine Art Museum (Volkhonka Street), which has one of the best collections of French art of this period in the world. Of particular note among the literary museums is the Lev Tolstoy House-Museum, the Moscow home of the author of *War and Peace* and *Anna Karenina* (21 L Tolstoy Street).

Excursions on the Moscow Metro are very popular with visitors. Although in recent years, the Metro has become somewhat less clean and spick and span, its marble, mosaics, plasterwork, sculptures and original designs continue to delight the eye. The first line, built in 1935, linked the stations of Sokolniki and Park Kultury. You are advised to pay special attention to the following stations: Komsomolskaya, Teatralnaya, Mayakovskaya and Kievskaya. The morning rush hour on the Moscow Metro lasts till about 10:00 am, and the evening rush hour starts after 4:00 pm. It is best to avoid using the Metro at these times for it is not a cultural experience that can be recommended to visitors.

Foreigners in Moscow tend to flock to Arbat Street. Here you will find old buildings, numerous shops, street traders selling souvenirs, buskers and artists. The Arbat, which is a pedestrian precinct, is always noisy and full of people.

Of the Moscow parks, I would especially recommend Sokolniki. Here there is plenty of space to get away on your own and breathe in fresh air. You can try the traditional pancakes and *shashlik*, and in the central part of the park, if you so wish, immerse yourself in a variety of different pleasures ranging all the way from merry-go-rounds to dancing in the open air.

From the Sparrow Hills (until recently the Lenin Hills), there is an unforgettable panoramic view of Moscow. Before you, as if on the palm of your hand, the whole of the central part of the city is laid out. Directly below you is Luzhniki, Moscow's largest sports stadium and the venue of the 1980 Olympic Games, and behind you is Moscow University, one of the so-called Stalin high-rise blocks. For all the different opinions as to the architectural worth of this building, its grandeur is most impressive.

Saint Petersburg

Saint Petersburg—the so-called second capital of Russia—is located at the Neva River, very close to the Gulf of Finland of the Baltic Sea. It was built by the order of Peter the Great at the beginning of 17th century and was meant to be the city of a new epoch, based on the Western model. It was called 'the window to Europe'. A beautiful city, it has European grandeur and Russian large scale—severe style and imperial gold, canals, bridges, palaces and lots of museums. It is here that the Winter Palace—home of the Russian emperors—is located, now turned into the world-famous museum the Hermitage. Saint Petersburg is best enjoyed in winter when the noble architecture is underlined by white background. In June, it has a period that in Russia is called 'White Nights' (midsummer night): in the midnight, it is almost as bright as during the day, and people gather at the Neva river to see the raising of bridges.

Saint Petersburg is full of picturesque sights. Featured here is the Beloselsky-Belozersky Palace, which used to serve as the Communist Party's district headquarters. It is now open to the general public and concerts and tours of the palace's beautiful interiors are organised throughout the year.

The Golden Ring

Historic towns of old Russia were united into the so-called 'Golden Ring'. It includes several towns, among them Sergiev Posad—monastery-fortress and the centre of Russian Orthodoxy, founded in the second half of 14th century by Sergi Radonezhski, one of the most reverend Russian saints. Pereslavl-Zalessky has an old cathedral in the central square, several monasteries and the museum of Russian fleet. It was here that Peter the Great started the Russian maritime glory by building the first battle ship. Rostov Veliky (the Great) is dominated by its Kremlin and is best known for its tower-bell music. Yaroslavl, Kostroma and Vladimir are regional centres; all have ancient monasteries, old buildings, fine architecture and lots of history. Suzdal is the smallest of the Golden Ring towns. It is full of churches and monasteries, good hotels and restaurants and traditional national entertainments (mostly preserved for foreign visitors but enjoyed by Russians as well).

Transsib

Transsib (Trans-Siberian Railway, or Great Siberian Road as it was called before) was opened at the very beginning of the 20th century and is still the most important railway connecting Central Russia and Far East. It is 9288.2 km (5771.4 miles) long and goes through eight time zones. You can take the train in Moscow and after six days you'll be at the opposite side of Russia, in Vladivostok on the shore of Pacific Ocean. Trains are relatively comfortable and travellers are rewarded for all inconveniences by the idea that they crossed all Russia from west to east, from Europe to Asia.

The Russian North

The Russian North is less known to foreign visitors but is worth seeing. Beautiful and quiet, it is full of ancient monasteries that were first to appear in these remote and uninhabited areas. Huge forests, slow rivers and the shores of the Northern Sea create an unforgettable atmosphere of this area. The most famous is the Vologda region and Solovki Island.

Siberia

Siberia, like a magnet, attracts travellers to Russia. It is considered to be the real Russia, with eternal cold, brave people and everlasting winter. It is worth visiting, although it may be really hot here in summer and people and their way of life are more or less the same as everywhere in Russia. There are not so many historical and architectural monuments as most of the towns were built rather late—in the 18th or 19th centuries—but if you are looking for wild and beautiful nature, that is the place to go. Great rivers, endless forests full of wildlife, huge trees, everything here is on a great scale.

General

Generally speaking, you will find more or less the same set of historical and cultural treasures in all the main regions of Russia: ancient monasteries, noble estates, very often architectural masterpieces, old churches and the birthplaces of prominent Russians—writers, philosophers, musicians, generals, saints and heroes.

SIGHTS

Russians are rightly proud of their culture. The country has many wonderful architectural, historical and artistic monuments. These include city buildings, churches, monasteries, pictures and works of the decorative and applied arts, not to mention the world-famous Russian classical music, ballet, theatre and literature. In short, there are things to see.

Unfortunately over the last few years, many monuments and museums have been in decline. The Soviet government destroyed churches and country estates, but supported museums and places connected with great people from the past. Nowadays, many museums, particularly those that are isolated and thus not commercially viable, lead a miserable existence based on ticket sales, or have closed completely. However, churches and monasteries which have been handed back to the Russian Orthodox Church are being actively restored.

Not everything is bad. Many museums are still open and they are wonderful. And the ticket prices, with the exception of those in the centre of the two capitals, are laughably low. Although it is true to say that they often do not have the range of services that are standard in the West, such as cafes, restaurants and shops with souvenirs, they do retain the spirit of their time.

Moscow's museums are one of its chief treasures. Here, you can become acquainted with Russian icons, the various Russian art movements and ultra modern art. There are also fine collections of Western European art, and you can learn about Russian history and about the life and work of Russia's leading writers, scientists and other outstanding men. In Moscow, there is a museum to suit all tastes.

Moscow theatres are of undoubted interest to visitors. Before the *perestroika*, their role in the cultural and spiritual life of the Russian people was enormous, and it now seems that this is gradually coming back. While in order to appreciate Russian drama, some knowledge of the language is necessary, Russian ballet and opera are accessible to everyone.

A visit to the Moscow baths is recommended. The bath-house occupies a fairly important place in Russian life. In the provinces and villages, it remains to this day the main means of keeping oneself clean; while in the major cities, it is regarded as a pastime that is both enjoyable and good for the health. For many Russians, the bath-house is a pleasure they would not dream of giving up. The Russian bath-house differs from the Scandinavian sauna (though the latter is becoming increasingly popular in Russia). A stone stove, high temperatures, a switch of dried birch leaves with which to massage the body in the steam room, contrast between the heat of the steam room and the icy cold temperatures of the pool or snow-drift (in winter)—such are the attributes of the Russian bath-house. A visit to one

In the last ten years, the cinema has lost its role as the 'entertainer' of the Moscow masses. The majority of cinemas are now let to commercial firms. Today in Moscow, there are a few fashionable cinemas of the Western type. In some of them, for instance the American House of Cinema at the Radisson-Slavyanskaya Hotel and The Cinema under the Dome at the Olympic Penta Hotel, you can watch films in the English language.

of the old Moscow bath-houses, for instance the Sandunov Baths (14 Neglinnaya Street), will also be of interest as a cultural experience.

The Moscow markets play a specific role in the capital's life. Even if you do not need to buy food, I would advise a visit to one of them. There you will see everything that is produced or grown in Russia. The most popular (and therefore the most expensive) market with foreigners is the Cheremushkinsky Market, where you can buy anything from meat to whatever berries are in season. There are markets of this sort in all the Moscow districts and in every big Russian town. Do not mistake these markets, however, for the flea markets where one can buy cheap goods, or the wholesale markets where one can buy things from all over the world and foodstuff which are cheaper than in the shops (though there is no guarantee of quality). The latter type of markets are a fairly new phenomenon in Russian life and have become very popular. Markets of the traditional type sell only agricultural produce which is mainly grown or produced by the seller.

The Russian shops today are a mixture of Western brand names and cheap goods from the East, plus a Russian style

The agricultural markets in Russia are interesting places to visit and will give you a glimpse of the local life of the Russians.

of trading. There are all sorts of shops in Moscow, ranging from exclusive Western boutiques to shops of the traditional Russian kind.

SOUVENIRS

The best buys in Russia are the traditional Russian souvenirs. Although today many of these may be found in any part of the globe, those sold in Russia are still the most attractive and cheapest. Moreover there are many fakes on sale, which, although similar in appearance and at a cheaper price, are a far cry from the genuine article, which always has a trademark and often the name of the artist who made it on its reverse side. We should start off by naming the various unique Russian folk arts and crafts. Among them are the famous lacquer wooden boxes made in the villages of Palekh, Mstera and Fedoskino. On these boxes, personages from Russian fairy tales and legends, as well as historical and literary characters, are depicted against a traditional black background. Miniature boxes are the most common: the smaller the box, the more expensive and valuable it is.

The blue-and-white ornamental china from Gzhel is equally well known and popular. Khokhloma are wooden articles

Souvenir sellers warm themselves from the Russian wind, while waiting for tourists to buy their items.

decorated with a red, black and gold geometrical design of berries and fruit. The Pavlovo-posad shawls have a brightly-coloured floral design against a traditional black ground. The Zhostovo trays with their fruit flower and berry designs are known throughout the world. Fine glassware is produced by the factory at Gus-Khrustalny and exquisite china by the Leningrad China Factory. Superb embroidery is made at the factory at Tarusa and those in many other Russian towns.

Always popular are the traditional Russian souvenirs, for instance the matryoshka wooden dolls (you will find a wider variety in Russia than anywhere else in the world), vodka (the purest and best quality vodka is stocked in leading Moscow shops) and furs, in which, as before, the Russian land abounds.

Among other good buys available in Moscow are good quality and cheap art books, particularly on Russian art, and music recordings including Russian classical music as well as Russian folk instrument recordings. In Moscow, you can buy unique works of art and antiques—often for a song—from people whose material circumstances force them to sell their family possessions.

Finally, among other good buys in Russia are gold and silver jewellery, and especially semi-precious stones from the Urals. Jewellery in different styles and varying enormously in price may be bought in Moscow shops. As a general rule, in Moscow and other Russian towns, it is best to buy items which are made locally; the closer you are to the place of manufacture, the cheaper the item in question.

FREE TIME

In Russia, most people spend their free time in exactly the same way as people in many other countries: at home in front of the television or with a book or a newspaper. But there are some specific Russian features that are worth a few words.

City-dwellers like to leave their city. Nowadays, many have a *dacha*, which is often a piece of land with a small house on it. Some of the things that people enjoy doing at their *dacha* are digging the garden, drinking tea from a *samovar*, having a barbeque outside with their friends (and a drink to warm you up), going fishing and enjoying the countryside.

There is another national passion: picking mushrooms. For many people, this is the best way of relaxing. On a

These Russians busy themselves with building a new *dacha*.

Saturday afternoon in August, there will be empty cars standing on the side of roads all over the country. Do not be afraid. Their occupants are wandering around the woods with baskets in their hands (for the mushrooms), in boots (against the mud and snakes), and with scarves or hats on their heads (to protect them from ticks and other insects), looking under leaves and branches for hidden mushrooms. It combines being out in the fresh air, doing something useful for the housekeeping, getting pleasure from the woods, which is always different and beautiful, and then you can eat fried mushrooms and potatoes in the evening, or pickled mushrooms in the winter.

And it really is a passion. I have known mushroom pickers who got so carried away that they wandered right into the very heart of the forest and had to spend the night under a tree, frightened by the howls of the animals and the rustling of leaves and clutching their prized basket full of the day's 'catch' tightly to their chest. But even the horrors that they had been through could not stop them, and soon they headed out into the woods again with their former fervour.

But *dachas* and mushroom picking are seasonal: they can only be done in the summer months through to the beginning of autumn. During the winter, there are other pastimes, for example ice skating or skiing. Or you can slide down snow-covered hillsides on sleds or a piece of cardboard. Children love playing snowballs, when whole battles are fought out. Yes, the Russians love winter.

One of the other favourite pastimes, as was mentioned earlier, is to go to the *banya* (bath-house). In many places, the *banya* remains the only way of washing. But many people go simply for the pleasure of it. The *banya* is always a wonderful occasion for talking with friends, relieving tension and relaxing. Nowadays, it is a small holiday festival in its own way.

And it is a festival which has its own traditions and rules. When you go into the sweat room, you need to be beaten with a *venik*, like a small brush made of birch, lime or oak twigs. This can only be done with somebody else. While you lie down on the bench in the sweat room, the other person beats you all over with the *venik*. It is not as painful as it sounds, and actually quite pleasant. It is like a massage using natural leaves.

Another rules states 'After the *banya*, steal if you have to, but have a drink.' Having come out of the steam room, many people consider it essential to have a glass of beer or a shot of vodka as part of the ritual relaxing. However, many people do not now observe this tradition as it is bad for your health, preferring instead a cup of fresh herbal tea.

Sports is an important part of Russian life, although it is predominantly a male domain. The most popular sports are probably football and ice hockey (note that in Russian, this is simply hockey as they do not play any other sort. In order to describe in Russian the game most often played in the UK, you have to specify that it is played on grass). Nowadays, more people watch sport than actually get involved. And the excitement aroused when favourite teams are playing knows no bounds.

Quite often, groups form as if spontaneously to play football. At specific times on weekends, people turn up at a stadium and just start to play. Sometimes, these traditions last for years. The players age, but continue to keep loyal to their teammates. Nobody organises these matches, they are just about having pleasure and a good time.

Nowadays new traditions are appearing, for example holidaying abroad. The world which is opening up to Russians brings with it new experiences. And a reasonably comfortable holiday in Russia will cost more than in many of the world's tourist spots. But despite this, the official figures for the country are not that high. They say that only 5–7 per cent of the population travel abroad.

LEARNING THE LANGUAGE

CHAPTER 8

'I talked to the Russians a good deal, just to be friendly,
and they talked to me from the same motive;
I am sure that both enjoyed the conversation,
but never a word of it either of us understood.'
—Mark Twain

THE RUSSIAN LANGUAGE

Russians like to study foreign languages. Anybody who can speak foreign languages can be sure of earning respect and of having a better chance of finding a good job. English is the most widespread of foreign languages in Russia. It is a compulsory subject in the majority of middle schools and you will undoubtedly hear a number of simple phrases from most people who pass you in the street. The second foreign language is German and then French.

Language is not always an important factor during travelling. If you are in a good mood, it is not even necessary. Mark Twain, while visiting Russia, wrote that you do not need to know words in order to understand and feel the surrounding world: 'I talked to the Russians a good deal, just to be friendly, and they talked to me from the same motive; I am sure that both enjoyed the conversation, but never a word of it either of us understood.'

However, if you are planning something slightly more than just a short tourist visit, it is better to have some idea of what Russian is like. You need to know at least the alphabet in order to find your way round town, since the names of streets and Metro stations are mostly written in Russian. Russians prefer not to put everything on show, and this also applies to different types of establishment. It is frequently impossible to see what is going on behind a sheet of impenetrable glass, and so it is sometimes only by reading

Most signboards and street names are in Russian, so it is good to learn the Russian alphabet and simple Russian words so you can get around more easily.

the sign that you know you are standing in front of a café or a hairdresser's.

The Russian language is a state language in the Russian Federation and this fact is fixed in the Constitution of RF. It belongs to the Slavonic group of the Indo-European family of languages, thus making English, German, French and Hindi its relatives.

The history of the Russian language is not very long comparatively. It is supposed that the Old Russian Language was formed some time around 6th century (although some scholars think it happened much earlier than that). It is believed that the written language was introduced to Russia by two brothers, Greek monks Constantine (Saint Cyril) and Methodius. They translated liturgical books into Old Slavonic (later called The Church Slavonic), thus introducing the Slavonic alphabet into Russia. Some people think that they just used already existing alphabet, but this idea still needs to be proved.

The eldest-known inscription in Russian dates back to the beginning of the 10th century, long before Russia was baptised.

It was found near the Russian town of Smolensk, written on a clay pot and said '*gorushna*'. Nobody knows for sure what that means, but a general assumption is that this pot had some spices in it, probably mustard (*gorchitsa* in Russian).

One of the first Russian books is the beautifully decorated *Ostromirovo Evangelie* (or *Ostromir Gospel*), written in 1056–1057. Since that time, book art became widespread in Russia. Books were beautifully decorated, with bright vivid illustrations, and even the manner of writing letters was beautiful.

One of the most interesting examples of written Russian documents was first found in Novgorod in the middle of the 20th century. A rich collection of birch-bark documents dating back to the 11th–15th centuries was dug out by archaeologists. The best thing about them was that they included lots of private letters and notes written by ordinary citizens, discussing their private matters. Such documents are very rarely found and usually easily disappear with time. Their existence proves that written Russian in medieval times was known not only to the chosen few.

Peter the Great started a new period in the history of Russian language. Starting from the 18th century, conditions were formed for the creation of a new modern language. Since then, the old Slavonic language became the language only of the Russian Church. Mikhail Lomonosov—founder of Moscow State University—published the first Russian grammar in the middle of the 18th century and invented the first Russian forms of versification (before that, only classical ancient Greek or Latin forms were used).

At that time, the Russian nobility were carried away by foreign languages. French, sometimes German or English, were used more than Russian, and the latter was considered by some of them to be uncultured and coarse. By the beginning of the 19th century, some of them even managed to forget their own native language. Famous Tatyana Larina from *Eugene Onegin* writes her love-letter in French! It became very important for some writers and thinkers to prove that Russian language is as beautiful as any other. Since that time, many foreign words were introduced and became part of the Russian language.

The Russian poet Alexander Pushkin is sometimes called 'the father of the Russian language', as it is in his works that we first find a modern Russian language that is almost the same as it is now. After him, there was no need to prove the glory and beauty of Russian. Ivan Turgenev, who spent most of his adult life abroad, wrote: 'At times of doubt, at times of deep thoughts about the fate of my Motherland, you are my only hope and support, the great, mighty, truthful and free Russian language.'

RUSSIAN AS A LANGUAGE OF INTERCULTURAL COMMUNICATION

Today, about 250,000,000 people in the world (inside and outside Russia) are considered to speak Russian either as their native or as a second language. Russia has been a multinational and multicultural state for more than 300 years. The Russian Empire, the Soviet Union and to a lesser extent the Russian Federation, under different names, united various—large and small— groups of people. Many of them have their own language, culture and traditions. Some of them got their alphabet only from the hands of 'the big Russian brother'. When different ethnic or national groups live together, they need a common language if they want to understand each other. Thus the Russian language became the language of intercultural communication for the peoples of Russia.

Since the break-up of the Soviet Union, there have been many speculations about the Russian language. It was even called the 'language of occupants' and the 'language of totalitarianism'. And many other bitter and even rude words were said at the collapse of the old system. Mainly it was not true. The Russian language has been taught as a second language in many schools all over Russia from the 19th century, but on a voluntary basis. Only in 1938, the Soviet government issued a resolution about the compulsory introduction of Russian language in secondary schools all over the Soviet Union. Although national languages were still learnt along with Russian, its position in the country had vividly strengthened.

When former republics became independent states, an unexpected problem arose: the citizens of new countries didn't know their state languages. Almost instantly, all paperwork, official negotiations and formal meetings were ordered to be conducted in national languages—Belarusian, Ukrainian, Kazakh—and the people found themselves facing a serious problem. Most of the educated people, officials and intelligentsia spoke only Russian (and many of them were Russians). Doctors, teachers, government officials and local authorities, many of them not very young, had to learn languages new to them in order to survive in a new system.

Whether the expansion of the Russian language was good or evil is debatable, but it is still a language of intercultural communication. It is used not only by Russian and non-Russian people when they want to understand each other, but by non-Russian and non-Russian as well. The only way to communicate for Georgians and Tadzhiks, or Armenians and Turkmen is to use the Russian language. The only alternative is English and the young generation likes this idea, but for the old and middle-aged, there are no doubts—it is Russian that makes conversation possible for people of different nationalities.

When the Soviet Union was strong and represented a possible threat to the Western world, the Russian language was very popular in different countries. The last display of interest was immediately after *perestroika*, but since then a decline of Russian language studies became quite noticeable. Some Russian departments were even closed (or rather merged with something else) in the universities of Australia, United Kingdom and even the USA, where Russian studies had long and renowned traditions.

However, interest in the Russian language is reviving in some countries. The language is important for business in some countries, in others for tourism (more and more tourists from Russia bring their money to the world). Even former socialist countries like Hungary and Poland, which were happy to get rid of Russian, seem to look at it more favourably now that their goods are in great demand in Russia but are not needed in Europe. However, fewer and fewer people are interested in Russian culture and literature.

THE RUSSIAN ALPHABET

A traditional name for the Russian alphabet is *Azbuka*. It originates from the names of the first two letters of the old Slavonic alphabet—*az* and *buki*. Modern ways of writing letters go back to the times of Peter the Great, who 'corrected' the old Russian alphabet by simplifying their writing and excluding some extra letters. The Russian alphabet ceased to be as beautiful as it was before, but it became accessible to everybody. There was no more need to have special painters drawing complicated letters for books. New letters became 'ready' for new, secular life. The last changes were adopted in 1917 by the new Soviet government, making things even easier.

The modern Russian alphabet consists of 33 letters. Foreign visitors sometimes laugh at the Russian people, stating that they do not remember their own alphabet by heart. That is not really true. The problem is with its last part: not many remember the right order of the last letters, especially as some of them are unpronounced.

Russian Letter	Transliteration	Pronounced As
А	a	*a* in *car*
Б	b	*b* in *bit*
В	v	*v* in *vine*
Г	g	*g* in *go*
Д	d	*d* in *do*
Е	e	*ye* in *yet*
Ё	yo	*yo* in *yolk*
Ж	zh	*s* in *pleasure*
З	z	*z* in *zoo*
И	i	*ee* in *see*
Й	j	*y* in *boy*
К	k	*k* in *kitten*

Russian Letter	Transliteration	Pronounced As
Л	l	*l* in *lamp*
М	m	*m* in *map*
Н	n	*n* in *not*
О	o	*o* in *folk*
П	p	*p* in *pet*
Р	r	*r* in *roll*
С	s	*s* in *see*
Т	t	*t* in *tip*
У	u	*oo* in *boot*
Ф	f	*f* in *face*
Х	kh	*h* in *house*
Ц	ts	*ts* in *sits*
Ч	ch	*ch* in *chip*
Ш	sh	*sh* in *shut*
Щ	shch	*sh* in *sheep*
Ъ	The hard sign	
Ы	y	*i* in *ill*
Ь	The soft sign	
Э	e	*e* in *met*
Ю	yu	*u* in *use*
Я	ya	*ya* in *yard*

LEARNING RUSSIAN

Russian has traditionally been considered to be a difficult language. It has its own alphabet and a large number of grammatical forms. There are three genders in it, each with different endings. As nouns and adjectives have different cases and declensions, their endings change according to the declensional class to which they belong. In order to use pronouns, you just have to learn the tables; there is no other way. Verbs in the past tense change their forms according to the gender of the subject. And there are always lots of exceptions. There is even a strange proverb in Russian: 'The exception only proves the rule', which seems to exist only to justify an enormous amount of exceptions from general rules in all spheres of Russian life.

To make things worse, Russians have a particular love for diminutive and endearing terms, which sometimes makes a word with all its suffixes, completely incomprehensible. They will hardly ever just say bread, or butter, or house, or flower but always use the diminutive form: *khleb—khlebushek*, *maslo— maslitse*, *dom—domik*, *tsvetok—tsvetochek*. Some people think that it proves their kind and soft nature, others consider it to be designed specially to humiliate foreign visitors.

The word order is not so important as it is in English. There may be sentences without a verb, or even consisting of one word. Various endings help the listener to understand what is going on.

Another problem is that there are some particular Russian words that cannot be translated and are very difficult to understand. There is the whole world behind them. *Dusha* is very important for every Russian. It is literally translated as 'soul', but in real translations is always changed for the much more materialistic 'heart'. In expressions like 'with all my heart' or 'in my heart', it is always 'soul' in Russian. And that is of course something really different. It is difficult to imagine that the soul can ache or can be out of place, but that is what happens to Russian people very often.

When this happens, they have a sudden feeling of *toska* another untranslatable notion. 'Melancholy' or 'depression' given by the dictionary do not transmit half of the depth and almost sacred feeling when you have *toska*. It is always unreasonable and often needs one remedy: a glass of vodka and long conversation after that.

Contrary to what dictionaries claim, *Smireniye* has nothing to do with humility or humbleness. The Russian word connotes something that is noble and honourable, something that everybody respects and considers to be the highest form of existence. If you have *smireniye*, your *dusha* will never ache and you won't feel *toska*.

Rude words are common with some groups of people. They are usually used while drinking alcohol or by people who are so addicted to drinking that they cannot communicate in any other way. It is said that some 'specialists' can have a long and informative conversation using only two or three roots with various suffixes, prefixes and endings.

Quoting From?

The Russian tradition to use lots of quotations is a somewhat unexpected problem for foreigners. The sources are numerous and diverse. Quotes are taken from popular films, sometimes very old, books, poetry, anecdotes, jokes, songs and even cartoon films. Just a couple of unintelligible words are pronounced, and everybody starts laughing except for the poor foreigners who do not understand what is going on. There is nothing in the words but there is a lot behind them—a funny episode, a ridiculous character or an absurd situation. In order to understand all this, it is important to start from the very beginning—children's books, television programmes, etc.

ADDRESSING IN RUSSIAN

Addressing people in Russia is an entirely separate problem, and a reasonably complicated one at that. Firstly, Russian retains two forms of 'you': *ty* (the intimate form) and *vy* (the more formal version). How to use them is a delicate question, and you should not insult somebody by being too familiar with them. Using the form *ty* can sound simply rude. Therefore, in order to avoid mistakes, it is better to use the form *vy* in all cases. People will never be insulted by *vy*, and if you are already on a sufficiently friendly footing, they themselves will offer to 'switch over to *ty*'.

There is a similar situation with names. Russians have not only the first name and surname, but also a patronymic, based on the name of their father: Ivan, son of Igor, is Ivan Igorevich; Maria, daughter of Valentin, is Maria Valentinovna. It is a sign of respect to refer to somebody by the name and patronymic, while with friends you can use just their name. Surnames are used for soldiers in the army, for schoolchildren, and sometimes for students. Usually people will offer the preferred form when introduced, so listen carefully. If you are not sure, just say, "I'm sorry, I didn't catch your patronymic." The person will answer either "Maria Ivanovna", in which

246 CULTURE**SHOCK!** RUSSIA

In Russia, it is not customary to address people by their titles; professor, doctor, engineer are not used very often. Addressing someone by his first name and patronymic shows much more respect than titles.

case that is what you need to call her, or "Don't worry, just call me Masha!"

The last problem with addressing people came to life after *perestroika*. During Soviet times, it was customary to address people (even unknown) in this way: men—*tovarishch* (comrade) or *grazhdanin* (citizen); women—*grazhdanka* (female citizen). Both forms became unpopular after the collapse of the Soviet system. Some people (especially 'new Russians' and 'new aristocracy') would even feel offended and may answer something like "we are not comrades with you" (or even ruder "goose is not swine's comrade", which is an old Russian proverb).

Nevertheless, in more simple situations like on public transport, on the streets or in shops, both addresses are still widely used without any communist meaning.

There are attempts to revive some old pre-Revolutionary forms. Old Russian *sudar* and *sudarynya* are used only with irony. Like a professor may say to his student: "*Sudar*, you are late to class", or a displeased parent to his daughter: "*Sudarynya*, where are you going, I wonder?" The same refers to foreign forms like Sir, Mister and Madame. In this case, they often have negative connotations and are used to underline that somebody feels himself or herself too important.

In business and official circles, *Gospodin* and *Gospozha* are now widely used. Both titles came from pre-revolutionary Russia, when they meant Master and Mistress. Many people enjoy this flattering form, feeling themselves part of the Russian nobility. But some, remembering their peasants roots, dislike it and may respond with: "I am not your Master…"

For addressing unknown people, two neutral forms are left. First, Russian language allows to avoid any address at all and to start conversation with impersonal forms, like: "please, tell me…" Second, *molodoi chelovek* (young man) or *devushka* (young woman) can be used to address people of all ages. But this form of address must definitely be avoided in official, formal or business situations.

NON-VERBAL COMMUNICATION

Gestures are not as common in Russia as in many other countries. Some people use their hands in animated conversation when they want to strengthen their point. They may wave their forefinger in front of someone's face or even poke one's chest. But this is considered to be only good for close friends.

There is not much respect for private space in Russia. People feel themselves quite comfortable standing near each other, even if they are strangers. During conversation, it is customary to touch a person with whom you are talking. This gesture is meant to create confiding atmosphere, but is not always rightly understood by foreigners considering it to be rather intimate.

The language of gestures in Russia is not as politicised as is usually thought. Endless books by foreign authors discuss certain gestures, supposedly in use in Soviet times. Two fingers touching your shoulder means there is a KGB agent present, raising your eyes to the ceiling means that we are being listened to, and so on. These myths were born not in Russia but abroad, and were necessary to support the concept about the difficulty of living under a totalitarian regime. It should be noted that if everybody really was being followed (and who knows today), then it would not have been so openly stupid. Ordinary citizens would not even have guessed and therefore would have had no need of a special language of gestures.

The national gestures which do exist relate to more pressing and eternal questions: tapping your neck to invite somebody for a drink, swivelling your finger on your temple to mean you're a fool, and raising your thumb for everything's okay.

BUSINESS IN RUSSIA

CHAPTER 9

'Trust, but verify.'
'When money talks, then truth stays silent.'
'The agreement costs more then money.'
—Russian proverbs

THE RUSSIAN BUSINESSMAN

The Russian businessman is a new phenomenon for our country. Up to the 1917 Revolution, people engaged in commerce were known as entrepreneurs, in the Soviet period as 'abettors of capitalism', but now in the post-*perestroika* era, the Western term 'businessman' has struck deep roots in the Russian language. The new name has given rise to a new form and content. Today, among the businessmen whom foreigners are most likely to come across, several types may be distinguished.

First, we should begin by saying a few words about the so-called 'New Russians', who are to be found among all types of businessmen. One of the main distinguishing traits of the 'New Russian' is the possession of big money. The amount of money necessary to qualify for such respected status varies and depends on social environment. For some, the latest model of Mercedes, a private residence along the Rublyovskoe highway (the most prestigious address in out-of-town Moscow) and a villa on the Mediterranean are a must; others are content with a secondhand Opel, a flat with Euro standard interior décor and a case of expensive, good-quality vodka to celebrate the holiday with. An all-important factor here is awareness of one's own wealth and the need to show it off to one's peers. 'New Russians' usually come into being quickly and suddenly cease to be.

...sia to begin with, the 'New Russians' aroused ...n and even malice: "There is nothing to eat, and they ...g their money around. What did they do to deserve it?" ...oday this attitude is changing and acceptance ("since he exists, he must be meant to be") and even pity ("you had better enjoy life while you can, poor devil: for you'll end up bankrupt or might even be murdered") are beginning to show through the negative reactions. Generally speaking, the Russian people are patient and compassionate.

Interest in the 'New Russians' has given rise to a huge number of anecdotes so popular in Russia, and which, better than anything else, illustrate the characteristics typical of, or rather attributed to, the 'New Russians'. The chief among these are:

- Senseless extravagance, as revealed in anecdotes of the type: 'Two New Russians meet in an automobile showroom. One buys a Mercedes-600, and the other asks him: "I say, you bought one of those a week ago. Have you smashed it?" "No, the ash-tray is full."'

- Stupidity, lack of education: 'Having bought himself a Lego model, a New Russian boasts to his friend: "Look, it says here 2–4 years, and I put it together in three months."'

- 'Face', the desire to upstage the neighbours in everything: 'Two 'New Russians' meet and one brags to the other: "Look at the tie I bought today for one grand!" " Idiot! In the shop next door, the same tie is on sale for one and a half grand!"'

In the West, all Russian businessmen tend to be referred to as 'New Russians', while in Russia, it is often a term used to describe the absurd personages of anecdotes, a derogatory and degrading nickname for those for whom what is important is not so much to clinch a deal as the desire to get one's hands on 'easy' money and spend it as quickly as possible.

As far as concerns the 'serious' Russian businessmen, here several groups are distinguishable. First, the representatives of the intelligentsia, graduates of the country's leading institutions of higher education, often with degrees and other academic titles, who have taken up business either due to the need to make money or to a liking for this activity, the new conditions giving them the opportunity to develop their abilities in this direction. For foreigners, contact with such people is, as a rule, quite straightforward: the Russian intellectual (member of the intelligentsia) is fairly cosmopolitan in his views, well educated (be ready to converse with a former engineer who has an excellent knowledge of American 19th century poetry and/or Italian Renaissance painting), speaks foreign languages and knows the world if only through literature, newspapers, the 'Voice of America' and Western films. Acquaintance with a businessman-intellectual, even if you are not linked by common business interests, will always be useful, since education in Russia is rated extremely highly. Moreover as a rule, an educated man has good contacts, is respected by those who surround him, including business circles, knows life well, can always help with advice and likewise suggest how to react to a particular situation or other.

The other numerous group of businessmen consists of the so-called 'old guard'. These are people who, having accumulated wide experience in administrative, party and organisational work in the Soviet period, have been able to readjust their bearings in the new historical conditions, to fall on their feet in the new life, putting their abilities to good use in a new sphere of activity. Such people, having 'gone through the mill', are hyper-cautious and take their time in conducting negotiations, doing so with feeling, deriving pleasure from the process as from a game of chess, and it is often difficult for foreigners (and not only foreigners) to foresee or gauge their thoughts and actions. They are very well connected and therefore have great potential, since 'contacts' play a major role in Russian life. Though now, instead of being made use of to obtain a pair of French boots or tickets to the Bolshoi Theatre, they are used to open a company, get round the law and secure a contract.

Such people will not deceive you in small things. Over the years, they have developed a peculiar code of honour of their own: they are capable of large scale intrigue, but

A foreign traveller in Russia in the 17th century tells how 'several Moscow merchants begged a Dutchman, who had cheated them of a large sum of money in business, to form a company with them and become their trading partner.' He notes with astonishment that there was no sign of anger at the Dutchman's duplicity, just respect for him and a wish to take a leaf out of his book.

will never take a risk in minor matters—'one has to think of one's reputation'. From the earliest times in Russia, major duplicity was regarded more as a virtue.

It is much easier to establish contact with the younger generation of businessmen. These are young men who, more often than not, have no experience of working in the Soviet period, but are well acquainted with the Western style of conducting negotiations, are happy to acquire new habits, more likely to speak foreign languages than the 'old-timers', and dislike procrastination or putting things off indefinitely. With some of them, you will feel as if you are in the company of your own fellow countrymen, with no differences in manners, clothes, interests, or even in pronunciation!

As a rule, it is usually fairly easy and pleasant to conduct negotiations with young businessmen. However, it is here that one is most likely to run up against deceit and petty swindling. Behind the outer veneer of Western-style efficiency, there may lurk a swindler, or more likely than not just an irresponsible fellow who has assimilated a somewhat Western style of behaviour and decides to take a risk in the hope he will get away with it. One often reads that it is easier to do business with the younger generation who are more pro-Western in orientation, less inclined to procrastination, quick to take decisions and so on. A quick-witted young man who has seen the world, speaks English, learnt (from guides for businessmen) what to say and how to conduct himself in a particular situation, makes a better impression than an elderly, respectable-looking businessman with the face of a party functionary. However, be warned: quick wits and haste may conceal deception, while slowness may derive from caution, experience and reluctance to take a risk.

One more piece of advice: have a laid-back attitude to the political convictions of your business partners. Forget your usual labels. A man who calls himself a communist (and in particular the man who talks nostalgically of the good old days) may be a first-class businessman, a reliable partner and intelligent, however contradictory this is of your view of the world. In Russian politics today, everything is very confused and it is extremely difficult to understand what is going on. Russian political life is not a division into black and white, as it is often seen to be in the West; it is all much more complex. Therefore, for the duration of your business negotiations, put aside your convictions and views.

BUSINESS ETIQUETTE

So-called business etiquette in Russia today is still in the process of taking shape, basing itself partly on pre-revolutionary, partly on Soviet, and partly on Western patterns. This explosive mixture—unstable, indeterminate and not always pleasant to the taste—determines at the present time the behaviour of the majority of Russian businessmen. One must constantly bear in mind that life in Russia, the business world included, changes with extreme rapidity. That which ten years ago appeared to be totally impossible, the concept of Russian business for instance, is today a commonplace feature of everyday life. Who knows what tomorrow will bring? Let us dwell on the more general tendencies and traditions characterising the behaviour of Russians in the conduct of business, and deriving first and foremost from national traits of character.

Preparatory work prior to a business trip to Russia is of vital importance. An exchange of faxes and emails setting out the aims and goals of the trip is useful practice. Do not count on the ordinary postal service, which is extremely unreliable in Russia: you will never find out at what stage your letters or parcels went astray.

In business correspondence, there are some peculiarities characteristic of Russian life. First, you should bear in mind that the people who correspond with you are not necessarily those who will be conducting the negotiations in Moscow. Therefore to be on the safe side, have with you a spare copy of letters and documents, for it is possible you will have to spend time fixing things you thought were already done. Second, don't write a novel. Remember that for the recipients, it is a foreign language and not all are completely fluent in it; list your main goals and formulate them as simply and clearly as possible. Finally, remember that in Russia, there exists a peculiar attitude to the printed word and to any kind of official document or instruction. Whereas in the Western world an official document carries a lot of weight, in Russia there is a favourite word 'formality', meaning that a given document, though formally essential, in effect signifies nothing. Often, not only are the instructions on it ignored, no one will bother to read it even.

Spoken Above the Written

An American professor received an official invitation from one of the faculties of Moscow University to read a lecture there. He was awaited with impatience, all details of the visit had been arranged and agreed at all levels of the university administration. The invitation necessary for him to be given a Russian visa was composed by a secretary and signed by one of the university bigwigs. Neither of them had ever heard of the professor in question (Let me remind you that Moscow University has 21 faculties, each of which have from 200 to 2,000 staff members, thus to keep track of everything that happens at the ground level is impossible. All official documents, however, have to be signed by one of the bosses on the university's general administrative board). As a result, a standard invitation was dispatched containing quite different conditions to those which had already been agreed. The professor took umbrage and did not come. The faculty staff sent him numerous faxes explaining that the invitation he had received was just a formal piece of paper necessary to obtain a visa at the embassy, while the conditions of his visit remained unchanged. In the end, the faculty staff also took umbrage at the professor's lack of comprehension. There is a simple moral to this story: if there is something out of order in the correspondence from your Russian business partners, clarify the issue before taking offence. It is possible that is not a mark of disrespect to yourself, but due to the carelessness of a secretary, the blunder of a minor bureaucrat, or simply a stupid misunderstanding (the wrong document being sent to you). This is possible in any country, but particularly in Russia, where no one takes such documents seriously.

Once all the preparatory work for your visit has been successfully completed, all the necessary documentation received, a visa stamped in your passport and a ticket lying in your pocket and you are full of firm resolve to set off for distant parts, try and understand the obvious truth that the success of your undertaking depends first and foremost on yourself and your state of mind. Russian businessmen know full well that many foreigners come to Russia determined to play the game in their own way and to follow their own rules of behaviour in conducting negotiations, anything else being regarded with distrust, scorn and disdain. It is for this very reason, for instance, that American businessmen in Russia are often considered to be too pushy and aggressive, overfamiliar and lacking in delicacy. Remember, you are encroaching upon a different world, a world, moreover, that today is fairly unstable and therefore particularly vulnerable.

BEST TIME FOR A VISIT

When planning a business trip to Russia, you should take into account seasonal features. Summer, which tends to be the most popular period with foreigners, is not necessarily the best time for Russian business, for it is the school and general holiday season when all are intent on escaping from the stuffy cities into the countryside—whether at home or abroad. Even if your business partner agrees to meet you during the summer period, you should bear in mind that other staff members may well be on leave, and that your negotiations could be held up because some big boss, without whose approval no final decision can be taken, has gone off to Cyprus, or that the secretary, whose job it is to stamp the documents, is away at her *dacha* planting potatoes.

It is not advisable to come to Russia a week before, during or after a holiday. The busiest holiday period in Russia is the New Year. For two weeks before 1 January, no one is in the mood for serious undertakings: there is too little time and therefore it is not worth getting started on anything. At offices, celebrations get underway at all levels, and as these never coincide, the whole period becomes transformed into one extended junket. People's minds are occupied with buying presents, getting food and with solving domestic and family problems. The holidays continue after 1 January: on 7 January, the Russians celebrate the Russian Orthodox

Christmas, and on 14 January the so-called Old New Year. This is not an official holiday, but for all that, many people reverently celebrate it.

The family and children play a major role in the life of the Russian, and for this reason, it is recommended to avoid the school holiday periods (1–10 November, 30 December–11 January and the last week in March). Many businessmen whom you know to be tough, serious trading partners will become as meek as lambs when their offspring demand to be taken to the sea or countryside.

The autumn and, however paradoxical this may sound, the winter (with the exception of the New Year holiday period) are good times for business visits. Only don't forget your fur hat and gloves! The Russian winter in Moscow is nothing to be frightened of; it is much milder and warmer than is commonly imagined. Added to which, Russian houses are usually beautifully warm inside, and many foreigners indeed often complain of stuffiness.

BUSINESS NEGOTIATIONS
Business negotiations in Russia are conducted in the office and only in the office. In Russia, it is definitely not the done thing to invite a colleague to a hotel room to talk business; this will cause bewilderment and at best be taken as a sign of the lack of serious intentions. Now, particularly among the younger generation of Russian businessmen, the habit of business lunches and even breakfasts is becoming more and more common. However, they are usually invariably accompanied by meetings in an official environment and are viewed just as a supplement to the latter.

But for all that, be prepared for the fact that Russians will talk business to you everywhere—at a slap-up meal in a restaurant, at a private home where you are guests, in the countryside over a barbecue, during an excursion to a museum, before the stove at a *dacha* and so on. The end of the working day does not mean the end of work for a Russian, particularly if he is carried away by a new project. Though your Russian colleague may be drunk, his discussion of the potential perspectives of your mutual cooperation will be lucid and to the point. Take note of what he says and ask questions. However, the next day you should clarify the points on which you have reached agreement once more. While many important issues in Russia are decided in an informal environment, final agreement, though, may be reached only in the office.

The beginning of the negotiations is of prime significance. Above all, bear in mind that in Russia, to be late for a meeting—even a business meeting—is not considered to be rude or a sign of disrespect. Certainly, the major Russian companies of statewide significance try today to conduct negotiations within precisely indicated time limits, but at a less important level, you will more likely than not constantly come up against disruptions to the timetable of your talks.

The Russians have a different attitude to time compared to the Westerners and a delay of 10–15 minutes is not regarded at all as being late.

Don't Mind the Wait!

One of my acquaintances, an American professor, was invited to a meal in a Russian home and it was arranged he should meet his hostess in the Metro at 7:00 pm. When at 7:20 pm she arrived at the appointed spot, having collected her child from the kindergarten after work and waited in a bus queue, the American was nowhere to be seen. And with that their acquaintance ended, for the professor considered that for his hostess to be late was unforgivable, while his hostess regarded his refusal to wait 20 minutes for her as bad manners. So if you arrive at a meeting which is delayed since your Russian partners have not yet appeared, don't be upset and remember about the differences in culture and traditions. Incidentally, you as a foreigner will be expected to be on time, so despite what has been said above, you had better not be late.

The Russians' special attitude to time is reflected in the way they conduct negotiations. It may often be that these are extended way beyond the time slot allotted to them, even if you have agreed, for instance, on a one hour long meeting. If your intentions are serious, don't hurry, don't fuss, relax and most importantly, don't pack your appointments too close together. Always leave a space between them, otherwise it may happen that you will have to leave just as you have begun to get down to brass tacks.

The Russian side will be introduced by the head of the organisation or his deputy, in which case the deputy will always introduce his boss first. Introductions are often made in order of diminishing importance; other variants are possible however, as per the seating order round the table for instance. In the latter case, the person making the introductions will almost certainly explain what he is doing so that no one gets hurt. Often, women are introduced first, irrespective of rank. The same goes for elderly people, even if their presence at the negotiating table is purely formal, in order to emphasise the importance of the moment or so that they should not feel left out.

Lending Weight

At the beginning of the 20th century, Anton Chekhov described the 'wedding generals': strangers who for a small sum were invited to a wedding, dressed up in uniform and medals to impart an air of solemnity to the occasion. Today too, people will often be invited to be present at negotiations who play no part in the taking of decisions, but who, in the opinion of the Russian side, lend weight and a sense of respectability to the proceedings.

Some of those present may not be introduced at all: this means they are either minor officials, or totally extraneous people who are there by chance and simply waiting their turn. You should be prepared for the fact that their presence at the negotiating table does not necessarily imply interest in the talks.

As far as concerns the foreign delegation, the senior member of the party should start speaking first and do the introductions, presenting all members of his team, describing their function and position and indicating the degree of importance of each in the taking of decisions. It is best to immediately put your Russian partners in the picture—about yourself, the aim of your visit and about those final documents you plan to sign.

Western guidebooks often write that for respectability's sake, it is essential to have a stock of gold-embossed visiting cards and an expensive suit for your visit to Russia. And there is a grain of truth in this. For in Russia, it is customary to start off any meeting with an exchange of visiting cards (the visiting card is still regarded as an indicator of status and position in society) and certainly an expensive dark suit will make a positive impression on your Russian partners. On the other hand, there is a popular Russian saying which goes 'you are judged by your appearance first, but by your mind later on' ('clothes count only for first impressions'). Thus your jeans, even if they disconcert the Russian businessman at first, will be forgiven and attributed to Western eccentricity if it emerges that you have serious and interesting propositions to put on the table.

On meeting and parting in Russia, it is customary to shake hands—firmly and with everyone around you—each time you meet, even if the negotiations continue for several days. Women are the exception to the rule here, for their hand is shaken only when you meet them for the first time. Incidentally in Russia, it is considered gallant to kiss a woman's hand, thus businesswomen should be prepared for this and accept it as a mark of respect and not as indicating a frivolous attitude towards the 'weaker' sex.

The presence of extraneous people at negotiations who are there purely by chance often complicates the all-important task of determining who is who, who takes the decisions, who will carry them out and so on. For not to observe the pecking order may result in seriously ruffled feelings and be taken as a mark of disrespect on your part. Here are some words of advice in such a situation:

- Meetings are usually held in the office of the most senior-ranking member of those present, though there is no guarantee that it is he who will make the final decision. The boss usually sits at the head of the table, and the rest often in order of diminishing importance: the further away you are from the boss, the less important your rank. The secretary, as a rule, serves tea by seniority.
- If you understand Russian, listen to how members of the Russian delegation address each other: *vy* plus Christian name-patronymic is a junior addressing a senior, *ty* plus Christian name is a senior addressing a junior.

- Even if you don't know the Russian language, observe how the Russians react to each other—who is asked most questions, who is looked at most—and follow their intonation. Respect and scorn are, as a rule, detectable even without understanding the words.

- On the whole, it is better not to pay anyone apart from the boss too much attention, so as to avoid mistakes, even if you find what his deputy says to be more interesting and it makes a greater impression on you. It is best you talk to him alone, outside his boss's office.

- To go out of your way to show consideration and respect for the leader of the Russian side is not just routine good manners. For it is his position that is often crucial: it is on his opinion, in the final count, that the success of the negotiations depends. For all that, attention to the middle and lower ranks of personnel can be very important. Often a lot depends on them—meetings, organisation and even the outcome of negotiations. A small souvenir and attention will, in the majority of cases, help you solve this problem. Every Russian knows that it is often more important to please the secretary than her boss.

- For all the outer appearance of strict hierarchy in the collective, the relationships between its members are much more democratic (internally) than one might think, and relations between the boss and his subordinates will often be closer and less formal than is the case in Western society. In Russia, over the years there has grown a view of the workplace community as a large family, whose head—though possessing great power and authority—is, for all that, a member of the same family. Today, many companies try to introduce a more Western style of relationships in the workplace community, establishing greater discipline and formality, but they do not always succeed in this.

Business Gifts

Many guidebooks tend to devote a paragraph or two to the presents which should be brought to Moscow for business meetings. And up to a point, this is correct—Russians like to be given presents and, to some extent, expect them. But Russians also love giving presents, so you may find yourself in an embarrassing position if you come empty-handed. In most books about Russia, however, the information on what to bring is out-of-date. Only ten years ago, small souvenirs which symbolised the forbidden Western world were for this reason greatly appreciated and of interest. Ever since, the authors of many guidebooks for businessmen have been under the delusion that trifles such as key rings, packets of cigarettes, biros and so on make good presents.

Life in Russia has undergone great changes since then, and for a businessman today, this type of present will be humiliating, putting him (if only in his own eyes) in the position of a native, who exchanges gold bars for the glass beads and small mirrors of European explorer-conquerors. Souvenirs bearing the company logo can and should be brought, but they should be presented casually, as a ritual and not as presents. I should like to put on record once more that Russians today are very easily hurt and they have a chip on their shoulder about being treated with respect. It is better to give nothing—you'll simply be thought inconsiderate and it will be put down to culture differences—than to give a worthless present which will give you the reputation of stinginess and mean you will be looked on with distrust.

What are good presents to give? It is good to have one official present: this may be a souvenir or some object reflecting local characteristics or bearing the insignia of your company. It should be quite big so that it can be displayed in the office. It is good to play it up: when you present it, for instance, you might bring it into a speech about contacts between countries or cooperation between companies. As far as concerns individual presents, men always appreciate alcoholic drinks (the best to give are spirits or drinks

An anecdote comes to mind. In Russia, there is a lovely tale about a little golden fish which is very popular: if you catch her, she will fulfill any three of your wishes. In the 'New Russian' version, it goes as follows: Once a New Russian caught a little golden fish and he asked her: "Tell me, what I can give you?"

typical in your country), women always appreciate sweets and everyone likes good quality stationary items: expensive fountain pens, leather folders, briefcases, etc. The quality and cost of your presents will depend on the size of your company and the scope of the proposed project.

It is best to give your presents at the end or in the middle of negotiations, but not right away—first you need to get to know each other.

Show gratitude for and make the right noises about the presents you are given, even if they seem to you to be unnecessary, bulky or cheap. It is quite possible that much effort has gone into their acquisition. A disparaging attitude on this issue will be very hurtful for your partners.

How to Behave During Negotiations

There is a direct link between the way business negotiations are conducted in Russia and the general cultural traditions and national character of its people. Negotiations usually proceed at a leisurely pace and are very thorough, all rituals being observed, even in those cases when the issue is a foregone conclusion.

The Russians like making speeches of welcome, which at first may seem to be totally irrelevant. For the Russian, it is vital to feel that in addition to making a fortune himself, he is at the same time doing something important and necessary for his country and its people.

One of my acquaintances who has started up his own business and is earning good money and thus can take frequent holidays in places which, in the old days, would have been beyond his wildest dreams, continues to yearn for the times he worked in a design office where he earned nothing, spent his leave staying with friends in the Moscow region but, for all that, felt himself to be part of a grandiose plan, designing unique planes which had their equal nowhere in the world.

I suggest you prepare a speech along the lines 'for peace and friendship among peoples'. Such a global approach will, in the majority of cases, be met with approval and support from the Russian.

During negotiations, be prepared to be patient and tolerant. The Russian language has a mass of sayings which condemn haste in the taking of important decisions: 'A tale is quickly told, but to do a job takes time', 'It's easier said than done', 'If you hurry too much, you'll make a fool of yourself', 'Haste makes waste', 'Slow and steady wins the race' and many others. During negotiations, be prepared to listen attentively, not showing signs of impatience, looking at your watch, yawning or drumming your fingers on the table, even when the discussion is obviously going off at a tangent or, in your view, too general and inconsequential.

Remember that the main guarantee of success in Russia is the establishment of personal contacts. It is, therefore, very important to be considerate to the people you intend to do business with. Qualities such as hard-headedness, precision and efficiency, which are highly rated in the USA and in the countries of Western Europe, are regarded in Russia more as failings. One of the main grudges of the Russian is that 'they don't respect me'.

Be ready to listen more than to talk. This has its advantages. During long speeches, you can study your partners, their relationships to one other, manner of behaviour and so on.

Today, the 'Western' style of negotiations—in the boss's office, in a relatively official environment—is becoming more and more widespread in Russia. But alongside this exists a more traditionally Russian style of organising meetings. Don't be surprised if, on arriving for business talks, you find a table covered with eats and drinks, irrespective of the time of day, and are met by a large, excited crowd. Such a situation does not indicate a lack of seriousness in your partners' intentions; it is just a display of traditional Russian hospitality.

Fairy Tale Hospitality

Hospitality has always been a distinguishing feature of Russian life. In one Russian fairy tale, one of the chief villains, the old witch Baba Yaga, plans to gobble up the hero, but is completely disarmed when the latter says to her : "First feed your guest, give him drink, put him to bed, and after that gobble him up". The need to fulfil her duty as hostess gets the better of her evil nature. And 'having fed him and given him drink', in other words established personal contact with him, there remains nothing else for Baba Yaga to do than to assist the hero in his battle.

Food and drinks are considered in Russia to be the best way of winning someone's trust and friendship. A typical situation: The Russian side organised a meeting for an important foreign delegation they were expecting. They put out the eats and drinks, gathered together as many people as possible, welcomed their guests, entertained them, fraternised with them and parted from them the best of friends. And afterwards they could not understand why the contract was signed not with them but with another less respectable and reliable company, which had conducted negotiations in a strictly official style. A laden table, informal atmosphere, prolonged drinking of toasts etc., by no means indicates a lack of business ability in your Russian partners, nor is it an attempt to buy you. It is a tribute to tradition and speaks rather of their respect and wish to show you consideration.

Even during official negotiations in Russia, it is customary to make ceremonial speeches and drink toasts. Don't miss the opportunity to answer and to toast back. Whatever you say will be received with approval. Incidentally, never make a point of refusing drink during an official meeting. Even if you don't want to drink, it is better all the same to make a show of clinking glasses, raising your glass to your lips and putting it down again. The same goes for food—don't refuse and praise everything, even if you are full.

During negotiations, it is best to conduct yourself in a reserved and collected manner, don't lounge in your chair or be too laid-back. Of course, the younger generation of businessmen may conduct themselves in this very manner, so be guided by circumstance. But even with the younger generation, reserve always makes a good impression: he may be a bit boring, but at least he is respectable.

Russians are very fond of jokes, anecdotes, informal contact and heart-to-hearts. But in an official atmosphere, everything has to be serious; It is a ritual of a sort, a game— we are engaged on serious business. If you are not very well acquainted with your partners, not experienced enough to easily adapt to a new situation, or not confident of your ability to quickly size up the characters of your Russian colleagues, then you had best adopt a serious, business-like air during your meetings. When they joke with you, smile, when they fill up your glass, clink glasses, and when they slap you on the shoulder, take it in good part. Remember, a man who is serious and says little always produces a good impression in Russia.

Smoking at Work

In Russia, many people smoke. Smoking today is part of the business image, and therefore in some cases, business talks may be an excruciating experience for you if you cannot stand the smell of tobacco smoke. However in certain companies, smoking in the office is forbidden, so if you want to smoke yourself, ask permission first.

All these varied, complicated and at times high-flown and pompous traditions of conducting negotiations in Russia make it difficult to gauge an all-important issue—namely, just how effective are your negotiations. Your partners may agree, nod their heads approvingly, but as yet this doesn't mean anything; they are just being polite. Not infrequently, the expression of obvious interest in your project may derive from the desire not to hurt your feelings. That having been said, the younger generation are often more open in displaying their enthusiasm, while older people tend to be more reserved and cautious, trying not to show their feelings.

Whom to believe and how to ensure that one is not taken for a person who is easily swayed—these are questions which have long worried Western entrepreneurs coming to Russia. Back in the first half of the 17th century, a German traveller wrote: 'Their cleverness and cunning come to the fore particularly in buying and selling, for they think up all manner of guile and sharp practice in order to hoodwink their neighbour. And he who wishes to deceive them, must have good brains...' As if in answer to this, an English connoisseur of Russian life in the middle of the last century noted that 'foreigners who go to Russia and embark in speculations without possessing any adequate knowledge of the character, customs and language of the people positively invite spoliation, and ought to blame themselves rather than the people who profit by their ignorance'.

Here is some practical advice.

External appearances are often deceptive. The following historical anecdote is well known:

When Catherine the Great decided to visit the Russian villages in order to see for herself how her people lived, Prince Potemkin in a very short time literally transformed a village lying in the middle of nowhere: the facades of the houses were freshly painted, the roads hurriedly strewn with earth, clean clothing distributed to the peasants and a table was laid out with festive fare in the largest hut. The empress was favourably impressed by the well-being of her subjects, and a new expression, 'Potemkin villages', entered the Russian language. Some modern Russian companies have grown out of the old state institutions, and therefore a smart building and oak furniture are not necessarily an indication of the company's reliability. In addition to which, Russians as a whole tend to be very impressed by external pomp, and 'face' is important for them. Not infrequently, a firm will spend its first profits on smart office furniture and equipment.

Don't Let Your Eyes Deceive You!

Several years ago at an international trade fair in Paris, I was witness to an amusing though characteristic episode. During President Mitterand's visit to the fair, a member of the Russian delegation, the representative of a publishing firm, with great difficulty elbowed his way through the large crowd to the French president's side. Some cunning photos taken by a colleague gave the impression that Mitterand and the publisher were engaged in conversation. After general laughter, the young publisher remarked: "they will look good in our advertising booklet." So it is not always wise to believe one's eyes; it is better to trust intuition and instinct.

The Russians themselves are afraid of being done down and not infrequently they will search for concealed traps in your proposals. And it is because of this fear that they sometimes play for time, while they try and check up on your reliability. But at the same time, they often won't ask you any direct questions, being afraid to offend you. So it is better that you prepare in advance a packet of documents confirming your respectability. Here we again come up against one of the paradoxes of Russian life—respect for a document and a deprecatory attitude to it. Your numerous well-printed and imposing officially-stamped documents, information materials and prospectuses—it is desirable, of course, to have at least something in Russian—will undoubtedly make a favourable impression on your Russian partner.

It is very important to make sure that the man who will make the final decision and sign the agreement is acquainted with the project and has approved it; it is advisable to have his signature on the draft agreement. Sometimes, a project may be wrecked by internal intrigue, power struggles and non-observance of subordination, even if this runs counter to common sense and to your Russian partners' advantage.

One major British company engaged in prolonged negotiations with a serious Moscow organisation. A great deal of effort, time and money was expended by both sides. However, when it came to the crunch, the head of the Russian organisation refused to sign the agreement, though at the outset he had given his verbal consent to it, not to the Englishmen, but in private conversation with his subordinates. He objected to the fact that all the negotiations had been conducted without his participation and, though the agreement was extremely advantageous to both sides, relations were broken off in one day, no explanation being given. Find out right at the start of negotiations whose decision is final and who will sign the agreement; a meeting with this person is desirable and even essential.

THE MAIN FEATURES OF RUSSIAN BUSINESS

And now for several general comments on some characteristic features of the way Russians conduct business. I hope that they may at least to some degree help you understand what is going on.

Russians love to take a risk. A favorite word is '*avos*' ('let's hope' or 'perhaps'). It means that one should put one's faith in fate: if one is lucky one will win, there is no need to think about what will happen if one loses though. The following are favourite Russian sayings: 'If you are frightened of wolves, don't go into the forest', 'If you play with matches, you can't be afraid of getting burned', 'Nothing ventured, nothing gained' (a variant is 'He who ventures nothing, doesn't drink champagne'), and 'Risk is a noble thing'. This particular feature of the Russian make-up applies to business relations too.

But at the same time, there are diametrically opposing traits in the Russian character—namely, overcautiousness and suspicion, which are revealed in equally popular sayings of the type: 'Measure seven times, cut once', 'Better safe than sorry', 'It's good to trust, but better still to check up', and 'Business and friendship (pleasure) don't mix'. These characteristics of the Russian businessman often mean that negotiations are unjustifiably drawn out and the making of the final decision put off again and again.

There is no need to be afraid of the broad sweep of the Russian imagination. The phrase 'We can do everything' does not always mean that this is not the case. So long as there is a will.... Here is a popular anecdote of business in New Russian style: Two Russian businessmen meet and one asks the other: "Will you buy a truckload of Snickers?" "Yes, I'll buy it," comes the answer. And they part company—one to search for a truckload of Snickers, the other for the cash to buy it with. Added to which Russians are spontaneous, impulsive and incapable of working to a timetable.

The Russians have an unusual attitude to money and wealth. Russian literature of the 19th century and Soviet ideology in the 20th instilled in effect one and the same thought: namely, that happiness does not lie in money and, worse still, that money is the source of all evil. Life today is undergoing rapid change, but very many Russians, as before, find conversation about money embarrassing. This is by no means to say that they do not need money. It's just that for a Russian, it is very important that his personal accumulation of wealth, at least in the eyes of the world, is seen to be combined with the good of society. This, I think, is a sensitive theme which requires careful handling.

There is a well-known saying: 'Russians take a long time to saddle up, but ride very quickly.' And nowhere is this demonstrated so graphically as in the sphere of business. In view of the overall instability of life in Russia, people prefer not to plan far ahead. A project which will begin to bring in profit—even if considerable—only after several years will hardly be in great demand in Russia today. Long negotiations are, as a rule, replaced by feverish activity in order to put plans into effect as quickly as possible.

Comparing Bureaucracies

The Russian bureaucracy is considered to be the worst in the world. I was of the same opinion until I began to travel in other countries. Generally speaking, the only difference between the Russian bureaucracy and its American, British, French, etc. counterparts, is that with the former one can come to agreement: either by playing on the emotions, such as pity, for example, or by giving bribes. Incidentally, it is best to leave the distribution of bribes to your Russian partners (or at least consult them); they know best whom to give a bribe to, when and how much it should be. And don't offend them by showing that you distrust or suspect them—Russians take umbrage easily, especially when people suspect them of being dishonest.

In conclusion, I would emphasise that your success will depend on a combination of your personal qualities and a number of external factors. An approximate recipe for successful business in Russia consists of a mixture of the following ingredients: common sense, business intuition and being observant, tolerance of and respect for foreign traditions and links and contacts in the country. Also desirable, of course, are several years of stability in Russia.

FAST FACTS ON RUSSIA

CHAPTER 10

'I had been afraid of Russia ever since I could remember.
When I was a boy its mass dominated the map which
covered the classroom wall...Where other nations—Japan,
Brazil, India—clamoured with imagined scents and colours,
Russia gave out only silence, and was somehow incomplete.'
—Colin Thubron, British travel writer

Official Name
Russian Federation (Russia)

Capital
Moscow

Flag
It consists of three equal horizontal bands of white, blue and red. The proportion of the flag's width to its length is 2:3. This flag was originally used as a naval flag, and then Peter the Great adopted it as a merchant flag in 1705. Between 1883 and 1917 (until the Revolution), it was the official national flag. On 21 August 1991, it was re-adopted as the state flag.

National Anthem
'*Rossiya—svyashchennaya nasha derzhava...*' ('Russia—Our Sacred State...'). Introduced in 2000 and based on the music and lyrics of 'Hymn of the Soviet Union' written in 1944.

Time
Russia is a vast country spanning 11 time zones from GMT + 2 (Kaliningrad) to GMT + 12 (Chukotka).

Telephone Country Code
7

Land

Russia is the largest country in the world, situated in the east of Europe and north of Asia. Ural mountains divide the Eurasian continent—and Russia—into Europe and Asia. One-fourth of Russian territory lies in Europe, the other part lies in Asia.

Area

Total: 17,100,000 sq km (6,602,346.9 sq miles)
Land: 16,995,800 sq km (6,562,115.1 sq miles)

Highest Point

Mountain El'brus: 5,633 m (18,481 ft)

Lowest Point

Caspian Sea: 28 m (91.9 ft)

Climate

Ranges from steppes in the south to humid continental in much of European Russia; sub-arctic in Siberia to tundra in the polar north. Winters vary from cool along the Black Sea coast to very cold in Siberia; summers vary from warm in the steppes to cool along the Arctic coast.

Natural Resources

Wide natural resource base including major deposits of oil, natural gas, coal, timber and many strategic minerals

Population

145,161,000 (2002 general census of the population)
Three-fourths of the population lives in the European part and one-fourth lives in the Asian part (Siberia and the Far East region).

Ethnic Groups

Russian 79.8 per cent, Tartar 3.8 per cent, Ukrainian 2 per cent, Bashkir 1.2 per cent, Chuvash 1.1 per cent, others from more than 100 ethnic groups 12.1 per cent (2002 general census of the population)

Religion

The most widespread is Russian Orthodoxy. Others include Islam, Buddhism, Catholicism and Judaism.

Official Language

Russian

Government Structure

Federal Republic with an elected president. The 1993 constitution created a dual executive consisting of a president and prime minister, but the president is the dominant figure. The Bicameral Federal Assembly or *Federalnoye Sobraniye* consists of the Federation Council or *Sovet Federatsii* and the State Duma or *Gosudarstvennaya Duma*.

Adminstrative Divisions

49 *oblasts*, 21 republics, ten autonomous *okrugs*, six *krays*, two federal cities and one autonomous *oblast*

Oblasts: Amur (Blagoveshchensk), Arkhangel'sk, Astrakhan', Belgorod, Bryansk, Chelyabinsk, Chita, Irkutsk, Ivanovo, Kaliningrad, Kaluga, Kamchatka (Petropavlovsk-Kamchatskiy), Kemerovo, Kirov, Kostroma, Kurgan, Kursk, Leningrad, Lipetsk, Magadan, Moscow, Murmansk, Nizhniy Novgorod, Novgorod, Novosibirsk, Omsk, Orenburg, Orel, Penza, Perm', Pskov, Rostov, Ryazan', Sakhalin (Yuzhno-Sakhalinsk), Samara, Saratov, Smolensk, Sverdlovsk (Yekaterinburg), Tambov, Tomsk, Tula, Tver', Tyumen', Ul'yanovsk, Vladimir, Volgograd, Vologda, Voronezh, Yaroslavl'

Republics: Adygeya (Maykop), Altay (Gorno-Altaysk), Bashkortostan (Ufa), Buryatiya (Ulan-Ude), Chechnya (Groznyy), Chuvashiya (Cheboksary), Dagestan (Makhachkala), Ingushetiya (Magas), Kabardino-Balkariya (Nal'chik), Kalmykiya (Elista), Karachayevo-Cherkesiya (Cherkessk), Kareliya (Petrozavodsk), Khakasiya (Abakan), Komi (Syktyvkar), Mariy-El (Yoshkar-Ola), Mordoviya (Saransk), Sakha [Yakutiya] (Yakutsk), North Ossetia (Vladikavkaz), Tatarstan (Kazan'), Tyva (Kyzyl), Udmurtiya (Izhevsk)

Autonomous *okrugs*: Aga Buryat (Aginskoye), Chukotka (Anadyr'), Evenk (Tura), Khanty-Mansi, Komi-Permyak (Kudymkar), Koryak (Palana), Nenets (Nar'yan-Mar), Taymyr [Dolgano-Nenets] (Dudinka), Ust'-Orda Buryat (Ust'-Ordynskiy), Yamalo-Nenets (Salekhard)

Krays: Altay (Barnaul), Khabarovsk, Krasnodar, Krasnoyarsk, Primorskiy (Vladivostok), Stavropol'

Federal cities: Moscow (Moskva), Saint Petersburg (Sankt-Peterburg)

Autonomous *oblast*: Yevrey [Jewish] (Birobidzhan)

Currency
Russian ruble (RUR)

Gross Domestic Product (GDP)
US$1.723 trillion (2006 est.)

Agricultural Products
Grain, sugar beets, sunflower seed, vegetables, fruits, beef and milk

Industries
Wide range of mining and extractive industries producing coal, oil, gas, chemicals and metals; all forms of machine building; defense industries, shipbuilding; road and rail transportation equipment; communications equipment; agricultural machinery, tractors and construction equipment; electric power generating and transmitting equipment; medical and scientific instruments; consumer durables, textiles, foodstuffs and handicrafts

Exports
Petroleum and petroleum products, natural gas, wood and wood products, metals, chemicals and a wide variety of civilian and military manufactured goods

Imports

Machinery and equipment, consumer goods, medicines, meat, sugar and semi-finished metal products

Airports

Total: 1,623
Paved runways: 616

FAMOUS PEOPLE
Alexander II (1818–1881)

Russian emperor since 1855 and son of Nicholas I. Alexander is famous for his liberal reforms. The most important among them was the abolition of serfdom in Russia in 1861, for which he was called Tsar-Liberator. Other reforms included administrative, juridical, military and educational ones. In 1867, he sold Alaska to the US (for which he is still widely criticised by many). Despite being one of the most liberal Russian *tsars*, he was persecuted by revolutionaries most of his life. He was finally killed by revolutionary terrorists.

Chekhov, Anton (1860–1904)

A novelist and playwright. His short stories are very popular in modern Russia. They are full of both humour and tragedy, showing different sides of life. He wrote about ordinary lives of ordinary people, penetrating into their inner world. Outside Russia, he is better known for his plays, which influenced drama all over the world during the 20th century. His four major plays—*The Seagul*, *Uncle Vanya*, *The Three Sisters* and *The Cherry Orchard*—are frequently staged in theatres all over the world.

Dostoevsky, Fyodor (1821–1881)

Great Russian writer. His most famous novels are *Crime and Punishment*, *The Brothers Karamazov*, *The Idiot* and *The Gambler*. His works focus on deep psychological penetration into the human soul, the search for eternal truth, suffering and revival. His ideas greatly influenced 20th century literature and philosophy.

Gagarin, Yuri (1934–1968)

The first Soviet cosmonaut. On 12 April 1961, Gagarin was the first to go around the earth in the spaceship *Vostok*. Gagarin, with his nice, open smile, became a symbol of the new victorious Soviet Russia that had conquered space. He tragically died in a plane crash.

Glinka, Mikhail (1804–1857)

Russian composer and the founder of Russian opera. Among his most famous operas are *Life for the Tsar* (about the episode in early 17th century Russian history when Russian peasant Ivan Susanin was killed by the Poles because he refused to show them the place where Tsar Mikhail was hidden) and *Ruslan and Ludmila* (based on Alexander Pushkin's poem).

Gorbachev, Mikhail (born 1931)

First and only president of the USSR (March 1990–December 1991). Being the general secretary of the Communist Party of the USSR, he started the so-called period of *perestroika*. In December 1991, he signed the treaty dissolving the Soviet Union. Very popular abroad as the Soviet leader of a new Westernised style and rather unpopular in his own country (probably for the same reason).

Ivan IV (the Terrible) (1530–1584)

The *tsar* of Russia known for his uncompromising politics towards his enemies. Enlarged the eastern boundaries of the Russian state by conquering Tartary and Siberia, and transformed it into a multinational and multicultural state. A controversial person whose reign was estimated accordingly: some think him to be one of the greatest Russian rulers, others one of the worst tyrants.

Kutuzov, Mikhail (1745–1813)

Russian military leader and diplomat. He is most well known for his role in the war with Napoleon in 1812. Although he is considered the main winner of this war, some people think that the idea to leave Moscow to the enemy was a wrong one. On the one hand, it allowed the Russian army to keep strength and to strike back; on the other hand, Moscow was burnt down by the French troops.

Lenin, Vladimir (1870–1924)

The leader of the Bolshevik Party and the founder of the Soviet state. His original surname was Ulyanov. He played an outstanding role in the Russian Revolution and during the first years of the new Soviet state. After his death, his body was laid in a specially-built mausoleum in Red Square. The influence of his personality and his ideas was great during the Soviet period of Russian history. His images were everywhere, his works were read at schools and universities and all Russian cities had a Lenin's Street and his monument in a central square. Since the collapse of the Soviet Union, his image has lost its grandeur, but he is still considered to be an important figure of Russian history.

Lomonosov, Mikhail (1711–1765)

Russian scientist and educator. The son of a fisherman from a remote northern village, he went on foot to Moscow to be educated. His life is considered to be an illustration of the idea that a strong will and eagerness to study can do miracles. Lomonosov became one of the most famous Russian scholars. He was knowledgeable about various subjects: literature, history, chemistry, physics, mathematics and art. He was one of the founders of the first Russian university in Moscow (1755), later named after him.

Mendeleev, Dmitri (1834–1907)

Russian chemist. He is renowned for creating the first periodic table of elements. He even managed to predict some of the elements yet to be discovered. Among other things, he is also praised for creating the modern type of Russian vodka (40 per cent of alcohol).

Nevsky, Alexander (1219/1220–1263)

Grand prince of Novgorod who became famous after his victory over the Teutonic knights in 1242 at the Chudskoe lake near Pskov. This battle became known as the 'Ice battle'.

He established good diplomatic relations with another great Russian great enemy of his time—The Golden Horde. This helped Russia to save its lands and people from new destructive battles. After his death, he was proclaimed a saint by the Russian Orthodox Church. Peter the Great moved his relics to the new Russian capital of Saint Petersburg in order to strengthen its importance. During Soviet times, Alexander became a symbol of Russian courage, patriotism and military strength. The famous film by Sergei Eisenstein *Alexander Nevsky* (1938) was very popular during the Second World War and the Order of Alexander Nevsky was one of the highest military decorations.

Nicholas II (1868–1918)

The last Russian emperor. His rule and personality received a somewhat contradictory evaluation. Some think him a weak ruler who was unable to manage the country during political turmoil or command its army in the First World War, which brought Russia to the Revolution. Others consider him to be a saint, suffering and struggling to save his dying country. Nicholas and his family were executed after the Revolution. In 2000, they were canonised by the Russian Orthodox Church.

Pavlov, Ivan (1849–1936)

Russian physiologist and physician. He was widely known for being the first to describe the phenomenon known as conditioning reflex in his experiments with dogs. He was also the first Russian to be awarded the Nobel Prize.

Peter I (Peter the Great) (1672–1725)

Russian *tsar* and the first Russian emperor (1721). Peter carried out the policy of Westernisation and expansion that transformed Russia into a major European power. His reforms in different spheres—in politics, administrative and military systems, education, religion, culture, mode of life—changed the Russian state completely and moved Russia to a new stage of development. He was an outstanding person—bright, energetic, fearless and unruly.

Pushkin, Alexander (1799–1837)

He was read and praised at all times—in *tsarist* Russia and even during Soviet times (during Stalin's rule, the celebration of the centenary of his death was one of the greatest national festivals). His fame survived in all its glory after *perestroika* (not so many other authors managed). His fairy tales are read to children, his poems are known by all Russians, and his short novels laid the foundation for Russian literature. His works lose a lot in translation so foreigners rarely understand this Russian passion. But if you want to know Russia and Russians, you need to read and love Pushkin.

Putin, Vladimir (born 1952)

The current president of the Russian Federation (2000, 2004). He was born in Leningrad (hence the rising power of this city) and served in the KGB (later FSB) for many years. The beginning of his political carrier was rather theatrical: he was announced by President Yeltsin to be his successor on the very eve of the New Year 2000. Virtually unknown at the beginning, he managed to win the presidential elections twice. In his politics, he tries to compromise and pacify different political groups.

Rublev, Andrei (died 1430)

The most famous Russian painter of the Middle Ages, whose icons became an example for many future generations of Russian artists. The best known is his *Trinity*, which is kept in Tretyakov Gallery. It is also possible to see his wall paintings in the Cathedral of Annunciation in the Kremlin and in the Assumption Cathedral in Vladimir. Andrei was canonised by the Russian Orthodox Church. In the 20th century, his fame was strengthened by Andrei Tarkovsky's film *Andrei Rublev*.

Seraphim Sarovsky (Saint Seraphim of Sarov) (1759–1833)

Monk of the Sarov Monastery, one of the most revered Russian saints and one of the first 19th century *startsy* (elders at Russian monasteries who were spiritual teachers and advisors). He spent his early life in continuous prayer as a hermit and for many years kept a vow of silence. He is considered to have had the gift of seeing the future. In his later days, he was visited by hundreds of pilgrims from all over Russia, and he tried to help everybody with advice, herb medicine or simply kind words. He is considered the patron saint of Russia. Seraphim was canonised by the Russian Orthodox church in 1903 at a very difficult time for the country, on the eve of revolutions and wars. His relics, lost during the Soviet period, were miraculously found in another time of trial in 1991. They were taken to the Sarov Monastery and are now visited regularly by many pilgrims.

Stalin, Joseph (1878–1953)
The leader of the Soviet Union from the mid-1920s to his death in 1953. His real surname is Dzhugashvili and he is one of the most controversial and talked-of figure in Russian politics. On the one hand, under his leadership the Soviet Union was transformed into a major world industrial power, won the Great Patriotic War (1941–1945) and became a global superpower. On the other hand, his rule was a period of arrests and executions, of his cult of personality and of strong dictatorship. The dispute about his role in history continues today: some people consider him the worst dictator of all time, while others see him as Russia's only saviour.

Stanislavsky, Konstantin (1863–1938)
Stage director and Russian theatre innovator. He was born to a wealthy merchant family (his real surname was Alexeyev) but devoted his whole life to the theatre. Stanislavsky was one of the founders of the Moscow Art Theatre (1898), one of the best Russian theatres. He is famous for his 'theatrical art system' and acting methods based on it. Stanislavski's system is focused on the development of realistic characters and the creation of stage worlds. It is still very influential in modern theatre across the globe.

Suvorov, Alexander (1729/1730–1800),
A Russian general, reckoned to be one of a few great generals in history who never lost a battle. He was famed for his

manual *The Science of Victory*, and noted for the saying 'Train hard, fight easy'. He was very popular in Russia and became a symbol of Russian military wit and strength (his image was widely used during the Second World War).

Tchaikovsky, Peter (1840–1893)

A Russian composer whose works were much more Western than those of his Russian contemporaries, as he effectively used international elements in addition to national folk melodies. Among his most famous musical works are the ballets *Swan Lake*, *Sleeping Beauty*, *The Nutcracker* and operas *Eugene Onegin*, *The Queen of Spades*, *Iolanta* and others.

Tolstoy, Leo (1828–1910)

A great Russian writer, probably one of the best known outside Russia and the most popular within the country. Among his greatest novels are *War and Peace* and *Anna Karenina*, famous for their realistic depiction of Russian life and knowledge of peoples' psychology. As a moral philosopher, he was notable for his ideas of non-violent resistance. For his denial of the official Russian church and a constant search of his own faith, he was excommunicated later in his life.

Vasily, Fool for Christ (Saint Basil) (around 1464–1552)

Yurodivy or holy fool, proclaimed a saint after his death. He was known to walk naked during both summer and winter, to tell the truth (even unpleasant things) to everybody including the Russian *tsar* Ivan the Terrible, to see the unseen world and to predict the future. Ivan the Terrible respected him a lot, asked for advice and after his death personally took his coffin to the grave. By his order, a beautiful cathedral was built in Moscow over Basil's grave and became known as Saint Basil's Cathedral.

Zhukov, Georgy (1896–1978)

Military commander, politician and marshal of the Soviet Union. Played an important role during the Second World War and occupied various important positions. Some people consider him to be the main organising military power during the war.

ACRONYMS

ChP ЧП	emergency чрезвычайное происшествие
CU ЦУ	important instructions ценные указания
DTP ДТП	road traffic accident дорожно-транспортное происшествие
FSB ФСБ	Federal Security Service of Russia Федеральная служба безопасности Российской Федерации
GAI \ GIBDD \ DPS ГАИ \ ГИБДД \ ДПС	state traffic inspector \ State Traffic Safety Inspectorate \ road police Государственная автомобильная инспекция \ Государственная инспекция безопасности дорожного движения \ Дорожно-патрульная служба
GUM \ CUM ГУМ \ ЦУМ	state department store \ central department store государственный универсальный магазин \ центральный универсальный магазин
KGB КГБ	Committee for State Security Комитет Государственной Безопасности
MGU МГУ	Lomonosov Moscow State University Московский государственный университет им. М.В. Ломоносова
SMI СМИ	mass media средства массовой информации
SNG СНГ	Commonwealth of Independent States (CIS) Содружество Независимых Государств

SSSR СССР	Union of Soviet Socialist Republic (USSR) Союз Советских Социалистических Республик
U.E. У.Е.	standard unit (usually American dollars) условные единицы

CULTURE QUIZ

SITUATION 1
You are invited to a party. There are lots of alcoholic drinks and people around you insist on you drinking every toast. How can you avoid getting drunk?

Ⓐ Try to explain that you have some health problem.
Ⓑ Say that it is not traditional in your country to drink that much.
Ⓒ Refuse to drink without explanation.
Ⓓ Pretend to drink and if found out try to make fun of this situation.

Comments
The correct answer is **Ⓓ**. When you refuse to drink, you offend your hosts and friends and destroy the atmosphere of closeness and confidence. Nobody wants you to be drunk, it is just the way of communication; so if you pretend to share in the company, that will be enough to satisfy your friends.

SITUATION 2
You are a businesswoman visiting a Russian company. You arrive to conduct business negotiations and find yourself surrounded by men who immediately start paying compliments, praising your good looks, smart clothes, young age, etc. Your reaction is:

Ⓐ You feel offended and don't try to hide it.
Ⓑ You try to explain that you have been in business for many years.
Ⓒ You say that it is not customary in your country to say compliments during business negotiations.
Ⓓ You laugh, say thank you and start talking about business matters.

Comments
Ⓓ would be the best reaction and will make the process of negotiation easier.

SITUATION 3

You have invited a Russian girl to go to a cinema. She came there with three other friends, saying that they also want to see this film. Your reaction is:

A You say that you don't feel like going and leave them alone.
B You tell a girl that it was not a good idea to bring her friends to your rendezvous.
C You go to a cinema with this company, but next time when inviting a girl, tell her that you want to be with her alone, underlining that it is something special for you.

Comments

Obviously **C** is the best option as she won't understand your negative reaction over such a simple matter.

SITUATION 4

You were invited to visit some people who are complete strangers to you. You were entertained fabulously, food was great and there were lots of drinks, talks and laugh. While saying goodbye, you:

A Immediately invite them to a restaurant the next day\week.
B Say how much you enjoyed your visit and hope to invite them to your house one day.
C Say thank you and later send them a thank you postcard.

Comments

The answer is **B**. Immediate invitation is not expected and thank you postcards are considered to be too impersonal.

SITUATION 5

After a party, you want to go home. It is late and you decide to go by taxi. You are told by your Russian friends that there are several options. What is your choice?

A You are told that the most popular way in Russia is to go to the nearest street and to catch a *chastnik* (a gypsy cab).

ⓑ You may call one of the big well-known taxi companies and ask them to send a car; it is the most expensive way.

ⓒ One of the guests says that he will give you a lift but you must wait a little.

ⓓ Your host suggests that he will call his friend and the friend will take you home.

Comments

The most sensible way to behave is **ⓑ**. You will pay more but feel safe. Waiting 'a little' for somebody at a party may last very long. And it is not polite to impose on your host's hospitality; he feels responsible for you especially as you are a foreigner.

SITUATION 6

You have an appointment with your Russian acquaintance and he is 20 minutes late. You are waiting for him at a tube station and feel very uncomfortable. What do you do in this situation?

ⓐ Go away without waiting any longer.

ⓑ Wait till he comes and make a scandal.

ⓒ Wait for him, be polite but stop all the contacts with this person.

ⓓ Wait for him and be patient and forgiving.

Comments

The best is **ⓓ**. You may mildly reprimand your acquaintance telling him/her that in your culture, being so late is a sign of disrespect. But keep in mind that in Russia, being late means nothing. He may be a good and reliable person and hold you in great esteem, but up to 30 minutes is not considered to be really late.

SITUATION 7

You are looking for a nanny for your children. How will you choose?

ⓐ Turn to advertisements in a newspaper.

ⓑ Go to a specialised agency.

G Ask your Russian friends for recommendations.

D Telephone a person who advertised herself in a street advertisement.

Comments

The cheapest are **A** and **D**, the most expensive is **B**, and they are all not very reliable. **C** is optimal as you have the recommendations of somebody who has already gone through this nanny's services.

SITUATION 8

During a business meeting in your Russian partner's office, your partner is constantly distracted from your conversation: the mobile rings, people come and go, the secretary brings urgent papers to be signed, etc. How do you respond?

A You stop the meeting, saying that you will come next time when he is less busy.

B You reproach your partner that he is not attentive enough about your matter and ask him to concentrate his attention.

C You continue your meeting but later stop having business with him.

D You continue your negotiations and business.

Comments

D is the most sensible, but next time try to organise your meeting in a different place and not in your partner's office, suggesting that it may be more fruitful and less time-consuming.

SITUATION 9

You have a very interesting and pleasant conversation with one of your Russian colleagues. Quite unexpectedly, he invites you for dinner for tonight, saying that he has already telephoned his wife telling her that he will bring his friend. He asks you several times and tries to persuade you. You are free and want to go but are shocked with the swiftness of your friendship. What do you do?

Ⓐ You refuse flatly, saying that you are not ready for this visit.

Ⓑ You refuse under some plausible pretext.

Ⓒ You say that in your culture, such spontaneous invitations are impossible and you can't go.

Ⓓ You say "thank you, how nice although rather unexpected", buy flowers for your friend's wife and go with him.

Comments

If you want to go, then go. If he insists, it means that it is not just politeness, he really means it. And it is almost for sure that his wife (even if she is not very happy) has already spent her time cooking something special.

SITUATION 10

It is the birthday of one of the Russian employees of the company where you work. During lunchtime, she lays the table for her colleagues. There are sandwiches, sweets, cakes, maybe wine on the table. You are asked by somebody to join the company. You know this person very vaguely and are not tempted at all by the food on the table. What do you do?

Ⓐ You say "no, thank you" and go to the buffet for lunch.

Ⓑ You say that you have health problems and must have a proper lunch.

Ⓒ You congratulate the person and go to another office to have your own sandwiches quietly.

Ⓓ You join the company.

Comments

Your choice must be **Ⓓ**. People are very sensitive about such situations. If you don't want to eat, have at least something and say that you are not hungry. This way, you will make friends and gain the respect of your colleagues. You may have your own food in the evening.

SITUATION 11

One of your colleagues rebuked you for calling him by his first name without patronymic. How do you respond?

Ⓐ You explain that there are no patronymics in your country and keep calling him this way.

Ⓑ You say that you don't know Russian and can't pronounce his patronymic.

Ⓒ You stop addressing this person at all.

Ⓓ You say that you know nothing about this Russian tradition and address him as he wants.

Comments

The answer is Ⓓ, for some people it is important.

DO'S AND DON'TS

DO'S

- Try to establish good personal contacts with Russians. This is the best way not only to survive in Russia but to enjoy your stay.
- Take presents with you if you are invited for a visit. They may be small—flowers, candies, chocolates or wine.
- Dress smart and look serious if you are going to an important meeting or business negotiation.
- Try to be sincere and open-hearted while communicating with people.
- Talk about your family if you want to create an informal atmosphere. Talking about family matters for Russians is like talking about the weather for the British.
- If you want to make friends, try more to listen than to speak.
- If you are a woman, even if you are travelling for business matters, be ready at being openly and emphatically courted and complimented by men.
- Don't be afraid to praise people, their families, their children, their homes, their city and their country. Russians have a soft spot for compliments even if they try to hide it.
- If you want to please your hostess, eat very much; if you want to please your host, drink very much.

DON'TS

- Don't be arrogant or aggressive even if you don't like something. Russians are very sensitive and in the present unstable situation easily hurt.
- Don't feel offended if your Russian friends or partners are late. It is not from the lack of respect but from a special cultural attitude to time.
- Don't refuse food and drinks. Try at least something and pretend to enjoy it even if you don't.
- Don't ignore presents given to you even if you don't need them.
- Don't expect the agenda to be followed during negotiations.

- Don't show impatience during negotiations, a meeting or informal gathering.
- Don't trust papers too much: they may be inadequate or outdated. A spoken word is often more reliable.
- Don't use a patronising tone even if you sometimes feel like a representative of a highly civilised country lost among barbarians.
- Don't criticise Russia in front of Russians. They may do it themselves but won't be glad to hear it from a visitor.
- Don't be afraid of asking questions and behaving like 'a foreigner'. That is what is expected from you.

GLOSSARY

Useful Words, Phrases and Expressions

Dobroe utro / dobriy den' / vecher	Good morning / day / evening
Spokojnoj nochi	Goodnight
Zdravstvujte / do svidan'ja / privet	Hello / goodbye / hello
Utro / den' / vecher / noch'	Morning / day / evening / night
Da / net	Yes / no
Menja zovut	My name is
Pozhalujsta	You are welcome
Pozhalujsta	Please
Spasibo	Thank you
Izvinite	I am sorry
Vchera / segodnja / zavtra	Yesterday / today / tomorrow
Den' / nedelja / mesjac / god	Day / week / month / year
Levyj / pravyj	Left / right
Horoshij / plohoj	Good / bad
Bol'shoj / malen'kij	Big / small
Deshevyj / dorogoj	Cheap / expensive
Gorjachij / holodnyj	Hot / cold
Staryj / novyj	Old / new
Otkrytyj / zakrytyj	Open / closed
Vy govorite po-anglijski?	Do you speak English?
Ja ne govorju po-russki	I don't speak Russian
Ja ne ponimaju	I don't understand
Chto jeto znachit?	What does it mean?
Ja hotel by…	I'd like to…
Gde nahoditsja…?	Where is …?
Pomogite, pozhalujsta	Please, help me

Weekdays	
Ponedel'nik	Monday
Vtornik	Tuesday
Sreda	Wednesday
Chetverg	Thursday
Pjatnica	Friday
Subbota	Saturday
Voskresen'e	Sunday

Months	
Janvar'	January
Fevral'	February
Mart	March
Aprel'	April
Maj	May
Ijun'	June
Ijul'	July
Avgust	August
Sentjabr'	September
Oktjabr'	October
Nojabr'	November
Dekabr'	December

Numbers	
Odin	1
Dva	2
Tri	3
Chetyre	4
Pjat'	5
Shest'	6
Sem'	7
Vosem	8

Numbers	
Devjat'	9
Desjat'	10
Odinnadcat'	11
Dvadcat'	20
Sto	100
Tysjacha	1000

RESOURCE GUIDE

IMPORTANT NUMBERS
- 01: Fire
- 02: Militia (Police)
- 03: Ambulance

COMMUNICATIONS
For international phone calls: press 8, wait for the beep sound, press 10, followed by the country code and the telephone number. At present, Russia is in a transitional period. It is said that soon it will be transferred to the European system and international calls will start with 00 as everywhere else. For calls within Russia: press 8, wait for the beep sound, followed by the city/town code and the telephone number. For local calls, just dial the telephone number.

Codes of Russian Cities:
- Moscow: 495 or 499
- Saint Petersburg: 812
- Vladivostok: 4232
- Novosibirsk: 3832
- Voronezh: 4732
- Kaluga: 4842
- Pskov: 8112
- Novgorod: 8162
- Arkhangelsk: 8182
- Murmansk: 8152

Internet
There are Internet cafes in all major cities, private users in smaller towns and no Internet facilities in the countryside.

HOSPITALS
Moscow
- **American Medical Center**
  1 Grokholskiy Pereulok
  Tel: 933-7700

- **Cardiology Institute**
  15a Cherepkovskaya 3-ya Ulitsa
  Tel: 140-9336 (Information)
      149-0717 (Registration)
- **Clinics of Moscow Medical Academy**
  5 Pogodinskaya Ulitsa
  Tel: 248-3400
- **International SOS Clinic**
  31 Grokholsky Pereulok
  Tel: 937-5760
- **Medexpress**
  124 Mira Prospect.
  Tel: 401-5470; 401-0382
- **Medical Emergency Assistance Center of Moscow**
  3 Koptelskiy 1-yy Pereulok
  Tel: 924-6472
- **Morozovskaya Children's Hospital**
  1 Dobryninskiy 4-yy Pereulok
  Tel: 958-8904
- **Moscow Ophthalmology Hospital**
  7 Mamonovskiy Pereulok
  Tel: 299-7970 (Reception)
      299-3020 (Information)
      299-6128 (Medical Emergency Care)
- **Moscow Physical Therapy Hospital**
  26a Talalikhina Ulitsa
  Tel: 276-7556
- **Municipal Hospital N 29**
  2 Gospitalnaya Ploshchad
  Tel: 263-1828
- **Municipal Urological Hospital N 47**
  51 Parkovaya 3-ya Ulitsa
  Tel: 164-6620
- **Municipal Hospital N 1**
  8 Leninskiy Prospect.
  Tel: 236-6535
- **Municipal Hospital**
  5 Botkinskiy 2-oy pr-d
  Tel: 252-9488

- **Municipal Hospital N 33**
  7 Stromynka Ulitsa
  Tel: 268-0906
- **Neurosis Clinic**
  43 Donskaya Ulitsa
- **Neurosis Clinic (branch)**
  2 Novorublevskaya Ulitsa Poselok Rublevo
  Tel: 414-3376

Saint Petersburg

- **American Medical Center (AMC)**
  Serpukhovskaya Ulitsa 10
  Tel: 326-1730
- **AviMed**
  11 Liniya V.O.
  Tel: 321-2490
  Fax: 321-2483
- **Emergency Medical Consulting**
  14 Izmaylovskiy Prospect
  Tel: 112-6512; 112-6510
- **EuroMED**
  60 Suvorovsky Prospect
  Tel: 327-0301
- **Eye Trauma Emergency Center**
  25 Liteynyy Prospect
  Tel: 272-5955
- **Family Medicine Clinic**
  49 Lunacharskogo Prospect
  Tel: 559-9455
- **International Clinic**
  19/21 Ulitsa Dostoyevskogo
  Tel: 320-3870
- **Institute of Emergency Medical Care
  n.a. I.I. Dzhanelidze**
  3 Budapeshtskaya Ulitsa
  Tel: 105-2970; 105-0779
- **Family Medicine Department**
  43 Zanevsky Prospect
  Tel: 528-8888

- **Polyclinic Complex**
  22 Moskovsky Prospect
  Tel: 316-5881; 316-5904
- **St. Petersburg Clinical Hospital**
  72 Prospect Morisa Toresa
  Tel: 553-3383
- **Saint-Petersburg Multiline Clinic**
  49/51 Bolshoi Prospect, V.O.
  Tel: 320-7000

SCHOOLS

There are schools for foreigners attached to many embassies in Russia. The best way to find this information is to contact the embassies directly.

- **Anglo-American School of Moscow**
  1 Beregovaya Street
  Tel: 231-4488
  Day school for English-speaking children of American, British and Canadian diplomats, as well as diplomats from other countries, members of the business community and Russian nationals.

EXPAT CLUBS

There is a good and useful Moscow expat site (in English): http://www.expat.ru

RELIGIOUS INSTITUTIONS

Moscow

Russian Orthodox Church (main Cathedrals):

- **Cathedral of Christ the Redeemer**
  Prechistenskaya nab
  Tel: 203-3823
- **Cathedral of Our Lady of Kazan**
  8 Nikolskaya Ulitsa
  Tel: 298-0131
- **Cathedral of the Epiphany**
  15 Spartakovskaya Ulitsa
  Tel: 267-7591

- **Intercession Cathedral** (known as St. Basil's Cathedral)
  4 Krasnaya Ploshchad
  Tel: 298-3304
- **St. Andrew's Anglican Church**
  8 Voznesenskiy Pereulok
  Tel: 229-0990
- **Catholic Chaplaincy of the Anglo-American School**
  78 Leninskiy Prospect
  Tel: 243-9621
- **Chapel of our Lady of Hope** (Catholic)
  7 Kutuzovskiy Prospect
  Tel: 243-9621
- **Church of Immaculate Conception of the Virgin Mary**
  (Polish catholic church)
  27 Mal. Gruzinskaya Ulitsa
  Tel: 252-3911
- **Eglise Catholique Romaine De Saint Louis des Francais Moscou**
  12 Mal. Lubyanka Ulitsa
  Tel: 925-2034
- **Armenian Apostolic Church of the Resurrection**
  10 Sergeya Makeeva Ulitsa
  Tel: 255-5019
- **New Apostolic Church**
  5 Malomoskovskaiya Ulitsa
  Tel: 282-9565
- **Lutheran Worship in Church of St. Peter and Paul**
  7 Starosadskiy Pereulok
  Tel: 928-3262
- **Georgian Orthodox Church**
  12 Bol. Gruzinskaya Ulitsa
  Tel: 254-0985
- **Moscow Protestant Chaplaincy**
  1 Mytnaya Ulitsa
  Tel: 143-3562
- **Choral Synagogue**
  10 Bol. Spasoglinishchevskiy Pereulok
  Tel: 923-4788

- **Marina Roshcha** (Moscow Jewish Religious Commune)
  5a Vysheslavtsev 2-oy Pereulok
  Tel: 289-9423
- **Central Moslem Administration**
  49 Ostozhenka Ulitsa
  Tel: 247-3100
- **Moslem Mosque**
  7 Vypolzov Pereulok
  Tel: 281-3866

SAINT PETERSBURG
Main Russian Orthodox Churches and Cathedrals
- **St Isaac's Cathedral**
  2-a Kanala Griboyedova Nab.
  Tel: 314-4096
- **Kazan Cathedral**
  2 Kazanskaya Ploshchad
  Tel: 314-5856
- **The Smolny Cathedral**
  Rastrelli Ploschad 3
- **Church of Resurrection of Christ**
  Naberezhnaia kanala Griboyedova
- **St. Nicholas' Naval Cathedral**
  Nikolskaya Ploshchad
- **Alexander Nevsky Monastery**
  1 Reki Monastyrki Nab.
  Tel: 274-1702
- **Spaso-Preobrazhensky Cathedral**
  1 Preobrazhenskaya Ploschad
  Tel: 272-3662
- **Anglican Chaplaincy of St. Petersburg, Church of England, Church of St.Catherine**
  Malaya Konyushennaya Street, 1-3
  Tel: 571-2081
- **Armenian Church**
  Nevsky Prospect 40
- **Baptist Church**
  Naberezhnaya Fontanki 46
  Tel: 351-1400

- **St. Catherine Roman Catholic Church**
  Nevsky Prospect 32-34
  Tel: 311-7170
- **Church of St. Peters and St. Paul** (Lutheran)
  Nevsky Prospect 22/24
  Tel: 312-0798
- **Church of St. Mary** (Lutheran Evangelical)
  Bolshaya Konyushennaya Ulitsa 8
  Tel: 314-7161
- **Mosque**
  Kronverksky Prospect 7
  Tel: 233-9819
- **Big Choral Synagogue**
  Lermonovsky Prospect 2
  Tel: 713-8186

BOOKSHOPS
Moscow
- **Anglia British Bookshop**
  6 Vorotnikovsky lane
  Tel: 299-7766
- **Biblio-Globus**
  6/3, Building 5 Myasnitskaya Ulitsa
  Tel: 781-1900; 928-3567

Bookberry:
- 87b,Varshavskoye Shosse
  'Varshavsky' entertainment center
  Tel: 981-4796
- Kaluzhskoe Shosse, MEGA
  Tel: 789-6502
- Leningradsky Shosse, 62a, Gallery Aeroport
  Tel: 771-7261
- Nikitsky Boulevard, 17
  Tel: 789-9187
- Leningradsky Proezd, 62a
  Tel: 771-7261
- Moscow district, Khimki, MEGA-Khimki
  Tel: 221-3142

- Marshala Biruzova Ulitsa, 32
  Tel: 955-1808
- Kutuzovsky Proezd, 10
  Tel: 243-6690
- Kirovogradskaya Ulitsa, 14, Global City
  Tel: 956-4239
- Dom Knigi, Novy Arbat Ulitsa, 8
  Tel: 789-3591
- Moskva, Tverskaya Ulitsa, 8
  Tel: 229-6483

Saint Petersburg
- **Anglia**
  38 Nab. reky Fontanky
  Tel: 579-8284
- **Dom Knigi**
  62 Nevsky Proezd
  Tel: 570-6402
- **DVK**
  20 Nevsky Proezd
  Tel: 312-4936
- **Staraya Kniga** (Old Book)
  3 Nevsky Proezd (in courtyard)
  Tel: 315-1151

NEWSPAPERS / MAGAZINES
Moscow
Foreign press is sold in many hotels and street stands, especially in the centre of Moscow. You can get almost any magazine or newspaper in English and in other languages in one of the following places:
- **Maxim's News Stand**
  2 Nizhnyaya Maslovska
  They have everything, and if they don't, you can order.
- **Arbat Supermarket**
  Novy Arbat Street, Novoarbatsky Supermarket
  Just next to the entrance, they sell some English-language magazines and fresh newspapers.

- **Bookberry**
  17, Street 1 Nikitskiy bulv
  Tel: 202-6679
  The new Moscow book supermarket has an extensive section of foreign magazines and newspapers at moderate prices.

The main English language newspaper published in Moscow is *The Moscow Times*. Other local English-language newspapers are the weekly *Russia Journal* and *The Moscow News*. A good English-language magazine is the *Go-Magazine*, which provides interesting information in English about the entertainment and arts in Moscow.

Saint Petersburg

You will find foreign press in all central hotels and some central bookshops.The main English language local newspaper is *The Saint Petersburg Times*.

FURTHER READING

The Icon and the Axe. James Billington. New York: Random House, 1970.
- A classical book about Russian culture universally acknowledged in the West. Many editions since 1966 when it was written.

The Russian Mind. Ronald Hingley. New York: Charles Scribner's Sons, 1977.
- A book about the Russian people, their attitudes and behaviour written with a good sense of humour.

Land of the Firebird, The Beauty of Old Russia. Suzanne Massie. New York: Simon and Schuster, 1980.
- Slightly idealised but beautiful image of Russia. The book is about Russian cultural life in the 19th century.

Understanding Imperial Russia. Marc Raeff. New York: Columbia University Press, 1984.
- Good and readable study of Russian history from Peter the Great till 1917.

A History of Russia. Nicholas Riasanovsky. New York: Oxford University Press, 1963 (Fifth edition, 1993).
- Still a very reliable book on Russian history although written years ago.

From Nyet to Da: Understanding the Russians. Yale Richmond. Boston: Intercultural Press, 1992.
- Very thorough and open-minded research on Russian life. Slightly outdated as it was written about the Soviet era, but is still very good for learning about constant, unchanged values.

Russia. Insight Guides. Washington: APA Publications, 1994.
- Good popular edition with lots of information.

Russian Fairy Tales. Aleksandr Afanas'ev. New York: Pantheon Books, 2006.
- Fairytales are an inexhaustible source of information about Russian life and people.

Russia. Donald Wallace. Princeton, New Jersey: Princeton University Press, 1984.
- This book about Russian life is a result of six years of travel in Russia in the 1860s. Russian correspondent for *The London Times* Sir Donald Mackenzie is much less known but a much more reliable source of information than Marquis de Custine, who travelled before him.

Xenophobe's Guide to the Russians. Elizabeth Roberts. UK: Ravette Books, 1993.
- Everyone and everything is made fun of in this series. But in the Russian language, there is a proverb: 'Every joke has a grain of truth'.

ABOUT THE AUTHOR

Anna Pavlovskaya is Doctor of History, Professor of Moscow State University, Head of the Department of Russian, European and American Studies and Director of the Centre of Cross-Cultural Studies. Among her books are *Russia and the USA: the Problem of interaction of Cultures* (in Russian), *How to Deal with Russians* (in Russian and in English) and *Education in Russia: History and Traditions* (in Russian). Her book *How to Deal with Russians* was awarded a Gold Medal of the All-Russian Exhibition Centre in 2003. In 2004, she started a new series devoted to the traditions, ways of life and manners of different European nations. The first books are *England and the English* (2004) and *Italy and the Italians* (2006). A series of films have been made based on the books.

INDEX